Global Environment
What You Don't Know?

Attention Authors

Manas Publications is fighting a war to tell the world that India can win the battle not only by the bullet but also by pen. We are converting fighters into writers. There is no dearth of intellectuals in our country. However, their knowledge is confined to them only. No sincere effort has been made by any other publisher to channelise their knowledge. That is why the talent of every intellectual remains latent. An author always presents the raw material in the shape of a manuscript and it is the job of the publisher to convert it into a completely finished book. Manas has been motivating intellectuals continually and publishing their manuscripts for more than three decades and would like to publish your manuscript too. If you or your colleagues have a manuscript ready for publication or are working on it, contact us with a detailed synopsis and list of contents. Manas can also suggest you a suitable title for writing related to your area of expertise. Manas is known for its publishing quality. We take utmost care in production and give wide publicity to the book and its author through our national and international distribution network.

Global Environment
What You Don't Know?

Thakur Shailendra Nath

Manas Publications
(We Convert Fighters into Writers)
New Delhi-110002 (INDIA)

MANAS PUBLICATIONS
(We Convert Fighters into Writers)
(Publishers, Distributors, Importers & Exporters)
4402/5-A, Ansari Road (Opp. HDFC Bank)
Darya Ganj, New Delhi-110 002 (INDIA)
Off. ☎ 23260783, 23265523, Res. 23842660
Fax: 011-23272766
E-mail: manaspublications@gmail.com
manaspublications@yahoo.com
website: www.manaspublications.in

2nd Impression 2014
First Published:

ISBN: 978-81-7049-412-6
₹ 695/-

Designed at
Manas Publications

Printed in India at
HS Offsets, Delhi and published by Mrs Suman Lata for
Manas Publications, 4402/5-A, Ansari Road,
(Opp. HDFC Bank),
Darya Ganj, New Delhi-110 002 (INDIA)

Contents

Preface

I am pleased to present the book titled "Global Environment: What You Don't Know" before the readers. I am not an environmentalist but I have an agriculturist background. I had a passion for gardening from my very childhood. Whenever I got an opportunity and available vacant land around our house even rented one, I used to convert it into small gardens by planting some flowers and vegetable plants. It was only after my accident in 1993, I was physically not able to exert in gardening, it appears the inner turbulence which was stored inside has outburst in shape of this book.

Global warming and climate change is a matter of concern for all of us. J&K's rising temperatures are a disturbing development and the Indian Institute of Tropical Meteorology informs that regions in the western Himalayas (J&K, Himachal Pradesh, and Uttarakhand in India) are badly hit. In March 2010, the temperature in J&K was eight to 12 degrees above normal. For Kashmiri Bakarwal nomads, global warming is a reality that they face everyday. The tribe traditionally wanders the region in search of good pasture for its flock. An unusual warm March 2010 caused loss of half of their newborn livestock. Rescheduling nomadic migration may have adverse consequences for the tribal economy and social set up. Sunita Narain, director of the Centre for Science and Environment, says: "Environmentalists had long feared this would happen to the Bakawals. There would be changes in the local ecology that could lead to changes in people's life style. This is the hidden tragedy of climate change." A recent report says all glaciers have completely disappeared in Kashmir. This, along with rampant deforestation has caused shortfall of rain and snow resulting in fall in water level of almost every river and stream. The Maldharis in Gujrat aren't sure if they will find pasture for livestock. Rising sea levels have forced many to leave Sunderbans in West Bengal. Fishermen in the Gulf of Mannar report smaller catches due to changing water temperature. Chilka Lake is threatened by rising sea levels, affecting the livelihood of the Kaunta and Khatia fishing communities. Chakhesang Nagas are forced to leave their land as more dams are built for the stated purpose of combating climate change.

It is profoundly disturbing that millions of innocent people in villages who live in close harmony with nature and rely on nature's bounties for their existence and survival, have to suffer for no fault of theirs. The world over, it is the poorest of the poor living around forest areas who defend the biodiversity as they are dependent for survival on these resources. They have shielded thickly forested areas from being converted into wastelands. The forest and the vegetation that they preserve, act as fresh water reservoirs that feed the rivers that quench the thirst of the people and are also used in irrigation of land. It is solely because of them that the ecological balance remains intact. They are more vulnerable to climate change including long spell of droughts and prolonged floods, unprecedented strength of typhoons and cyclones, worsening food and water insecurity, increase in water borne-diseases, pest invasion, destruction of traditional cultures linked with nature. At this point of time, we all need to do our bit to save the planet, earth, rivers and all natural resources. If we continue to exploit our resources at the same pace, then we will not be left with anything in the future. We will have to realize that if we destroy the environment, we destroy ourselves. Thus we are required to be more sensitive towards environment issues, their consequences and the resources that are available to us. We have to initiate positive actions and get the citizenry involved at each level. We should figure out ways wherein we can use our natural resources minimally.

When the rapidly deteriorating environment is going to adversely affect all of us, why leave the fighting bit to just the Government or specialists. Every individual will have to think and contribute towards it by investing in an eco-friendly house. Experts have refuted the charge that the cost of eco-friendly house and a regular one is almost the same and also one stands to gain a lot from the former. Only one needs to know the factors that make an eco-friendly home, use of local and natural materials, rain water harvesting arrangements, water treatment systems, solar water heaters and photo-voltaic, good ventilation and day lighting, high roofs to keep the house cool are some aspects that can be checked and ensured while constructing or purchasing a house. Our forefathers never used air-conditioners. They used ample of open space in their homes and buildings and plenty of natural light. We see the Mughal architectures, those buildings are still standing tall and strong. It is true that now population has grown and there is scarcity of land, as a remedial measures flat culture has developed still we can add insulation to the walls, get double glazing, insulated window frames, high efficiency appliances, energy efficiency tube lights and CFL, make provisions for waste water re-cycling to make our home energy efficient.

Rich countries are emitting much CO_2 than developing and poor countries. For example there are 765 vehicles per thousand population in US whereas 12 in India and only 2 in Bangladesh. (In 1930, it was 200 vehicles/1000 population in US). Similarly power, 1460 per capita watts/day in US and only 50.7 and 14.7 per capita watts/day in India and Bangladesh respectively. And west says India, and China are not doing enough for climate.

The moral leadership at the Copenhagen meet was on 14th December 2009 wrested by the African countries when, in a show of strength and solidarity, they stalled the climate talks and walked out as the rich industrialized countries began demanding the Kyoto Protocol be set aside and discussions be held on only a single new track. In short, Africa erupted in outrage when the rich countries refused to provide money and technology to poorer countries as enshrined in the Kyoto Protocol. Under Kyoto, the rich are expected to reduce their emissions too. Until now, the leadership in this fight was being provided by emerging economies like India and China. On 14th December, they followed the African countries and staged a walkout along with other G-77 members, barring a small ginger group of island countries. Once the African nations had decided to give as hard as they were getting from the industrialized countries, the BASIC four countries India, China, South Africa and Brazil rallied behind them. They confronted the president of the negotiations, the host Danes, on the seeming logjam. They registered their protest that the schedule of talks for the day had been engineered in a way that discussions on the Kyoto Protocol had been marginalized in favour of industrialized countries demand that negotiations on Long Term Cooperative Action be prioritised. The solidarity of G-77 forced the Danes to back down. With the climate talks hitting a roadblock, the rich countries relented for the moment and included Kyoto in the talks.

I am obliged and indebted to my department and senior officers who have provided necessary help and guidance in writing this book. I am thankful to NACEN for providing me assistance and facilities of library in writing this book.

The help extended by M/s Gupta Services, Gwalior in typing of this book cannot be forgotten.

I owe a deep debt to my family members - my wife Prabha, my eldest daughter Anzulica and son-in-law Anunay, Shrutica and Jaishika for their reverential and encouraging attitude. I would not have found a congenial environment at home for undertaking the onerous task of writing a book in difficult times, covering a wide range of complex issues of environment.

I shall welcome criticism and suggestions for improving the quality of contents of this book from readers.

Thakur Shailendra Nath

Introduction

Earth, my mother,
Set me securely with bliss in full accord with heaven,
O Wise One,
Uphold me in grace and splendour!

— Atharva Veda

O Allah, You are the
Lord of the Universe,
You are the Creator
of everything.
You take care of everything.
O Allah, please take
care of me.

O Allah, have mercy
on me.

—Saniyasnain Khan

I am a Banyan tree,
Standing here,
For hundred and
three years,
Breathing, Watching!
A silent witness
To many stories,
events and people...

—Geeta Radhakrishna

While climate change has recently emerged as a clear priority for policymakers in many countries, in many others the focus has quite understandably been elsewhere—especially on development and the alleviation of poverty. The focus on ending poverty must remain and be sharpened. But we must guard against falling into the trap of seeing the protection of the environment and development of the economy as alternatives. They are, in fact, two sides of the same coin.

No longer can any country or city pursue its interests in isolation. Today, the emphasis is very much on interconnection, interdependence and co-operation. While history reveals that humans sometimes struggle to succeed in these respects, we must not be deterred from seeking a better future. One challenge that has been a lot for the last couple of years, and which is relevant to many developing countries, is the question of how to save what remains of the world's tropical rainforests.

These incredible ecosystems harbour more than half the earth's terrestrial biodiversity, on which, whether we like it or not, human survival depends. They generate rainfall;

they are home to many of the world's indigenous peoples; and they help meet the needs of hundreds of millions of other people. They also hold vast quantities of carbon, and their clearance is causing massive greenhouse gas emissions, accounting for a fifth of the total.

India has achieved many environmental gains through her ambitious afforestation programmes, the science also tells us of the urgent need to stop forests being cut down in the first place. This is precisely why Rainforests Project has made a great effort during the last two years to help facilitate a consensus on increasing international co-operation to deforestation. And happily, the efforts are being successful.

A new working group of more than 30 governments has set out proposals on how it would be possible to provide countries with financial rewards for their positive efforts to curtail deforestation. New financial incentives could be used in rainforest nations to implement strategies for sustainable development without having to rely so heavily on the kind of economic activities that cause deforestation. At the same time, money would be available for new health and education programmes, as well as genuinely integrated rural development models. In return, the world would sustain the vital ecosystem services upon which we all rely for our economic, physical and spiritual survival.

The idea that the world should pay in some way for the essential utility services provided by the rainforests (after all, we already pay for our water, gas and electricity) is not a new one. However, many would agree that it is an effective way to quickly reduce emissions and, thus, buy urgently needed time in the battle against catastrophic climate change.

While initiatives like this will need to be a part of the solution as we are getting alienated from nature, and more reliant on technological inventions to solve our problems, we have become less able to see our predicament for what it really is, i.e., being utterly out of balance, having lost any sense of harmony with the earth's natural rhythms, cycles and finite resources.

Forging a reconnection with nature and reintegrating our societies and economies with her capacities is very much a part of the challenge to which we must rise. The Copenhagen summit contributes to a shift at this deeper level, as well as set out the plan for transition to a low carbon economy and the means to ensure that the countries least responsible for this problem can be helped to adapt to the already inevitable change.

Mahatma Gandhi observed how "the difference between what we do and what we are capable of doing would suffice to solve most of the world's problems".

Climate change is a breaking story. Just over 30 years ago the experts were at loggerheads about whether Earth was warming or cooling, unable to decide whether an icehouse or a greenhouse future was on the way. By 1975, however, the first sophisticated computer models were suggesting that a doubling of carbon dioxide (CO_2) in the atmosphere would lead to an increase in global temperature of around five degrees Fahrenheit. Still, concern among both scientists and the community was not significant. There was even a period of optimism, when some researchers believed that extra CO_2 in the atmosphere would fertilize the world's croplands and produce a bonanza for farmers.

But by 1988, climate experts had become sufficiently worried about CO_2 to establish a panel staffed with the world's leading experts, to report on the issue twice each decade. Their third report, issued in 2001, sounded a note of sober alarm, yet many governments and industry leaders were slow to take an interest. The transition to a carbon-free economy is eminently achievable because we have all the technology we need to do so. It is only a lack of understanding and the pessimism and confusion generated by special interest groups that is stopping us from going forward. One of the biggest obstacles to making a start on climate change is that it has become a cliché before it has even been understood. What we need now is good information and careful thinking, because in the years to come this issue will dwarf all others combined. This year is likely to be the fifth-warmest on record and the first decade of this century the hottest since records began, according to the world Meteorological Organization. Australia had its third warmest year since record dating began in 1850, "with three exceptional heat waves", China saw the worst drought in five decades that affected millions, and poor rains caused severe droughts in India while there were massive food shortages due to a big drought in Kenya.

More recently we have been hearing complaints from women in Kumaon region villages about how they can't obtain water for sheer survival needs. On the one hand, water level in the Kosi river has reduced considerably and recent research has warned that if the present trend continues, river could dry up. On the other hand, village women told us that hotels were taking away such huge quantities of water that the basic needs of villagers could not be met. The police were sent in to ensure that urban needs would be prioritized. For us the protection of rivers is also associated with the water rights of villagers as we feel that their essential supplies should be protected as a priority. Protection of Himalayan Rivers is crucial not just for the hill villages but also for the vast plains below.

Protection of Himalayan Rivers is closely related to the protection of forests. Our mahila mandals in Kosi river basin have been active in protecting forests. Starting by themselves, they are now careful that collection of fuel and fodder do not damage the forests. They are determined to protect forests from fires. At the same time forest officials have to change their management practices so that trees with broader leaves get their due place in Himalayas. Those tree species that are better for soil and water conservation and also provide more and better fodder to villagers should be planted. Villagers in Uttarakhand have suffered greatly due to the dam-construction work: the enormous scale of the construction of dams, tunnel-dams and other hydel projects in remote villages. These have been undertaken without any prior consultation with the affected people. Villagers and their environment have been devastated by the blasting of the hills, takeover of their farmland, pastures and forests as well as disruption of community life. When villagers and activists from various parts of Uttarakhand met and exchanged notes on the situation of their area, a fuller picture of the devastation emerged and it was to check this devastation that we started a statewide campaign for protection of rivers.

This *Nadi Bachao Abhiyan* (campaign to protect rivers) has taken the form of yatras in affected areas and also led to a high level dialogue with government representatives. But it appears that very powerful vested interests and corruption marred the success of these efforts.

Shimla, Queen of the Hills a customary summer retreat, experienced its second hottest March since 1901. "Both minimum and maximum temperature were above normal. The all-time high since 1901 was recorded, on March 27, 2004, when the maximum was 27.2 °C.

The Centre has announced Rs. 5 crore package to save from extinction, Assam's Majuli, the largest riverine island in south Asia, swathes of which are eroded by annual floods in Brahmaputra. Environment and forest minister Jairam Ramesh, on a recent visit also promised the island would be declared "eco-sensitive" soon.

Grazing cuts laughing gas emissions

Grazing by cows or sheep can cut emissions of nitrous oxide, a powerful greenhouse gas, in grasslands from China to the US, says a new study in the journal *Nature* which points that the livestock can help limit microbes in the soil that generate the gas, also known as laughing gas.

$133m to fight Niger hunger

The United Nations said it needed $133 million to fight hunger in Niger after poor rainfall and harvests have led to serious food shortages in the West African nation. The UN estimates at current levels -3.78 1akh people will suffer acute malnutrition in Niger in the next 12 months.

Deforestation

While the air in a clear sky is nearly transparent to the visible wavelengths coming in from sunlight, air absorbs the infrared radiation emitted by the Earth fairly strongly. This absorption is not caused by the main components of the atmosphere, molecular nitrogen and oxygen: these gases are as transparent to infrared radiation as they are to visible light. Rather, the absorption comes from several minor atmospheric constituents, principally water vapour and CO_2. By absorbing and re-emitting infrared radiation throughout the atmosphere, these gases impede the passage of radiation from the Earth's surface to space. This process warms the Earth's surface and lower 10 km of the atmosphere, while cooling the atmosphere at higher altitudes. Ever since this natural warming mechanism was first described in the nineteenth century, it has been widely called the "greenhouse effect". More recently, it has been compared to wrapping a blanket around the Earth. Neither of these analogies is really accurate; however, since both blankets and greenhouses mainly work by slowing the physical escape of warm air rather than by disrupting the passage of radiation. The power of these "greenhouse gases" to warm the Earth's surface is awesome. Although these gases are present in the atmosphere in minute concentrations, they warm the surface by nearly 35°C. Their power becomes even clearer if we compare the climate of the Earth to that of the neighbouring planets, Mars and Venus.

Deforestation causes around fifth of greenhouse gas emissions every year, more than all the forms of air and surface transport combined. This is because trees absorb carbon dioxide as they grow, so every time forests are chopped down it reduces the Earth's ability to absorb the greenhouse gas. Therefore if the world wants to reduce emissions, it must stop deforestation. It is also a relatively easy way to reduce carbon dioxide, compared to the effort required in asking the world to stop driving cars and running factories. The big question is how you stop poor people in rainforest nations like Brazil, Indonesia and the Congo chopping down trees to feed their families. Or indeed to produce beef, palm oil and timber to export to countries like Britain. The answer lies in an innovative scheme that would pay the poor countries not to chop down trees. REDD or Reducing Emissions from Deforestation and Degradation has been talked about for years but the summit at Copenhagen is the first opportunity to see it implemented on a global scale. Richer countries would need to put forward money to set up the mechanisms such as a satellite monitoring service to ensure countries being paid not to chop down trees are keeping their promises. There will also be a need for cash to help provide alternative incomes for people in and around the forests. WWF is calling for funding around £27 billion per year by 2020 to keep the forests standing. The money could be raised by making forests part of the carbon markets. This would mean industries could pay to protect forests to offset some of their pollution. People could even buy 'forest bonds' that grow in value over time as polluting becomes more expensive. However there are serious concerns. Many of the rainforest nations are dogged by corruption and there are fears that they could end up in the wrong hands. If the scheme is not set up correctly, it is in danger of causing more deforestation because logging simply shifts elsewhere. Indigenous people who rely on the forests need to have a say in how their homeland is managed but in many countries they are marginalized. The Prince of Wales is leading the world in his fight to make sure trees are worth "more alive than dead". He points out that trees not only absorb carbon dioxide but provide 'water services' by regulating rainfall and 'ecosystems services' in maintaining wildlife. "If we lose the battle against tropical deforestation, we lose the battle against climate change", he warns.

Patrick Michaels, a member of the International Panel on Climate Change (IPCC), has accused the climate establishment of trying to manufacture a consensus in peer-reviewed academic journals by censoring or squeezing dissenters. He should know he is a victim. IPCC scientists, who won the Nobel Peace Prize, are not unanimous on climate change. A few like Patrick Michaels and John Christy say fears of global warming are greatly exaggerated. The climate establishment dismisses most dissenters as the equivalent of holocaust deniers. It cannot so easily dismiss Michaels or Christy, who are distinguished members of the Nobel Prize winning team.

Climategate is the recent scandal revealing that establishment scientists like Phil Jones and Michael Mann, at the Climate Research Unit (CRU) of East Anglia University, sought to destroy emails, hide data, and evade freedom of information requests in order to thwart dissenting voices. Mann and Jones claim that the censorship attempts were minor, and do not affect the truth on climate. These clumsy censorship attempts are merely the tip of the iceberg, says Michaels in a *Wall Street Journal* Op-Ed. The Bible of scientists is peer-reviewed literature in academic journals. Establishment scientists now seek to squeeze dissenters out of these journals, and close down journals that do not toe the line. This attempt to fix the academic literature and manufacture a bogus 'scientific consensus" suggests there might be something to hide.

The academic climate literature, including IPCC documents, held in the 1990s that the medieval warm period around 1100 AD was warmer than the twentieth century. Then, in 1999, Mann proposed the 'hockey stick' hypothesis. Using multivariate statistics and questionable data, he wiped out both the medieval warm period and the subsequent 'little ice age' (a cold period from the late sixteenth century to the mid-nineteenth century), leaving only the twentieth century warming as a big temperature outlier. The IPCC establishment eagerly embraced this rewriting of the entire history of climate change. In any other discipline, the hockey stick thesis would have gone down as one more plausible hypothesis. But the IPCC has in effect wiped out all the earlier historical literature in one stroke.

Then *Climate Research,* a referal journal, published two papers offending the establishment. One paper in 2003 by Willie Soon and Sallie Baliunas (of the Harvard-Smithsonian Center for Astrophysics), analyzed dozens of "paleoclimate" studies and concluded that twentieth century temperatures could not confidently be considered warmer than those a thousand years ago. This reaffirmed the existence of the medieval warm period. The establishment also disliked a paper by Michaels in *Climate Research* in 2002, showing that the magnitude of warming in CRU's own data was not as great as predicted by the IPCC models. This suggested that the models might be exaggerating the impact of atmospheric carbon dioxide. Normal academic practice would have required the establishment to rebut these views. Instead, Mann suggested putting *Climate Research* out of business, or at least hiding information from it. He wrote in one of his emails, "Perhaps we should encourage our colleagues in the *Climate Research* community to no longer submit to, or cite papers in this journal. We would also need to consider what we tell or request of our more reasonable colleagues who currently sit on the editorial board". After establishment scientists threatened a boycott of publications and reviews, half the editorial board of Climate Research resigned. Scientists like Michaels found it increasingly difficult to get published. Some dissenters like Sallie Baliunas stopped trying, "Tiring of summary rejections of good work by editors scared of the mob".

Geophysical Research Letters (GRL) is another popular referal journal. Climategate exposed emails between establishment scientists wanting to oust one of the editors of *GRL* suspected of climate scepticism. "It's one thing to lose *Climate Research.* We can't afford to lose *GRL*". The establishment succeeded in ousting the editor, and then exulted in an email, "the *GRL* leak may have been plugged up now *w/*new editorial leadership there".

Regrettably, the IPCC itself is now getting tainted by this attempt to capture academic journals and censor dissenting views. Objecting to some dissenting papers, Mann is reported to have said: "I can't see either of these papers being in the next IPCC report. Kevin and I will keep them out somehow even if we have to redefine what the peer-review literature is".

As a UN body, the IPCC must not allow itself to be captured by one scientific faction or another. It needs to give fair representation to all views. Indeed the IPCC is supposed to take into account all peer-reviewed literature, including dissenting views.

Scientific methodology usually beats attempts at manipulation. The problem here is that the IPCC has won a Nobel Prize. Establishment scientists are only human, and can be expected to spin everything and anything to prove that they did indeed deserve the award. That will seem to them a more worthwhile goal than mere scientific truth. Here lies the danger.

Nations are at an inflection point as they face their energy futures: with effective policy, swift implementation of new technologies and effective use of international forums, India cannot only firmly establish its position as an innovator and thought leader, but also create an environment for an energy revolution that has the potential to rival the internet revolution.

Energy is unlike any other commodity. The entire economy depends on access to dependable, affordable energy. Without this, nothing else can be successful.

Our energy options, in turn, are dependent on the development and adoption of new technologies. The incumbent technologies, on the whole, burn fossil fuels, and don't do that very well: most of today's power plants, factories and automobile technologies waste energy, generate "massive amounts of pollution accelerate climate change and leave the nation dependent on imported oil and coal. New technologies will give India far more control over her destiny, and reduce each of these problems".

Solar photovoltaic and centralized solar thermal generate electricity directly from the sun. Wind is becoming a mainstream energy source. Village-scale biomass and rural photovoltaic systems can offer energy services to the 40 per cent of Indian population that is currently left behind. And in all cases, energy efficiency is a bonanza: the best technologies can save terrific amounts of energy and money at the same time. These findings have been confirmed by the Confederation of Indian Industry, Teri, and McKinsey and in a number of IIT studies. We have a genuine opportunity to build clean energy prosperity, if we act decisively.

Take advantage of efficiency and renewable energy technologies that are available today, and do so with scale and speed. Inefficient lighting condemns householders to high energy bills, and their cumulative waste condemns our cities to blackouts. Simple policies can help bring about change. India should adopt standards for efficient lights, compact fluorescents and LEDs. Dr Jayant Sathaye of Lawrence Berkeley National Laboratory calculates that aggressive energy efficiency would save this nation over Rs. 2.4 million crore by 2017, by eliminating blackouts that cripple the economy.

Let us accelerate the implementation of programmes to drive the adoption of clean technologies, such as solar. Germany and Spain have special prices, called 'feed-in tariffs' that have made solar and wind mainstream options. These are being contemplated in India's solar mission. They should be established quickly, with scale, and with a long time period. Long-term government-backed power purchase agreements will create the appropriate environment for financing, thereby enabling the private sector to develop innovative solutions.

India should lead in the negotiations before and during environment summit. The government has made the points, dearly and correctly, that India cannot accept a cap, and that the ultimate carbon abatement, per capita, must provide converge for the rich and poor nations. But we need to do more. We need to identify and commit to the policies that are in India's self-interest, and offer these as serious commitments in a global regime. We decide what we need to do so to prosper, then we commit to doing it in an international forum. It is a key sticking point that must be repaired to enable a global deal. And a successful global deal will be good for India in two ways: it will reduce global climate impacts that will ultimately disproportionately impact the poor, and it will unleash serious money from the rich countries for expanded clean energy deployment in India. The developed nations in general, have their own sticking points. They need to commit to serious reductions, and serious finance. India has no reason to back down from insisting on that. But we need to become leaders in progressing ahead with conservation, and the best way to do this is to take our self-interest seriously, then commit to it internationally.

According to a recent report published by an international think tank, if whole mankind were to live life the way Americans do, we'd need an additional four earths to support us. Americans and many others do live wastefully, as the report suggests, but convincing people to renounce their creature comforts is an unpopular task. This is where technology can help. Green tech can allow people to keep their lifestyles with only a few minor adjustments, while substantially reducing their ecological footprints encompassing carbon, water and many other substances we use in our daily lives or generate as by-products. Embracing green tech will involve a complete re-orientation of lifestyles and production systems, bringing about perhaps even more sweeping changes than those ushered in by the IT revolution. And it will require large-scale government as well as civil society initiatives, while the IT revolution took place largely on its own. As the US is also innovative in terms of spawning new technologies, it's a large part of the problem as well as the solution. In this context, the commitment of Barack Obama to cut the US emissions by 17 per cent of 2005 levels by 2020 is a step in the right'direction, although more would have helped.

The solutions are both big and small. Scientists in several nations are trying to develop new sources of electricity that do not rely on fossil fuels, and to harness renewable energy from various sources so that it may provide a viable alternative to coal and gas. Automobile manufacturers are developing electric cars, which produce far fewer pollutants than their petrol or diesel alternatives. Governments across the world need to incentivize their production and build the supporting infrastructure, such as charging stations. Cities of the future will have to be planned so they do not sprawl outwards but grow vertically, while the infrastructure for mass transport needs to be prioritized so as to discourage use of personal vehicles. The construction of green buildings that account for the climatic conditions where they are situated should be encouraged via tax benefits. The biggest challenge for clean technology is what Vinod Khosla, one of Silicon Valley's foremost venture capitalists, calls the Chindia test: the price at which China and India will adopt a technology without subsidies. Governments need to foster a regulatory climate that encourages companies to develop technology that passes that test not more than the US, which is, after all the world's largest polluter.

According to Gresham's Law, bad money drives out good. In debate on complex policy issues, ideas sometimes suffer the same fate as money. The debate on climate change offers a good example. Many specious ideas have come to occupy public policy space. These must be exposed and clarity restored.

Meaningful mitigation is not possible without China and India accepting mitigation obligations. The US Congress has adopted this position and many commentators based in Europe and the US embrace it. Two arguments are offered in its support. First, China and India are such large emitters that without their participation, mitigation effort will not succeed. Second, unless these countries accept emission caps, developed country carbon-intensive industries will simply migrate to them with no net reductions in emissions. The fallacy in the first argument is that India is a small emitter and not in the same league as China whereas the latter accounts for 21 per cent of global emissions, India's share is only 4 per cent. In per capita terms, India ranks a low 137th. The fallacy in the second argument is that empirical evidence contradicts the hypothesis that absent emission caps in China and India developed-country dirty industries would migrate to them. Even the US Environmental Protection Agency estimates such migration to have at best a tiny effect.

India risked being isolated in Copenhagen unless it agreed to accept mitigation obligations as per the US demands. This is the most treacherous assertion. As a preliminary matter, it was not clear why disagreement with the the US should automatically translate into isolation especially when there exist good justifications for India's position. The fact that more than two-thirds of the humanity is on the same side as India and that Europeans do not neçessarily share the US view should matter as well. China, whose current position is not drastically different from that of India, does not see itself as being isolated either. Therefore, this idea can appeal only to those who view India as a tiny Latin American country unable to assert against the US rather than a rising global power. A separate point is that sometimes isolation may serve the national interest better than acquiescence.

India did not create the global warming problem; therefore, it has no responsibility to help solve it. This is a popular argument with left wing commentators in India. It is based on the observation that India has contributed only two per cent of the existing stock of carbon in the environment. The problem with the argument is two fold. First, India is currently emitting proportionately more than in the past and its share is rising. Second, and more important, India cannot ignore global warming because the expected cost to it in terms of increased frequency and severity of extreme events such as heat waves, droughts, floods and cyclones is high. You do not refuse to treat a wound just because someone else inflicted it on you. True, accepting mitigation targets in the next two or three decades would not serve well the country's interests since it will undermine its fight against poverty. But once this objective is achieved, India must do what it can to combat global warming. Indeed, even in the interim, it must continue its efforts at reforestation, reduced indoor pollution and regulation of urban pollution, which are consistent with its immediate development goals.

Developed countries cannot be held responsible for the environmental damage caused by the emissions. The reason given is that at that time in the past the countries did not know that their actions would lead to global warming. Philosophically, the argument is flawed: just because those committing acts of cruelty against Dalits two centuries ago did not know they were harming the future generations of the latter does not mean no affirmative action is called for today! The practice of tort laws in the US also allows for retroactive compensation.

The Comprehensive Environmental Response, Compensation, and Liability Act of 1980, popularly known as the Superfund Act, imposed retroactive fines on the firms responsible for dumping toxic waste at several sites as far back as the 1920s. The revenues so collected were then used to clean up the sites.

India can cap its emissions without sacrificing its growth and poverty alleviation objectives. While not asserted explicitly, the undercurrents of this argument could be felt in the statements Hillary Clinton made during her visit to India. While urging India to embrace mitigation targets, she simultaneously stated that the US "will not do anything that would limit India's economic progress".

In reality, as distinguished economist Gunnar Eskeland of Norwegian School of Economics and Business

Administration points out, mitigation is a highly costly activity. This high cost is the principal reason why developed countries have done so litttle to date to mitigate. Eskeland argue that genuine progress in mitigation requires massive R&D investments in the development of green sources of energy and mitigation technologies. Even the talk of access to technology is not meaningful when the real problem is the absence rather than diffusion of such technology.

Given the lumpy and highly risky nature of R&D investments in this area, private sector has been hesitant. This is why the proposal by Professor Jagdish Bhagwati for the creation of a large fund through contributions by developed countries as compensation for past emissions assumes special importance. Contributing countries can use the proceeds from this fund to finance research on green sources of energy and mitigation technologies. Because rich country firms will be the beneficiaries of such financing, the creation of the fund is likely to be politically acceptable. At the same time, given that research will be publicly funded, its fruits could be shared by all, including developing countries.

Climate change and its imperatives across the globe have moved beyond the immediate compulsions of rising mercury levels on planet Earth. It is today a debate among nations on geopolitics, and the shift in economic balance from the developed countries to the emerging economies. The rhetoric by global leaders thus needs to be taken with a pinch of salt for it is not all about climate change concerns.

The changing axis of economic power to the east and emerging countries of Asia will perhaps take a while to sink in. Developing economies like India are just beginning to take little steps on the global stage and industry and entrepreneurship will have to go a long way. Millions of households in India still have to depend on firewood and kerosene to light up their homes even as scores of Indians die every year for want of basic health amenities.

The priority for such a nation is meeting basic needs, providing food, health and education rather than spending large portions of its GDP on importing technologies to cut emissions, scientists argue. India needs to do its bit, but on its own terms and at its own pace. Simply put: India ranks just one rank below the US—sixth in the world pecking order—in greenhouse gas emissions, yet its per head carbon emission is a mere tenth of that of a US citizen.

With China declaring a voluntary deduction in carbon intensity by 40–45 per cent by 2020, the pressure on reluctant players like the US to act and commit just got higher. The Chinese move to voluntarily reduce its carbon intensity days ahead of the summit in Denmark has large implications. One, it will be difficult for developed countries like the US and Obama's Congress to oppose commitments to reduce greenhouse gases. China and India have often been cited as examples of countries that are unwilling to address these global concerns. Second, China has made it clear that it would go ahead with reductions in carbon intensity only on its own terms as per the requirements of its economic needs. This will come as a major boost to India as it echoes New Delhi's stated position on carbon emissions.

Close on the heels of China, India has announced its decision to set a target of cutting down its carbon intensity by 20–25 per cent, domestically. This is achievable even with a GDP growth of 8–9 per cent with the application of right technologies and fiscal measures that encourage energy efficiency. The crucial differentiator in the stand taken by China and India is that of setting an individual target that is not bound by an international or external cap. More importantly, India has made it clear that it is not ready to subject itself to international verification. The targets set by the country will be in accordance to its resources and social and economic priorities. Scientists argue that while technology may be available to leapfrog some hurdles, one has to keep in mind the costs involved in adapting such technologies.

Indian policymakers and environment think tanks that have worked closely with the government in finalizing the blueprint and actionable points on this front believe that the guiding principle of the United Nations Framework

Convention on Climate Change (UNFCCC) of 'common but differentiated responsibilities' is the only way forward. Countries across the globe are stakeholders of the planet and it is in their interest to make the world a better place to live in. But the crucial question is about the stake held by each nation and the actions thereof.

The UNFCCC that was signed and approved by more than 192 countries lays out how industrialized countries contributed to the biggest chunk of human emissions in history. Scientists argue that both China and India, considered to be amongst the biggest growing carbon emitters in the world have for years together given the environmental space to the developed countries, such as the US or in Europe. If, there were a cap for every country in accordance with its historical performance, industrialised economies may have already used up their respective portions of greenhouse gas emissions.

Lifestyles in these developed countries still remain largely unchanged as the wealthy continue to live in large villas, drive around in gas-guzzling SUVs and use high energy-consuming equipment for daily household chores. India may be the world's sixth-biggest greenhouse gas producer, but it has a per head emission of just two tons of carbon dioxide—66th in the world—whereas the US is the fifth in the world with a per head emission of 20 tons of carbon dioxide equivalent. This is precisely 10 times that of India, which is expected to have the same caps on emissions as developed countries like the US. This is totally against the principle of 'differentiated responsibility'. The solar mission, national water mission, sustainable habitat mission and urban transport mission are among the programmes that the government and India Inc are working on to meet some of its carbon-intensity reduction targets.

World fish stocks risk collapse

Nowadays, with massive trawlers dragging 60 km nets scooping up a dozen jumbo jets worth of fish in one go, that adage is looking rather shaky. Not only is overfishing the single greatest threat to the ecosystems of our oceans, but as fish are caught much faster than they can reproduce, it is driving traditional fisherman out of business. They can no longer rely on their skills to feed themselves for a lifetime. Such is the scale of the problem that sometime ago Cheers star Ted Danson weighed in to slam subsidies that promote unsustainable fishing practices.

As many as 20 million tons of fish are caught every year by bottom trawling. It's a non-selective method that takes no prisoners. Powerful boats trudge metal weighted nets across the ocean floor, scooping up turtles, sharks, dolphins, endangered species and young fish. "The holes in the mechanized nets are very, very small and so fish don't get a chance to breed", says a Machimar Kuti Samhiti representative. "There are no fish left for traditional fishermen". According to a 2004 study by the United Nations Environment Programme, almost a quarter of the fish pulled out from the sea never even find their way to the market. Meanwhile the oceans, once considered an inexhaustible resource, are running out of fish. "The fish don't stand a chance", says the World Wildlife Fund.

If we act now to bring overfishing under control by using restrictive gear, closing areas to fleets and limiting the total allowable catch, there is a hope. A study published this year in the journal Science found that in a few select regions such as Iceland and Australia, careful management of marine ecosystems has allowed fish stocks to recover. "Our oceans are not a lost cause", says Boris Worm, a marine biologist at Dalhousie University and a co-author of the report. However, he cautions that the trend, although far from irreversible, is far from being reversed. "Across all regions we are still seeing a troubling trend of increasing stock collapse", he says.

Efforts to deal with the problem are continually hampered by ineffectual regulation at an international level. According to the 1982 UN Convention on the Law of the Sea, every nation maintains sole fishing rights within its 'exclusive economic zone'. The high seas, however, are known as the common heritage of mankind, a heart-warming term evoking images of international co-operation that in reality has entirely the opposite effect. In many areas, illegal and unregulated fishing is on the rise weakening national and regional efforts towards sustainability. "Regional fisheries management organizations, the cornerstones of international fisheries governance, are struggling to fulfill their mandates despite concerted efforts to improve their performance", the UN Food and Agriculture Organization has found. The problem arises in part from "a lack of political will to implement decisions in a timely manner". It is, after all, hard to light a candle in the wind.

An international consensus has emerged on the need to combat the environmental crime of illegal, unregulated and unreported fishing by blocking illegal stocks from entering international trade, thus removing the financial incentive. However, eliminating illegal fishing whilst a necessary first step, is not enough to avert the on coming crisis.

When the criminal element has been removed, what remain to be challenged is that legal methods will continue to devastate the oceans. As such, it is imperative that we eliminate bottom trawling by catch and discards. In Maharashtra, a ban on fishing is in place from June 1 to August 15. "This should be increased to 90 days nationwide to allow fish stocks to replenish", says the president of the National Fishermen's Forum. At the same time, marine sanctuaries must be established in which fishing is prohibited. "Cat fish, Bombay duck and pomfret are now rare, and hammerhead sharks are diminishing", he says.

Whilst governments around the world have responded to the pressing need to preserve endangered species and habitats on land, existing marine parks account for less than one per cent of the world's oceans. Increasing this percentage is the only way to ensure breeding grounds for fish are maintained and to safeguard the livelihoods of fishermen.

Of course, it is not simply a problem of production. It is one of consumption that can be alleviated only by reducing demand as eating less fish, avoiding species like cod and tuna, or altogether fish from our diets removing. Can we end the reliance on destructive methods of mass fishing?

Rise in Night Temperature

In an ominous sign of climate change hitting home, India has seen accelerated warming in the past few decades and the temperature-rise pattern is now increasingly in line with global warming trends. The most up to date study of temperatures in India, from 1901 to 2007, has found that while it's getting warmer across regions and seasons, night temperatures have been rising significantly.

According to the study, the rise in night temperatures by 0.2 degrees Celsius per decade since 1970 could have potentially adverse impact on yields of cereal crops like rice. The paper also finds that warming has been the highest in post-monsoon and winter months (October to February).

"Until the late 1980s, the minimum (or night) temperatures were trendless in India. India was an odd dot in the global map as most regions worldwide were seeing a rise in night temperatures in sync with growing levels of greenhouse gases. Our analysis shows the global trend has caught up with India", said K Krishna Kumar, senior scientist and programme manager at IITM, Pune.

Regional factors seem to be getting overridden by warming caused by greenhouse gases, For instance, the cooling trend in much of north India seen in the 1950s and 60s has been reversed, possibly because the effect of aerosols in the air can no longer compensate for greenhouse gas warming.

A study on temperatures has found evidence of accelerated warming in India. The study—Surface air temperature variability over India during 1901-2007 and its link with ENSO – by IITM scientists DR Kothawale and AA Munot besides Kumar is a comprehensive analysis of temperature data gathered from 388 weather stations in the country and has been accepted for publication in the international *Climate Research Journal.*

"The rising night temperatures are a major cause of worry" said Jagdish K Ladha, principal scientist in the India chapter of International Rice Research Institute, "Minimum temperatures have a link with rice fertility. At higher than normal night temperatures, rice grains aren't properly filled up, leading to a drop in yield".

During 1901-2007, the all India mean, maximum and minimum annual temperatures rose at the rate of 0.51, 0.71 and 0.27 degrees Celsius per 100 years respectively.

However, post 1970, the rise has been sharper with mean and minimum temperatures both increasing at the rate of 0.2 degree per decade, faster than the maximum temperature which rose by 0.17 degree.

Among regions, the hardest hit seem to be the western Himalayas encompassing portions of Jammu & Kashmir, Himachal Pradesh and Uttarakhand. Here the mean temperature rise in the last century was 0.86 degree while, more recently, temperatures have been going up by as much as 0.46 degree per decade. The rapid warming of the region would have obvious fallouts on glacier melts.

On a seasonal scale, winter and post-monsoon temperatures show significant warming trends in recent decades though temperatures in other months have also been rising more modestly.

The Central Pollution Control Board (CPCB) that monitors air pollution levels in Delhi says that between 2009 and 2010, the levels of SPM and RSPM I (respirable SPM) have risen significantly. A fall was seen in February but that, officials say, could be due to a change in weather which brought some rain that month. Besides, the fall has not been uniform across the city; four of the seven stations monitored recorded increase.

"Dust has become a huge problem for Delhi and we do not see any respite unless a construction work is over. The levels of the two pollutants (SPM and RSPM) should be peaking right now as the there is some construction taking place almost in each part of the city", said SD Makhijani, director, CPCB.

Anumita Roychowdhury, director of the Right to Clean Air programme of the Centre for Science and Environment, visited Beijing before the Olympic Games to study how the Chinese were managing their problems of air pollution. She said that the Chinese capital had much the same problems as Delhi but the government there had a systematic management programme in place to deal with the pollution, something that Delhi lacked.

"Beijing had a plan for each of its sectors, from industries to transport to water. They had sprinklers at construction sites (which used to be covered), trucks going into construction areas would be washed so that no dust would travel on. During the Olympic Games, they had millions of cars off the road. Delhi seems to have no such plan and I wonder if they will be able to meet the air pollution norms especially since the norms have been tightened", she said.

Experts also point out that greening the city should be a priority for the government, since trees would provide some relief from the heat and dust. Ravi Agarwal, director of Toxics Link, says that the problem is only going to get more acute in summer. "Places where there are trees could be slightly better but then most of the city is dug up. Even the trees are coated with dust and that will settle only during the monsoon", he said.

Until then, however, residents will continue to suffer. Doctors say the number of patients with allergic rhinitis and pharyngitis, throat and nasal problems, are on the rise. "Problems of acute wheezing and allergic conjunctivitis are also being reported much more frequently these days. Pollen and dust are major contributors to chronic respiratory problems and the city is quite dusty right now", said Dr. Sandeep Budhiraja, HoD (Internal Medicine), Max Hospital.

River

The importance of the river cannot be overstated in the history of the country, or the development of the nation.

The state of India's main rivers reflects the callousness and ineptitude with which we approach the issue of managing our natural resources. Thanks to a lack of long-term river conservation or water management policies; several rivers across the country have either run dry or resemble rivulets. And those which still flow fine are wracked by pollution, and often resemble giant drains. Two of India's most important rivers—Ganga and Yamuna—are the filthiest. Decades long efforts by the government to breathe life into them through massive clean-up programmes have come to naught. Consider this: over Rs. 1,000 crore have been pumped into the Ganga Action Plan I and II between 1985 and 2000, but India's holiest river is still polluted.

Similarly, hundreds of crores have been spent on the Yamuna Action Plan, but there's little to show for the expenditure. It's literally money being sent down the drain. A rough estimate by the Planning Commission indicates that the National River Conservation Plan projects all over India would cost up to Rs. 33,000 crore, with almost Rs. 7,000 crore needed to fix Ganga's problems alone. Meanwhile, the government is now seeking an additional Rs. 833 crore from Japan International Cooperation Agency—in partnership with WHO it implements the Yamuna Action Plan—to fund the third phase of the project. But merely throwing more money is not going to solve the crisis.

A combination of factors has led to the extensive pollution of Ganga and Yamuna. Industrial effluents and sewage contribute the most to their pollution as well as certain practices people follow in the name of religion, like throwing holy offerings that are often packaged in non-degradable plastics. Therefore, any successful attempt to clean up these rivers mandates that citizens partner the government or even take the lead. It goes without saying that the government should formulate strict pollution norms for industries that are situated on river banks and enforce them, as well as boost sewage treatment capacities along the course of these rivers. On our part, we would do well to stop treating our rivers and other water resources as garbage dumps. There are examples from around the world where active public-private partnerships have brought dying rivers back to life. The Thames project in England is a good example where the public was made a stakeholder in the river's sustenance.

Ganga, the Holy River

Ganga, one of the holiest rivers of India is 2510 km long and sustains the lives of about 400 million people, either along its banks or in the river basin area; the populous river basin of the world as it journeys eastward into Bangladesh and empties itself into the sea in the Bay of Bengal. For those who look upon Ganga as goddess, she is more than just a river: she is a life giver, sustainer and purifier as well as the one whose water arms the dead—entrusted as ashes or half burnt bodies. Despite Ganga being so central to the lives of the millions of people and despite the river being worshipped as goddess, the river is in a sorry state of affairs because of heavy pollution. We believe our gods dwell in the mighty Himalayas, now home to one of the most fragile ecosystems threatened by climate change and global warming. Approximately 80 millions liters of sewage reportedly flows into the river from towns that are on its bank. Add to this, disposal of half burnt human bodies, mass bathing rituals and ritual pujas that involve making offerings to the river. We need to rethink our rituals and try to improve over them so that further pollution of the Holy River is stopped.

The fragile nature of the environment and ecology of the Himalayas and the Ganga in particular is causing immense concern among not just policymakers and research scientists, the fraternity of spiritual leaders and their followers too are cottoning on to the fact that the Holy River might not always remain so holy if rescue operations are not pressed into service. Swami Agnivesh says, "Ganga is the symbol of our environment, we need to save it". And he is trying to call a religious parliament over it. The body is made of five elements including earth, air, and water. Keeping them pollution free is important. Water has a special place in most religious rituals. If Hindus consider their rivers sacred, Christians need water for Baptism. Dominic Emmanuel, an environmentalist says, "All religions give importance to water and nature has provided it to us free. Today, some companies are selling water for a price. There might come a time when people will start selling bottled air. We have to stop polluting the environment. While some gurus lay emphasis on creating awareness, others stress on the need for introspection and changing development paradigms. We will have to change our lifestyles from consumerism and follow Vedic philosophy. Dalai Lama says, "The economy is important and spirituality is also equally important. Money can provide physical comfort, but it can't buy happiness or peace of mind. Our life is so complex that we need to take care of our body and our emotions and for this ecology is important". The Uttarakhand Government has launched the Sparsh Ganga Project; the programme appears to be action oriented. The Andrew Cohen's Clean Himalaya Project is a comprehensive waste management programme. The work of this project has been widely appreciated and rewarded.

Saving the river is to save ourselves. This is the trend theme of ongoing efforts today to rescue Ganga from overzealous devotees as well as mindless dumpers of toxic waste materials and effluents.

Chapter - 1

Global Warming and Ozone Depletion

The Earth's atmosphere is made up of different layers. The layer closest to the surface is called the troposphere which extends from the Earth's surface up to about 10 kilometers. The ozone layer is located above the troposphere in the stratosphere (10 km to about 50 km high). Stratospheric ozone is Earth's natural protection for all life forms, shielding our planet from harmful ultraviolet-B (UV-B) radiation. UV-B radiation is harmful to humans, animals, and plant life. The ozone layer is being destroyed by certain industrial chemicals including ozone depleting refrigerants, halons, and methyl bromide, a deadly pesticide used on crops.

Ozone depletion describes two distinct, but related observations: a slow, steady decline of about four per cent per decade in the total volume of ozone in Earth's stratosphere (the ozone layer) since the late 1970s, and a much larger, but seasonal, decrease in stratospheric ozone over Earth's polar regions during the same period. The latter phenomenon is commonly referred to as the ozone hole. In addition to this well-known stratospheric ozone depletion, there are also tropospheric ozone depletion events, which occur near the surface in Polar Regions during spring.

Ozone depletion damage gets much worse when the stratosphere is very cold. This has been the case in the past two years, causing extensive ozone depletion. This past winter, ozone depletion reached the most severe levels ever recorded over the Northern Hemisphere. Western United States ozone levels also continue to drop 3-4 per cent per decade. Even if all of our efforts to stop harmful emissions are successful, the ozone layer is not expected to begin recovery until around 2020 at the earliest.

Montreal Protocol

Under the auspices of the United Nations Environment Programme (UNEP), nations have co-operatively taken action to stop ozone depletion with "The Montreal Protocol on Substances that Deplete the Ozone Layer," signed in 1987.

The United Nations has developed a framework the "Kyoto Protocol on Climate Change," signed in 1997 convention on global warming and climate change. The adoption of the Kyoto protocol strengthens the framework with new policies and measures including quantified limitation and reduction objectives to greenhouse gas emissions not covered by the Montreal Protocol.

Scientists' are concerned that continued global warming will accelerate ozone destruction and increase stratospheric ozone depletion. Ozone depletion gets worse when the stratosphere (where the ozone layer is), becomes colder. Because global warming traps heat in the troposphere, less heat reaches the stratosphere which will make it colder. Greenhouse gases act like a blanket for the troposphere and make the stratosphere colder. In other words, global warming can make ozone depletion much worse right when it is supposed to begin its recovery during the next century.

The detailed mechanism by which the polar ozone holes form is different from that for the mid-latitude thinning, but the most important process in both trends is catalytic destruction of ozone by atomic chlorine and bromine. The main source of these halogen atoms in the stratosphere is photodissociation of chlorofluorocarbon (CFC) compounds, commonly called freons, and of bromofluorocarbon compounds known as halons. These compounds are transported into the stratosphere after being emitted at the surface. Both ozone depletion mechanisms strengthened as emissions of CFCs and halons have increased.

CFCs and other contributory substances are commonly referred to as ozone-depleting substances (ODS). Since the ozone layer prevents most harmful UVB wavelengths (270–315 nm) of ultraviolet light (UV light) from passing through the Earth's atmosphere, observed and projected decreases in ozone have generated worldwide concern leading to adoption of Montreal Protocol that bans the production of CFCs and halons as well as related ozone depleting chemicals such as carbon tetrachloride and trichloroethane. It is suspected that a variety of biological consequences such as increase in skin cancer, cataract, damage to plants, and reduction of plankton populations in the ocean's photic zone may result from the increased UV exposure due to ozone depletion.

Ozone cycle

Three forms (or allotropes) of oxygen are involved in the ozone-oxygen cycle: oxygen atoms (O or atomic oxygen), oxygen gas (O_2 or diatomic oxygen), and ozone gas (O_3 or triatomic oxygen). Ozone is formed in the stratosphere when oxygen molecules photodissociate after absorbing an ultraviolet photon whose wavelength is shorter than 240 nm. This produces two oxygen atoms. The atomic oxygen then combines with O_2 to create O_3. Ozone molecules absorb UV light between 310 and 200 nm, following which ozone splits into a molecule of O_2 and an oxygen atom. The oxygen atom then joins up with an oxygen molecule to regenerate ozone. This is a continuing process which terminates when an oxygen atom recombines with an ozone molecule to make two O_2 molecules: $O + O_3 \rightarrow 2\,O_2$. The overall amount of ozone in the stratosphere is determined by a balance between photochemical production and recombination.

Ozone can be destroyed by a number of free radical catalysts, the most important of which are the hydroxyl radical (OH•), the nitric oxide radical (NO), atomic chlorine (Cl) and bromine (Br). All of these have both natural and manmade sources; at the present time, most of the OH and NO in the stratosphere is of natural origin, but human activity has dramatically increased the levels of chlorine and bromine. These elements are found in certain stable organic compounds, especially chlorofluorocarbons (CFCs), which may find their way to the stratosphere without being destroyed in the troposphere due to their low reactivity. Once in the stratosphere, the Cl and Br atoms are liberated from the parent compounds by the action of ultraviolet light, e.g. 'h' is Planck's constant, 'v' is frequency of electromagnetic radiation.

$$CFCl_3 + hv \rightarrow CFCl_2 + Cl$$

The Cl and Br atoms can then destroy ozone molecules through a variety of catalytic cycles. In the simplest example of such a cycle,[4] a chlorine atom reacts with an ozone molecule, taking an oxygen atom with it (forming ClO) and leaving a normal oxygen molecule. The chlorine monoxide (i.e., the ClO) can react with a second molecule of ozone (i.e., O_3) to yield another chlorine atom and two molecules of oxygen. The chemical formulae (shorthand) for these gas-phase reactions are:

$$Cl + O_3 \rightarrow ClO + O_2$$

$$ClO + O_3 \rightarrow Cl + 2\,O_2$$

The overall effect is a decrease in the amount of ozone. More complicated mechanisms have been discovered that lead to ozone destruction in the lower stratosphere as well.

A single chlorine atom would keep on destroying ozone (thus a catalyst) for up to two years (the time scale for transport back down to the troposphere) were it not for reactions that remove them from this cycle by forming reservoir species such as hydrogen chloride (HCl) and chlorine nitrate ($ClONO_2$). On a per atom basis, bromine is even more efficient than chlorine at destroying ozone, but there is less bromine in the atmosphere at present. As a result, both chlorine and bromine contribute significantly to the overall ozone depletion. Laboratory studies have shown that fluorine and iodine atoms participate in analogous catalytic cycles. However, in the Earth's stratosphere, fluorine atoms react rapidly with water and methane to form strongly bound HF, while organic molecules which contain iodine react so rapidly in the lower atmosphere that they do not reach the stratosphere in significant quantities. Furthermore, a single chlorine atom is able to react with 100,000 ozone molecules. This fact plus the amount of chlorine released into the atmosphere by chlorofluorocarbons (CFCs) yearly demonstrates how dangerous CFCs are to the environment.

The most pronounced decrease in ozone has been in the lower stratosphere. However, the ozone hole is usually measured not in terms of ozone concentrations at these levels (which are typically of a few parts per million) but by reduction in the total column ozone, above a point on the Earth's surface, which is normally expressed in Dobson units, abbreviated as "DU". Marked decreases in column ozone in the Antarctic spring and early summer compared to the early 1970s and before have been observed using instruments such as the Total Ozone Mapping Spectrometer (TOMS).

Reductions up to 70 per cent in the ozone column observed in the austral (southern hemispheric) spring over Antarctica and first reported in 1985 (Farman et al. 1985) are continuing. Through the 1990s, total column ozone in September and October have continued to be 40–50 per cent lower than pre-ozone hole values. In the Arctic, the amount lost varies every year to a greater extent year-to-year than in the Antarctic. The greatest declines, up to 30 per cent, are in the winter and spring, when the stratosphere is colder.

Reactions that take place on polar stratospheric clouds (PSCs) play an important role in enhancing ozone depletion. PSCs form more readily in the extreme cold of Antarctic stratosphere. This is why ozone holes first formed are deeper, over Antarctica.

In middle latitudes it is preferable to speak of ozone depletion rather than holes. Declines are about 3 per cent below pre-1980 values for 35–60°N and about 6 per cent for 35–60°S. In the tropics, there are no significant trends.

Ozone depletion also explains much of the observed reduction in stratospheric and upper tropospheric temperatures. The source of the warmth of the stratosphere is the absorption of UV radiation by ozone; hence reduced ozone leads to cooling.

CFCs in the atmosphere

Chlorofluorocarbons (CFCs) were invented by Thomas Midgley Jr. in the 1920s. They were used in air conditioning/ cooling units, as aerosol spray propellants prior to the 1980s, and in the cleaning processes of delicate electronic equipment. They also occur as by-products of some chemical processes. No significant natural sources have ever been identified for these compounds – their presence in the atmosphere is also due to various manufacture units set by man. As mentioned in the ozone cycle overview above, when such ozone-depleting chemicals reach the stratosphere, they are dissociated by ultraviolet light to release chlorine atoms. The chlorine atoms act as a catalyst, and each can break down tens of thousands of ozone molecules before being removed from the stratosphere. Given the longevity of CFC molecules, recovery times are measured in decades. It is calculated that a CFC molecule takes an average of 15 years to go from the ground level up to the upper atmosphere, and it can stay there for about a century, destroying up to one hundred thousand ozone molecules during that time.

Verification of observations

Scientists have been increasingly able to attribute the observed ozone depletion to the increase of man-made (anthropogenic) halogen compounds from CFCs by the use of complex chemistry transport models and their validation against observational data (e.g., SLIMCAT, CLaMS). These models work by combining satellite measurements of chemical concentrations and meteorological fields with chemical reaction rate constants obtained in lab experiments. They are able to identify not only the key chemical reactions but also the transport processes which bring CFC photolysis products into contact with ozone.

The ozone hole

The Antarctic ozone hole is an area of the Antarctic stratosphere in which the recent ozone levels have dropped to a low of 33 per cent of their pre-1975 values. The ozone hole occurs during the Antarctic spring, from September to early December, as strong westerly winds blow around the continent and create an atmospheric container. Within this polar vortex, over 50 per cent of the lower stratospheric ozone is destroyed during the Antarctic spring.

The primary cause of ozone depletion is the presence of chlorine-containing source gases (primarily CFCs and related halocarbons). In the presence of UV light, these gases dissociate, releasing chlorine atoms, which then go on to catalyze ozone destruction. The Cl-catalyzed ozone depletion can take place in the gas phase, but it is dramatically enhanced in the presence of polar stratospheric clouds (PSCs).

These polar stratospheric clouds (PSCs) form during winter in the extreme cold. Polar winters span for three months without sunlight. The lack of sunlight contributes to a decrease in temperature and the polar vortex traps and chills air. Temperatures hover around or below minus 80 °C. These low temperatures form cloud particles. There are three types of PSC clouds; nitric acid trihydrate clouds, slowly cooling water-ice clouds, and rapid cooling water-ice (nacerous) clouds that provide surfaces for chemical reactions that lead to ozone destruction.

The photochemical processes involved are complex. The key point observation is that ordinarily most of the chlorine in the stratosphere resides in stable "reservoir" compounds, primarily hydrochloric acid (HCl) and chlorine nitrate ($ClONO_2$). During the Antarctic winter and spring, however, reactions on the surface of the polar stratospheric cloud particles convert these "reservoir" compounds into reactive free radicals (Cl and ClO). The clouds can also remove NO_2 from the atmosphere by converting it to nitric acid, which prevents the newly formed ClO from being converted back into $ClONO_2$.

The role of sunlight in ozone depletion is the reason why the Antarctic ozone depletion is greatest during spring. During winter, even though PSCs are at their most abundant, there is no light over the pole to drive the chemical reactions. During the spring when the sun comes out, it provides energy to cause photochemical reactions, and melt the polar stratospheric clouds, thereby releasing the trapped compounds. Rising temperatures at the end of spring around mid-December break up the vortex. As warm, ozone-rich air blows in from lower latitudes, the PSCs are destroyed, the ozone depletion process shuts down, and the ozone hole closes.

Most of the ozone that is destroyed is in the lower stratosphere, in contrast to the much smaller ozone depletion through homogeneous gas phase reactions, which occurs primarily in the upper stratosphere.

While the effect of the Antarctic ozone hole in decreasing the global ozone is relatively small, estimated at about 4 per cent per decade, the hole has generated a great deal of interest because of the reasons stated below:

- The decrease in the ozone layer was predicted in the early 1980s to be roughly seven per cent over a 60 year period.

- The sudden recognition in 1985 that there was a substantial "hole" was widely reported in the press. The especially rapid ozone depletion in Antarctica had previously been dismissed as a measurement error.
- Many were worried that ozone holes might start to appear over other areas of the globe but to date the only other large-scale depletion is a smaller ozone "dimple" observed during the Arctic spring over the North Pole. Ozone at middle latitudes has declined, but by a much smaller extent (about 4–5 per cent.)
- If the conditions became more severe (cooler stratospheric temperatures, more stratospheric clouds, more active chlorine), the global ozone may decrease at a much greater pace. Standard global warming theory predicts that the stratosphere will cool.
- When the Antarctic ozone hole breaks up, the ozone-depleted air drifts out into nearby areas. Decreases up to 10 per cent in the ozone level have been reported in New Zealand in the month following the break-up of the Antarctic ozone hole.

Effects of Ozone Depletion and Global Warming

UV-B radiation causes skin cancer, cataract and a weakend immunity in both animals and humans. UV-B also damages plants including hardwood forests, and phytoplankton (an alga which is the building block of the oceanic food chain).

Since the ozone layer absorbs UVB ultraviolet light from the Sun, ozone layer depletion is expected to increase surface UVB levels, which could lead to damage, including increases in skin cancer. This was the reason for the Montreal Protocol. Although decreases in stratospheric ozone are well-linked to CFCs and there are good theoretical reasons to believe that decreases in ozone will lead to increases in surface UVB, however, there is no observable evidence linking ozone depletion to higher incidences of human skin cancer. This is partly because UVA is linked with some forms of skin cancer; UVA is not absorbed by ozone, and it is almost impossible to control statistics for lifestyle changes in the populace.

Ozone, not so significant a constituent in the Earth's atmosphere, is responsible for most of the absorption of UVB radiation. The amount of UVB radiation that penetrates through the ozone layer decreases exponentially with the slant-path thickness/density of the layer. Correspondingly, a decrease in atmospheric ozone is expected to give rise to significantly increased levels of UVB near the surface.

Increases in surface UVB due to the ozone hole can be partially inferred by radiative transfer model calculations, but cannot be calculated from direct measurements because of the lack of reliable historical (pre-ozone-hole) surface UV data, although more recent surface UV observation measurement programmes do exist, at Lauder, New Zealand.

Because it is this same UV radiation that creates ozone in the ozone layer from O_2 (regular oxygen) in the first place, a reduction in stratospheric ozone would actually tend to increase photochemical production of ozone at lower levels (in the troposphere) although the overall observed trends in total column ozone still show a decrease, largely because ozone produced at the lower levels has a naturally shorter photochemical lifetime, so it is destroyed before the concentrations could reach a level which would compensate for the ozone reduction higher up.

The main public concern regarding the ozone hole has been the effects of increased surface UV and microwave radiation on human health. Typically so far, ozone depletion in most locations has been a few per cent and, as noted above, no direct evidence of health damage is available in most latitudes. Were the high levels of depletion seen in the ozone hole ever to be common across the globe, the effects could be substantially more drastic. As the ozone hole over Antarctica has in some instances grown so large as to reach southern parts of Australia, New Zealand, Chile, Argentina, and South Africa, environmentalists have been concerned that the increase in surface UV could be significant.

UVB (the higher energy UV radiation absorbed by ozone) is generally accepted to be a contributory factor to skin cancer. In addition, increased surface UV leads to increased tropospheric ozone, which is a health risk to humans.

1. *Basal and Squamous Cell Carcinomas* – The most common forms of skin cancer in humans, basal and squamous cell carcinomas, have been linked strongly to UVB exposure. The mechanism by which UVB induces these cancers is well understood—absorption of UVB radiation causes the pyrimidine bases in the DNA molecule to form dimers, resulting in transcription errors when the DNA replicates. These cancers are relatively mild and rarely fatal, although the treatment of squamous cell carcinoma sometimes requires extensive reconstructive surgery. By combining epidemiological data with results of animal studies, scientists have estimated that a one per cent decrease in stratospheric ozone would increase the incidence of these cancers by two per cent.

2. *Malignant Melanoma* – Malignant Melanoma—another form of skin cancer—is much less common but far more dangerous, being lethal in about 15–20 per cent of the cases diagnosed. The relationship between malignant melanoma and ultraviolet exposure is yet not well understood, but it appears that both UVB and UVA are involved. Experiments on fish suggest that 90–95 per cent of malignant melanomas may be due to UVA and visible radiation whereas experiments on opossums suggest a larger role for UVB. Because of this uncertainty, it is difficult to estimate the impact of ozone depletion on Melanoma. One study showed that a 10 per cent increase in UVB radiation was associated with a 19 per cent increase in Melanoma for men and 16 per cent for women. A study of people in Punta Arenas, at the southern tip of Chile, showed a 56 per cent increase in Melanoma and a 46 per cent increase in nonmelanoma skin cancer over a period of seven years along with decreased ozone and increased UVB levels.

3. *Cortical Cataract* – Studies suggest a nexus between ocular cortical cataract and UV-B exposure, using crude

approximations of exposure and various cataract assessment techniques. A detailed assessment of ocular exposure to UV-B was made in a study on Chesapeake Bay Watermen, where increases in average annual ocular exposure were associated with increasing risk of cortical opacity. In this highly exposed group of predominantly white males, the evidence linking cortical opacities to sunlight exposure was the strongest upto date. However, subsequent data from a population-based study in Beaver Dam, WI suggested the risk may be confined to men. In the Beaver Dam study, the exposures among women were lower than exposures among men, and no association was seen. Moreover, there were no data linking sunlight exposure to risk of cataract in African-Americans although other eye diseases have different prevalence among different racial groups, and cortical opacity appears to be higher in African- Americans compared with whites.

4. *Increased Tropospheric Ozone* – Increased surface UV leads to increased tropospheric ozone. Ground-level ozone is generally recognized to be a health risk, as ozone is toxic due to its strong oxidant properties. At this time, ozone at ground level is produced mainly by the action of UV radiation on combustion gases from vehicle exhausts.

November 2010 report by scientists at the Institute of Zoology in London found that whales off the coast at California have shown a sharp rise in sun damage, and these scientists fear that the thinning ozone layer is culpable. .

The study photographed and took skin biopsies from over 150 whales in the Gulf of California and found "widespread evidence of epidermal damage commonly associated with acute and severe sunburn," having cells which form when the DNA is damaged by UV radiation. The findings suggest "rising UV levels as a result of ozone depletion deserve blame for the observed skin damage, in the same way that human skin cancer rates have been on the increase in recent decades".

An increase of UV radiation would be expected to affect crops. A number of economically important species of plants, such as rice, depend on cyanobacteria residing on their roots for the retention of nitrogen. Cyanobacteria are sensitive to UV light and they would be affected by its increase.

Policy

The full extent of the damage that CFCs have caused to the ozone layer is not known and will not be known for decades; however, marked decreases in column ozone have already been observed (as explained before).

After a 1976 report by the United States National Academy of Sciences concluded that credible scientific evidence supported the ozone depletion hypothesis, a few countries, including the United States, Canada, Sweden, Denmark, and Norway, moved to eliminate the use of CFCs in aerosol spray cans. At the time this was widely regarded as a first step towards a more comprehensive regulation policy, but progress in this direction slowed in subsequent years, due to a combination of political factors (continued resistance from the halocarbon industry and a general change in attitude towards environmental regulation during the first two years of the Reagan administration) and scientific developments (subsequent National Academy assessments which indicated that the first estimates of the magnitude of ozone depletion had been overly large). The United States banned the use of CFCs in aerosol cans in 1978. The European Community rejected proposals to ban CFCs in aerosol sprays, and in the US, CFCs continued to be used as refrigerants and for cleaning circuit boards. Worldwide CFC production fell sharply after the US aerosol ban, but by 1986 had returned nearly to its 1976 level. In 1993, DuPont shut down its CFC facility.

The US Government's attitude began to change again in 1983, when William Ruckelshaus replaced Anne M. Burford as Administrator of the United States Environmental Protection Agency. Under Ruckelshaus and his successor, Lee Thomas, the EPA pushed for an international approach to halocarbon regulations. In 1985, twenty nations, including most of the major CFC producers, signed the Vienna Convention for the Protection of the Ozone Layer which established a framework for negotiating international regulations on ozone-depleting substances. That same year, the discovery of the Antarctic ozone hole was announced, causing a revival in public attention to the issue. In 1987, representatives from 43 nations signed the Montreal Protocol. Meanwhile, the halocarbon industry shifted its position and started supporting a protocol to limit CFC production. The reasons for this were in part explained by Dr. Mostafa Tolba, former head of the UN Environment Programme, who was quoted in the 30 June 1990 edition of *The New Scientist*, "...the chemical industry supported the Montreal Protocol in 1987 because it set up a worldwide schedule for phasing out CFCs, which [were] no longer protected by patents. This provided companies with an equal opportunity to market new, more profitable compounds."

At Montreal, the participants agreed to freeze production of CFCs at 1986 levels and to reduce production by 50 per cent by 1999. After a series of scientific expeditions to the Antarctic produced convincing evidence that the ozone hole was indeed caused by chlorine and bromine from manmade organohalogens, the Montreal Protocol was strengthened at a 1990 meeting in London. The participants agreed to phase out CFCs and halons entirely—aside from a very small amount marked for certain "essential" uses, such as asthma inhalers— by 2000 in non-Article five countries and by 2010 in Article 5 less developed signatories. At a 1992 meeting in Copenhagen, the phase-out date was deferred to 1996. At the same meeting, methyl bromide (CH3Br), a fumigant used primarily in agricultural production was added to the list of controlled substances. It should be noted that for all substances controlled under the Protocol, phase-out schedules were delayed for less developed ('Article 5(1)') countries, and phase-out in these countries was supported by transfers of expertise, technology, and money from non-Article 5(1) signatories to the Protocol. Additionally, exemptions from the agreed schedules could be applied for (under the) Essential Use Exemption (EUE) process for substances other than methyl bromide and under the Critical Use Exemption (CUE) process for methyl bromide. See Gareau and DeCanio and Norman for more detail on the exemption processes.

To some extent, CFCs have been replaced by the less damaging hydrochlorofluoro carbons (HCFCs), although concerns remain regarding HCFCs also. In some applications, hydrofluorocarbons (HFCs) have been used to replace CFCs. HFCs, which contain no chlorine or bromine, do not contribute at all to ozone depletion although they are potent greenhouse gases. The best known of these compounds is probably HFC-134a (R-134a), which in the United States has largely replaced CFC-12 (R-12) in automobile air conditioners. In laboratory analysis (a former "essential" use) the ozone depleting substances can be replaced with various other solvents.

Ozone Diplomacy, by Richard Benedick (Harvard University Press, 1991) gives a detailed account of the negotiation process that led to the Montreal Protocol. Pielke and Betsill provide an extensive review of early US government responses to the emerging science of ozone depletion by CFCs.

More recently, policy experts have advocated for efforts to link ozone protection efforts to climate protection efforts. Many ODS are also greenhouse gasses, some significantly more powerful agents of radiative forcing than carbon dioxide over the short and medium term. Policy decisions in one arena affect the costs and effectiveness of environmental improvements in the other.

Since the adoption and strengthening of the Montreal Protocol has led to reductions in the emissions of CFCs, atmospheric concentrations of the most significant compounds have been declining. These substances are being gradually removed from the atmosphere—since peaking in 1994, the Effective Equivalent Chlorine (EECl) level in the atmosphere had dropped about 10 per cent by 2008. It is estimated that by 2015, the Antarctic ozone hole will have reduced by 1 million km^2 out of 25 (Newman et al., 2004); complete recovery of the Antarctic ozone layer is not expected to occur until the year 2050 or later. Work has suggested that a detectable (and statistically significant) recovery will not occur until around 2024, with ozone levels recovering to 1980 levels by around 2068. The decrease in ozone-depleting chemicals has also been significantly affected by a decrease in bromine-containing chemicals. The data suggest that substantial natural sources exist for atmospheric methyl bromide (CH_3Br). The phase-out of CFCs means that nitrous oxide (N_2O), which is not covered by the Montreal Protocol, has become the most highly emitted ozone depleting substance and is expected to remain so throughout the twenty-first century.

When the 2004 ozone hole ended in November 2004, daily minimum stratospheric temperatures in the Antarctic lower stratosphere increased to levels that are too warm for the formation of polar stratospheric clouds (PSCs) about 2–3 weeks earlier than in most recent years.

The Arctic winter of 2005 was extremely cold in the stratosphere; PSCs were abundant over many high-latitude areas until dissipated by a big warming event, which started in the upper stratosphere during February and spread throughout the Arctic stratosphere in March. The size of the Arctic area of anomalously low total ozone in 2004–05 was larger than in any year since 1997. The predominance of anomalously low total ozone values in the Arctic region in the winter of 2004–05 is attributed to very low stratospheric temperatures and meteorological conditions favourable for ozone destruction along with the continued presence of ozone destroying chemicals in the stratosphere.

A 2005 IPCC summary of ozone issues concluded that observations and model calculations suggest that the global average amount of ozone depletion is almost stable now. Although considerable variability in ozone is expected from year to year, including Polar Regions where depletion is largest, the ozone layer is expected to begin to recover in coming decades due to declining ozone-depleting substance concentrations, assuming full compliance with the Montreal Protocol.

Temperatures during the Arctic winter of 2006 stayed fairly close to the long-term average until late January, with minimum readings frequently cold enough to produce PSCs. During the last week of January, however, a major warming event sent temperatures well above normal—much too warm to support PSCs. By the time temperatures dropped to near normal in March, the seasonal norm was well above the PSC threshold. Preliminary satellite instrument-generated ozone maps show seasonal ozone buildup slightly below the long-term means for the Northern Hemisphere as a whole although some high ozone events have occurred. During March 2006, the Arctic stratosphere pole ward of 60° North Latitude was free of anomalously low ozone areas except during the three-day period from 17–19 March when the total ozone cover fell below 300 DU over part of the North Atlantic region from Greenland to Scandinavia.

The area where total column ozone is less than 220 DU (the accepted definition of the boundary of the ozone hole) was relatively small until around 20 August 2006. Since then the ozone-hole area increased rapidly, peaking at 29 million km^2 on 24 September. In October 2006, NASA reported that the year's ozone hole set a new area record with a daily average of 26 million km^2 between 7 September and 13 October 2006; total ozone thicknesses fell as low as 85 DU on 8 October. The two factors combined and 2006 witnessed the worst level of depletion in recorded ozone history. The depletion is attributed to the temperatures above the Antarctic reaching the lowest recording since comprehensive records began in 1979.

On October 2008, the Ecuadorian Space Agency published a report called *HIPERION*, a study of the last 28 years data from 10 satellites and dozens of ground instruments around the world among them their own, and found that the UV radiation reaching equatorial latitudes was far greater than expected, climbing in some very populated cities up to 24

UVI, the WHO UV Index standard considers 11 as an extreme index and a great risk to health. The report concluded that the ozone depletion around mid latitudes on the planet is already endangering large populations in these areas. Later, the CONIDA, the Peruvian Space Agency, conducted its own study, which found almost the same facts as the Ecuadorian study.

The Antarctic ozone hole is expected to continue for decades. Ozone concentrations in the lower stratosphere over Antarctica will increase by 5 per cent - 10 per cent by 2020 and return to pre-1980 levels by about 2060–2075, i.e., 10–25 years later than predicted in earlier assessments. This is because of revised estimates of atmospheric concentrations of Ozone Depleting Substances — and a larger predicted future usage in developing countries. Another factor which may aggravate ozone depletion is the draw-down of nitrogen oxides from above the stratosphere due to changing wind patterns.

Effect on Infectious Diseases

Most infectious diseases are transmitted by insects and rodents. Transmitters of a disease are called vectors, e.g, mosquitoes transmit malaria, dengue and viral encephalitis (inflammation of the brain). Like other animals and plants, vectors are accustomed to certain climate conditions. If the climate becomes warmer, the mosquitoes will try to fly to new places where they can survive and expose more people to the disease. Changes in sea surface temperature and sea level can lead to higher incidence of water-borne and toxin-related infectious diseases, such as malaria, cholera , dengue which infection is characterized by severe pains in the joints and back), and leishmaniasis (skin ulcers).

Human susceptibility to infections can be compounded further by malnutrition. UV-B radiation from ozone depletion damages both plants and animals. UV-B harms amphibian eggs, midge larvae and trout. Crops that are damaged will reduce food availability. UV-B also can damage mammalian immune systems which makes humans and other animals more susceptible to infectious diseases.

Approximately, 92 million people are expected to become refugees from global warming and climate change by 2100, excluding those added from population growth.

Effects on Earth's Food Chain

Ozone depletion and global warming have harmful effects on plants and animals. If it is allowed to continue, our food chain will be disrupted seriously. For example, phytoplantktons are tiny floating algae in the ocean which are the base of the marine food chain. In Antarctica, there has been more than 50 per cent ozone depletion. This means that an unusually high amount of UV-B radiation has reached the Earth's surface in the Antarctic region. UV-B harms the productivity of phytoplanktons, thereby reducing the available food for animals that feed on them. Krill eat phytoplankton and penguins eat krill. From a climate change perspective, phytoplanktons normally absorb a lot of carbon from the air. As phytoplanktons perish due to UV-B radiation, the carbon is no longer absorbed. This means that more carbon will be left in the atmosphere, contributing to greater global warming. It can increase ozone depletion, which kills more phytoplankton, and the process repeats itself.

"Total Environmental Impact" of Refrigerants

Six parameters define the "total environmental impact" of refrigerants on our environment.

- Ozone Depletion Potential (ODP)
- Global Warming Potential (GWP)
- Atmospheric Life
- Energy Use
- Equipment Emission Rate
- Refrigerant Charge

Approximately, 70 per cent of the world's electricity is generated by the burning of fossil fuels. For every additional kWh used, there are more greenhouse gas emissions generated by electric utility power plants. This is the indirect effect of global warming refrigerants. The environmental impact of even small changes in chiller energy use has an impact. There is a need to use refrigerants that minimize both ODP and GWP to address global environmental concerns. If the efficiency of every centrifugal chiller in the world were increased by 0.08 kW/tons, power plant-generated greenhouse gas emissions would be reduced by literally billions of pounds. This is an amount equal to removing nearly two million cars from the road each year, or to planting nearly a half billion trees every year.

Action Plan for Organizations Using Refrigerants

Most refrigerants used in air conditioning and refrigeration contribute to global warming in addition to ozone depletion. Even the new non-ozone depleting alternative refrigerants add to the global warming problem. Businesses and organizations using refrigerants are encouraged to take action now to do what's right for both their organization and for the environment. Persons responsible for HVAC and/or environmental concerns in their company or organization need to take immediate corrective actions to reduce ozone depletion and global warming.

Minimize emissions of ozone depleting (ODP) and direct global warming (GWP) refrigerants used by you. The most effective way to start reducing emissions is to implement a refrigerant management plan and ensure that it complies with EPA's Section 608 Refrigerant Recycling Regulations. Refrigerants should be handled as a controlled substance. A defined leak management programme, including leak monitoring and leak repair policies is essential. Provide Refrigerant Management and Regulations Compliance training to responsible employees. Organizations using refrigerants should review and implement best practices in refrigerant management to minimize emissions at every stage of refrigerant handling. Implement a process to keep with current regulatory changes to ensure that compliance requirements are met.

Reduce energy consumption of HVAC systems using refrigerants to reduce indirect global warming emissions. Conduct a building tune-up to reduce your heating, cooling, and electrical loads, and thus your overall energy consumption.

Replace older HVAC systems containing high ozone depleting and/or global warming refrigerants with newer, more efficient systems. Frequently, HVAC systems are oversized. The operating costs of a high efficiency system may offer an attractive payback of investment. Evaluate HVAC systems on a total cost of ownership basis, rather than first cost.

Chapter - 2

Environment and Customs

Jean Monnet, one of Europe's founding fathers, said "People only accept change when they are faced with necessity, and only recognize necessity when a crisis is upon them." We cannot escape the fact that we have to change and modernize. It is only by thinking positively, by building brick by brick, by showing respect for the values of efficiency, modernity, transparency and honesty that we will create conditions conducive to greater efficiency, weather the storm, change the course of events and grasp the opportunities afforded to us by international trade. Success begets confidence, and confidence begets success.

The global economy is undeniably in a state of crisis, and the impact on the international Customs community is manifold. The word "crisis" crops up in every speech and appears in the media everyday. However, if we wish to pull ourselves out of the prevailing slump then we ought to veto the use of this word until the global economy picks up again. We will then be able to refer to the "crisis" in the past tense and stop blaming the state of the economy for all the evils in the world.

Even during this period of turmoil there are achievements being made, local and regional initiatives being taken, systems which are working, projects which are moving forward and programmes which are developing? The theme of WCO for 2009 was protection of the environment. Stepping up the fight against environmental crime is a huge challenge requiring resources, determination and willpower commensurate the scale of the environmental threat facing us.

As per World Customs Organization Press Release:-

> A joint global Customs initiative across Europe, Asia/Pacific region and Africa netted more than 30000 tons and 1,500 pieces of illegal hazardous waste in 57 seizures, ranging from household waste and scrap metal to discarded electronic goods and used vehicle parts. Between March and May 2009, Customs administrations from 64 countries launched Operation Demeter targeting the illicit cross border shipment of hazardous and other waste en route from Europe to countries in Asia/Pacific region and Africa. This fifty-day operation which was co-ordinated by the WCO Secretariat was aimed at increasing information exchange among Customs administrations: a vital element in tackling environmental crime at the border.

Customs officials at over 300 seaports and other selected points intensified their risk profiling and physical controls to identify high risk shipments and notified each other of any suspicious shipments across the continents. They were supported by their national environmental agencies, the Secretariat of the Basel Convention, the EU Network for Implementation and Enforcement of Environmental Law (IMPEL), and the seven WCO Regional Intelligence Liaison Offices (RILO) located in the participating regions. Officers in European exporting countries also followed up investigations of illegal exporters based on feedback from countries in Africa and the Asia/Pacific. CENcomm, the WCO's secure communication tool, was used by these officials to exchange over 500 intelligence messages during the operation.

The majority of seizures took place in European countries such as Netherlands, Belgium, and Italy before the waste could be shipped. Iron scrap destined for Asia topped the list in terms of quantities seized. Africa remained the destination of choice for household waste such as used refrigerators containing CFCs and old television screens with over 1100 of the approximately 1500 pieces seized destined for countries on the continent. On 9 June, 2009, Lagos Customs officers opened a container at a terminal after it had been under surveillance for exactly one month based on intelligence provided by their Customs counterparts in Europe. The container was fully loaded with waste television sets, but remained unclaimed.

WCO Secretary General, Kunio Mikuriya, said, "The international Customs community and its partners cannot allow the illicit trade in environmentally sensitive goods to continue unabated when it has such devastating affects on the health and safety of people around the globe", he added, "Rising international concerns about the fragility of the environment spurs us on to strengthen Customs border controls through focused capacity building initiatives and enhanced exchange of information as this will ensure that the illegal activities of syndicates involved in this trade are dealt a massive blow." Mr. Mikuriya further added, "Although most of the hazardous waste can be used as secondary raw material, it can still do detrimental damage to the environment if not recycled in an environment friendly manner which is often the case in developing countries lacking proper facilities, a fact which criminals use to their advantage." In conclusion the Secretary General said, "The success of Operation Demeter can be attributed to our desire to protect the environment for future generations, the strong political will and commitment of WCO Member

Customs administrations, and excellent co-operation with our partners at the national, regional and international level in fact the WCO is now even more determined to bolster the partnership further as co-ordination, co-operation and communication are the enemies of those who profit from this trade."

Under the Basel Convention which regulates the transboundary movement of hazardous wastes and their disposal, parties have the right to prohibit the import of waste. Parties are also prohibited from exporting waste without consent of importing countries. Where this occurs without consent, it is regarded as illegal trafficking and exporting countries are obligated to take the waste back or dispose it off properly in accordance with the terms of the Basel Convention.

The Executive Secretary of the Basel Convention Ms Katharina Kummer Peiry said, "Operation Demeter has confirmed the critical role of Customs authorities, the crucial importance of effective information sharing systems and the necessity for international co-operation to combat the illegal traffic of hazardous wastes. I note that the vast majority of seizures took place in European countries before the export actually took place a positive signal as it means earlier intervention in the illegal traffic waste chain", she added, "The outcomes of the Operation also provide very useful information on the types of waste that are the object of illegal traffic as well as on the countries of destination of these wastes." In conclusion Peiry said, "The Secretariat of the Basel Convention is grateful to have had the opportunity to collaborate with the World Customs Organization in this Operation and looks forward to continued co-operation."

The WCO will continue to co-operate closely with its partners in the Green customs initiative as the Organization remains of the firm belief that environment crime can be combated effectively only through concerted action on all fronts. These actions include even more capacity building for Customs officials working on the frontline, the development of enhanced tools to support these officials and global Customs operations aimed at squeezing the lifeblood out of this illegal trade.

About Green Customs

Environmental crime is a significant and increasingly lucrative business. National and international crime syndicates worldwide earn an estimated US$ 20–30 billion dollars annually from hazardous waste dumping smuggling prescribed hazardous materials and exporting and trafficking protected natural resources illegal international trade in environmentally-sensitive commodities such as ozone depleting substances (ODS) toxic chemicals hazardous wastes endangered species and living modified organisms is an international problem with serious consequences. It directly threatens human health and the environment contributes to species loss results in revenue loss for governments and undermines the success of international environmental agreements by circumventing agreed rules and procedures.

The need for action

Customs and border protection officers constitute the front line of every country's defence against transboundary illegal trade. They are the first link in the "compliance and enforcement chain" and without adequate capacity to prevent or detect illegal trade; the test of the chain will be considerably less effective. Building the capacity of these officers is therefore vital. Training is a key component of capacity building, but can be time-consuming and expensive when delivered separately for the wide range of issues customs officers must cover. An effective solution is co-ordinated training, and this is where Green Customs comes in.

Helping to address the problem— the Green Customs Initiative

The Green Customs Initiative is an unprecedented partnership of international organizations co-operating to prevent the illegal trade in environmentally sensitive commodities and facilitation of the legal trade in these. Its objective is to enhance the capacity of customs and other relevant enforcement personnel to monitor and facilitate the legal trade and to detect and prevent illegal trade in environmentally sensitive commodities covered by the relevant conventions and multilateral environmental agreements (MEAs). These include ozone depleting substances (ODS), toxic chemical products, hazardous wastes, endangered species and living-modified organisms. This is achieved through awareness rising on all the relevant international agreements as well as provision of assistance and tools to the enforcement community. Green Customs is designed to complement and enhance existing customs training efforts under the respective agreements.

UNEP's Governing Council expressed concern over the increasing environmental damage caused by illegal traffic in endangered species and dangerous and harmful substances and products. It also recognized that continuous efforts must be undertaken by all countries and relevant organization and agencies concerned with ensuring compliance and enforcement of relevant international agreements. The Green Customs Initiative is a partnership actively addressing these concerns (Council Decision 21/27 on Compliance with and enforcement of multilateral environment agreements, February 2001).

Green Customs Partners

The partners of the Green Customs Initiative comprise the secretariats of the relevant multilateral environmental agreements (Basel, Cartagena, CITES, Montreal, Rotterdam Stockholm), Interpol, the Organization for the Prohibition of Chemical Weapons, UNEP, the United Nations Office on Drugs and Crime (UNODC) and the World Customs Organization. The Green Customs Initiative also works closely with a number of other regional and international organizations.

Benefits of Green Customs

For Customs Officers:

- Increased knowledge about environmental issues, particularly those related to MEAs.
- Enhanced skills required to enforce national environmental commitments.
- Better recognition of the role of customs officers in environmental protection.

For Countries:

- Increased detection of smugglers and illegally-traded commodities by national customs officers, and facilitation of legal trade.
- Strengthened capacity for national compliance and enforcement of MEAs through monitoring of trade.
- Increased opportunity for dialogue with regional trade partner countries on illegal trade issues.
- Sustained capacity building through integration of Green Customs into national customs training curricula.
- Prevention of loss of revenue from tax and duty avoidance associated with smuggling Increased integration of environment into the security agenda.

For Partners:

- Increased opportunity for synergies in implementation between MEAs.
- Shared training infrastructure and experience developed by the Secretariats.

For Global Environment:

- Decrease in environmental crime, control of toxic chemicals and wastes, better species protection leading to a less polluted and more sustainable environment.

Green Customs Tools:

Green Customs Guide

Green Customs Guidebook is a book for trainees and trainers

to be used as a core element during the training courses and as a post-course reference document.

Workshops to train customs officers

Many Green Customs training workshops have been held all around the world. These have ranged from regional workshops to subregional and national workshops.

Green Customs website and materials

Information and more details on the Initiative can be found on website, including links to training materials and information on partner organizations.

Environmental crime, perceived by some as a low priority than smuggling of drugs or weapons, or in the context of today's financial crisis, is a growing and increasingly lucrative business.

Environmental crime can have grave health, environmental and financial consequences and as such deserves serious attention. Such illegal activities are carried out by national and international crime syndicates worldwide and can earn an estimated US$ 20–30 billion annually" said Rajendra Shende head of UNEP's Ozon Action Programme which hosts the Green Customs Initiative Secretariat.

It is recognized that customs officers are in the front line of a countries defence against transboundary illegal trade and therefore need the knowledge, capacity and tools to enable them to best fulfill their important role as protectors of the environment.

"The WCO recognizes the importance of the role of customs authorities around the world in tackling environmental offences and has therefore assigned a high priority to these issues; with 2009 being an year in which environment is a priority" said Mikuriya Secretary General of the WCO Secretariat, "Our increased commitment is demonstrated through activities such as this training workshop organized by the WCO under the banner of the

Green Customs Initiative, the first of its kind, as well as a number of other initiatives and tools such as joint operations and communication tools designed to assist our colleagues around the world."

The Green Customs Initiative provides co-ordinated and cost-effective delivery of training and awareness rising of customs officers and enforcement personnel that is delivered through an umbrella partnership involving multiple organizations with diverse mandates.

At this workshop, which was entitled Environment boarder protection, the Government of India launched two major initiatives demonstrating the country's commitment to combating environmental crime. India is the first county in the world to officially incorporate the Green Customs Initiative into the National Customs Training curricula, thereby building the capacity of customs officers to detect and prevent illegal trade in environmentally sensitive items such as toxic and ozone depleting chemicals, endangered species and living modified organisms, as well as facilitating the legal trade in these items. It was also announced that an e-learning tool, developed in co-operation with the United Nations Environment Programme and NACEN, Faridabad to train customs officers in the monitoring and controlling the trade in ozone depleting substances was released today. The WCO welcomes these efforts to regionalize and nationalize Customs training curricular.

The Green Customs Initiative

The Green Customs Initiative is an unprecedented partnership of international organizations co-operating to enhance the capacity of customs and other relevant enforcement personnel to monitor and facilitate the legal trade and to detect and prevent illegal trade in environmentally sensitive commodities covered by the relevant conventions and multilateral environmental agreements (MEAs). These include ozone depleting substances (ODS), toxic chemical products, hazardous wastes, endangered species and living-modified organisms.

The Green Customs Initiative achieves its aims through awareness rising on all the relevant international agreements as well as provision of assistance and tools to the enforcement community. Green Customs is designed to complement and enhance existing customs training efforts under the respective agreements.

Environmental Protection – Scope and its components

The topic of environmental protection is rather broad in scope having many components. The important ones are the matters relating to the CITES (Convention on International Trade in Endangered Species of Wild Flora and fauna), Ozone Depleting Substances (ODS) and Hazardous Wastes and Materials.

Plants and animals hold medicinal, ecological, aesthetic/ recreational, agricultural and commercial value. A study has revealed that about forty per cent of all medicines are formulated from the natural components of different species, and some of them are life saving drugs. Plant and animal species are the foundation of healthy ecosystems. Human beings depend on ecosystems such as coastal estuaries, grasslands and ancient forests to purify air, clean water and supply them with food. With many vital species becoming endangered, the health of these ecosystems has started deteriorating. Plants and animal species and their ecosystems supply recreational, spiritual Seized – Organ Pipe Coral and quality of life values, and thus provide the support system for the tourism industry. In the field of agriculture, there are an estimated 80,000 edible plants on this terra firma, and 90 pei cent of the world's food comes from agriculture. Besides, the wild relatives of some of the common crops provide essential disease-resistant materials. As for commercial value, various wild species of both flora and fauna are raised commercially, thus directly contributing to local and regional economies. It is, therefore, our onerous responsibility to ensure that endangered species are protected so that our future generations can continue to experience their presence and gain from their value. Customs can contribute in this effort of conservation by preventing cross border smuggling of these goods.

India Customs and Environment Protection

India is one of the mega biodiversity centers in the world and has two of the world's 18 biodiversity hotspots located in the Western Ghats and in the Eastern Himalayas. The sheer diversity of its terrestrial, marine and other aquatic ecosystems ranging from the vast beaches (over 7500 km of coastline), extensive forests, soaring mountains, sprawling deserts, wetlands and coral reefs is breathtaking. The country has a fascinating presence of close to 49000 plant species and 81000 animal species representing 12.5 per cent of the world's flora and 6.60 per cent of its fauna.

However, the pace of environmental change that is presently taking place is so rapid that most of the plant and animal species are unable to adapt to environmental variation, leading to extinction of species. Over the last century, a great deal of damage has been done to the existing biodiversity. Increasing human population, increasing consumption levels and unabated pollution are some of the causes that have led to overexploitation and degradation of ecosystems. The adverse consequences on climate change, species becoming extinct or endangered, besides the adverse economic consequences are visible to the common man today. Thus the importance of protecting the environment and fostering sustainable development cannot be overemphasized.

The Customs administrations play a key role in the fight against environmental crimes since one of the crucial elements is to combat this crime at the international borders. Considering the over arching importance of protecting the environment and the significant role played by Customs, the Worlds Customs Organization (WCO) has declared the theme of the year 2009 and of the International Customs Day 2009 as "Customs and the Environment: Protecting our natural heritage."

With a total staff strength of over 72,000, which includes officers working in the areas of Customs, Anti-smuggling, Central Excise, Service Tax and Narcotics, Indian Customs man around 36 international airports, 91 Ports, 136 functioning Land Customs Stations (LCS) and a number of Inland Container Depots/Container Freight Stations/Foreign Post Offices. India is a party to a number of International Conventions relating to environment and implement these conventions through the Customs Act 1962, Foreign (Trade and Development Regulation) Act 1992 and other relevant Acts.

India has been a proactive participant in the development, acceptance and implementation of many of the treaties and conventions relating to the preservation of global environment. The Customs and Central Excise Department has also been active equally in putting in place the necessary training in enforcement for its officers to combat environment related offences and play a pioneering role in training not only for Indian customs officers, but also those of other countries in detecting and enforcing the Montreal Protocol on Ozone depleting substances. Several significant seizures have also been affected by the officers of the department, as reflected in the information that is provided later in this article.

India will continue to play a proactive role in combating this heinous crime against the environment and biodiversity by continued action and further linkages with other governmental agencies nationally and also by participating in international efforts in this area.

Customs administrations play a vital role in environmental protection at borders. They ensure compliance with the provisions of Multilateral Environmental Agreements (MEAs) and national legislation. They also undertake the task of monitoring the trade in certain environmentally sensitive goods and endangered species, identifying and detecting smuggling and other offences, and helping to raise users awareness of this illicit trade. For a long time now, and at its Members' request, the WCO has been involved in efforts to combat environmental crime. The Secretariat is operating on all fronts in this domain. Not only are all the technical directorates participating, but also the WCO's regional structures (RILOs and ROCBs).

Likewise, close co-operation has been forged with other international organizations having responsibility for environmental issues, such as the CITES and Basel Convention Secretariats and UNEP.

Lastly, in order to raise users' awareness of the importance of protecting the world's natural heritage the WCO had chosen "Customs and the environment are protecting our natural heritage" as the theme for 2009. As a result international Customs Day on 26 January 2009 focused protecting the environment.

Environmental crime affects all of our society, for example poaching of endangered species affects the income of rural populations and has driven some species to the brink of extinction. Deforestation caused by illegal logging is a major contributor to almost 20 per cent of greenhouse gas emissions thus leading to climate change. Ozone Depleting Substances (ODS) destroy the ozone layer thus suppressing the human immune system, causing skin cancer and even cataracts. Hazardous waste causes long-term poisoning of soil and water, affecting people's health and living conditions. Increasingly unscrupulous trade in waste which is criminal under the Basel Convention has become a serious concern.

Environmental crime by its nature is transboundary and in many cases involves cross-border criminal syndicates. Globalization at the same time facilitates movement of environmentally harmful commodities unpunished. A tiger skin or an ivory tusk passes through many hands from the poaching site to the final buyer. A tree sawed down illegally can travel around the world to end up as luxury furniture. In many cases, endangered species and tropical timbers are shipped from less developed countries to the developed world and vice versa. The raw material is finally converted into goods and the entire process also results in to hazardous waste.

Environmental crime is not new for Customs. Customs have done a lot of work in this area for more than a decade.

The WCO Council Sessions have adopted several recommendations on fighting against environmental crime, and the latest recommendation approved in June 2008 calls for all members to continue their efforts to combat environmental crime and to ensure that the environment remains a priority issue for Customs across the globe.

Headings and subheadings in the Harmonized System (HS) for environmentally sensitive commodities have also been amended or inserted with a view to identifying and monitoring the most traded commodities. Data elements for hazardous wastes have been incorporated in V.3 of the WCO Data Model to facilitate not only Customs in their control and identification of imported and exported hazardous wastes but also to disseminate this information via the Single Window environment to the responsible government agencies.

The WCO Customs Enforcement Network (CEN) has been widely used for information exchange and the seizure database for border environmental enforcement. Seizures of endangered species and hazardous waste reported globally by Customs are stored in the CEN. The ODS seizure database will also be available in the near future Alerts trend analysis, as well as information from other organizations to keep global Customs officers alert on emerging illegal trafficking trends. Detailed Risk Indicators on endangered species ODS and hazardous waste developed by the Secretariat support frontline officers in their daily work for identifying illegal trafficking.

The WCO Regional Intelligence Liaison Office (RILO) network has been very active in collecting, analyzing seizure information, and hosting training on environmental border protection.

The first lesson of "Customs and CITES" is now available on the WCO e-learning platform. The course benefits not only Customs officers, but also other parties involved in the trade in CITES. The ODS e-learning programme jointly developed by the Secretariat and the UNEP is also available since 2009.

The Secretariat has been working very closely with international organizations based on Memoranda of Understanding, such as the CITES Secretariat, the Basel Convention Secretariat and UNEP, to maximize our joint efforts in the fight against environmental crime.

Since 2001, the WCO has been an active partner with the Green Customs Initiatives (GCI), which is a series of collaborative activities such as workshops, training materials, and joint actions, by partner organizations aimed at raising the awareness of Customs officers to environment issues.

A joint project called Sky-Hole Patching launched in 2006 by 20 Customs administrations in Asia Pacific and supported by the RILO AP and UNEP regional office in Thailand led to seizures of 155 tons of ODS, and 116 seizures of almost 20,000 tons of hazardous wastes, ranging from e-waste to used clothing and waste oil.

All WCO members launched a one-day intensive control operation targeting trafficking in endangered species. The Secretariat set up the CEN COMM for the operation to facilitate smooth and secure transmission of information.

The Secretariat has proposed to launch a joint operation in 2009 to intercept illegal movement of hazardous and other waste. The operation involves more than 100 Customs administrations in Europe, Asia Pacific and Africa, with the support of seven WCO Regional Intelligence Liaison Offices (RILOs), and national environmental authorities as well as several international organizations.

In the wake of the 21st century, Customs is faced with enormous challenges, but one thing is for sure, they take things seriously and engage themselves more in the fight against environmental crime at the border. The Customs community shares the responsibility to protect the only planet we live on for our next generation. Luxuries can be reproduced, but endangered species like tigers cannot afford to wait too long. When they are gone, they are gone forever. If we do nothing, more waste dumping like the tragedy in Abidjan, Cote d'lvoire in August 2006 might happen again. Customs has done a lot, but more action is needed to stop environmental crime and protect our natural heritage.

Even as revenue collection continues to be the core competence of Indian Customs, equally important are certain agency functions relating to prevention of illegal trafficking of 'goods' across borders, Customs being an important organization in the scheme of border control. The 'goods' cover a wide range antiques, objects of art and literature, arms and ammunition, counterfeit currency, narcotic drugs, Ozone Depleting Substances (ODS), hazardous waste and material and endangered species of flora and fauna. Over the years, illegal trade in wildlife and its products has become a matter of serious international concern. It undermines the conservation efforts of all nations, and it has led to near extinction of some species. Further, wildlife smuggling being as profitable as narcotics smuggling without the attendant risk of severe punishment as in case of drug smuggling, organized crime groups armed with highly sophisticated smuggling techniques have entered this illegal trade. This makes the job of Customs even more challenging.

There is, therefore, the need for the national Customs organizations to increase efforts to combat cross border environmental offences jointly.

ROCB AP'S contribution to Customs and the Environment

Regional co-operation and capacity building for enforcement officers are playing a very important role in dealing with illegal traffic of environmentally hazardous goods, such as Ozone Depleting Substances (ODS), Hazardous Waste, endangered animal and plants, etc. Since July 2005, WCO ROCB AP has established a very close relationship with UNEP Regional Office for Asia and the Pacific (ROAP) to support their networking and capacity building for enforcement officers. ROCB AP also became a member of the Regional Partner's Forum from the beginning with UNEP, UNODC, RILO AP, the NGO Environmental Investigation Agency (EIA) and Interpol, etc., The forum has exchanged information relating to the MEAs (Multilateral Environmental Agreements), illegal trade trends, and discussed future plan for capacity building etc.

Using these occasions, ROCB AP has tried to promote awareness and capacity building on environment protection among customs administrations in the region. An important activity of WCO ROCBs is organizing seminars/ workshops on the Harmonized System (HS), which thanks to the close co-operation between UNEP and WCO, now always draw attention to specific Harmonized System codes (HS codes) for ODS and other environmental goods. Furthermore, how to control the illegal movement of goods in Free Trade Zones, and how to share the information through intelligence networks, were topics also covered at the workshops.

To raise higher awareness of Customs Training departments, the ROCB invited UNEP to attend the Regional Training Center meetings in 2006. This became an important avenue for enhancing training on enforcement for the illegal trade in environmental goods and gains their support for the Green Customs Initiative, Project Sky Hole Patching, etc. Actually, this helped to establish a close relationship between UNEP and the Shanghai Customs College (SCC). The SCC hosted the Green Customs train-the-trainer workshop in May 2007 which was attended by regional customs experts and MEA secretariats. Workshops organized by UNEP and other related organizations were actively attended by the ROCB AP who introduced the enforcement tools developed by the WCO.

Keeping the project Sky-Hole Patching Mechanism

RILO A/P is determined to protect the environment. The success of Project Sky-hole Patching has marked an important milestone to curb illegal trade in Ozone depleting substances (ODS) and hazardous waste in the Asia Pacific region. Though the Project was completed on 1 November 2007 after 14 months' operation, it does not end the reporting and monitoring mechanism. The reporting and monitoring mechanism is still ongoing and continually contributes to huge numbers of detection of hazardous waste detections - 2,677,164 kg in 126 seizures since November 2007. The project has a high international reputation and customs influence has extended across the globe. In 2008, RILO A/P continued its active participation in international seminars and has begun discussion on the expansion of international co-operation. International co-operation is paramount to the effectiveness of ongoing protection of the environment globally.

German Customs uses specially trained Endangered Species Detection Dogs

Hundreds of tiny turtles in a washbag, parrot eggs hidden in underwear, birds squeezed into narrow plastic tubes or poison dart frogs in drinks bottles along with drugs and weapons, endangered species make for some of the most lucrative smuggling worldwide. Interpol estimates the volume of illegal trade in plants and animals at around USD 20 billion a year. German Customs has responded to this phenomenon with specially-trained endangered species detection dogs.

At Frankfurt Airport alone, the year 2007 witnessed 561 seizures encompassing some 111,838 items. These included 5,599 living animals as well as products such as snake-leather bags, caviar, furs or cobras preserved in alcohol. The damage done by this smuggling is dear: it is a threat to the very survival of rare species.

To stay a step ahead of the highly-professional wildlife mafia, German Customs has trained a number of specialized endangered species detection dogs in ten-week courses at one of its customs dog training centers. The dogs are able to detect even very faint-smelling objects and so are ideal for quickly controlling luggage, packages or entire shipping containers.

Hazardous Waste Management in Cote d'lvoire

Designated to answer several shortcomings that were highlighted by the dumping of hazardous waste from the vessel Probo Koala in Abidjan's residential areas in August 2006, the two-year project was implemented by the Basel Convention Regional Center for French speaking Countries in Africa, based in Senegal, and executed by the ministry of environment in Abidjan, in co-operation with the Basel Convention Secretariat.

Funded under the Strategic Approach to International Chemicals Management (SAICM) Quick Start Program, this project developed tools for the analysis of gaps in national legislation as related to international agreements for parties in Africa possessing port facilities. It aimed to enhance the capacity of Cote d'lvoire to implement and enforce, through a comprehensive and integrated approach, international and national laws relating to the control of transboundary movements (in particular import and transit) of hazardous waste and chemicals in compliance with the obligations, standards and objectives of the Basel Convention, the International Health Regulations (WHO 200S), MARPOL 73/78, the Rotterdam Convention, and the Stockholm Convention.

The 1989 Basel Convention on the Control of Transboundary Movements of Hazardous Wastes and their Disposal has two pillars; first, it regulates the transboundary movements of hazardous and other wastes; second, the Convention obliges its Parties to ensure that such wastes are managed and disposed off in an environmentally sound manner. To this end, parties are required to minimize the quantities that are moved across borders, to treat and dispose off wastes as close as possible to their place of generation and to prevent or minimize the generation of wastes at source.

Strong controls have to be applied from the generation of a hazardous waste to its storage, transport, treatment, reuse, recycling, recovery and final disposal.

The Basel Convention has 14 Regional and Co-ordinating Centers, with one or more operating on every continent.

Environment Protection

The RILO supports trade-related MEAs and co-ordinates input of data on seizures of relevant goods into the CEN system by customs services of the region. Co-operation is maintained with UNEP and the Regional Ozone Network for Europe and Central Asia in combating illegal trade in ozone-depleting substances. The RILO translated the "Guide for Enforcement Officers on Combating Illegal Trade in ODS" and prepared the brochure "Illegal transportation of ODS in 2007."

In 2005–08 two bulletins and a brochure on CITES seizures were published.

For 2009 the RILO planed bulletins on seizures of CITES and nuclear radioactive and hazardous goods.

Summary of Major Conventions and Agreements

Vienna Convention

The Vienna Convention for the Protection of the Ozone Layer is a multilateral environmental agreement agreed upon at the Vienna Conference of 1985 and entered into force in 1987. It acts as a framework for the international efforts to protect the ozone layer. However, it does not include legally binding reduction goals for the use of CFCs, the main chemical agents causing ozone depletion.

Montreal Protocol

Montreal Protocol is an international treaty designed to protect the ozone layer by gradually decreasing and eventually phasing out the production of a number of substances (halogenated hydrocarbons) believed to be responsible for ozone depletion over a period of time. At present, 193 of 196 United Nations member states have ratified the original Montreal Protocol though only 144 countries have signed the latest (Beijing-1996) Amendment. India signed the Montreal Protocol in 1992 and has ratified the Beijing amendment. India prepared its Country Program in 1993 to phase out ODS in accordance with its national industrial development strategy.

The Central Board of Excise and Customs issued a Notification in 2001 exempting the goods required for the substitution of Ozone Depleting Substances (ODS) and setting up of new capacity with non-ODS technology. Indian Customs authorities prevent and detect illegal movement and smuggling of ODS at its borders especially between India and Nepal, India and Bhutan, India and Myanmar etc. A large number of seizures of CFC gases smuggled in through these points have been affected.

Basel Convention

The Basel Convention is designed to reduce the movements of hazardous waste between nations, and specifically to prevent transfer of hazardous waste from developed to less developed countries besides ensuring environmentally sound management of wastes as closely as possible to the source of generation. There are 170 signatory parties to the Convention. The Convention has set up a very strict control system based on prior written consent procedure.

The Indian Government signed the Convention on 15th March, 1990 and ratified it on 24th June 1992. Every importer wishing to import hazardous waste must fill up a Form along with required fee, 125 days in advance, to the State Pollution Control Board/Central Pollution Control Board. The Customs authorities are empowered to verify the documents submitted by the importers under Rule 13(6) of Hazardous Wastes Management and Handling Rules, 2000 and inform the ministry of environment and forests, Govt. of India of any illegal traffic as per requirement of Rule 15 of the above Rules. CBEC has issued Notification no.

35/2004-Customs in this regard. CBEC has issued Circular no. 31/2004 dated 26th April 2004 on the directions of the Honourable Supreme Court of India dated 14.10.2003 in the matter of Writ Petition No. 657/95 in which the apex court has given directions on various issues relating to import of hazardous wastes of various kinds for action and implementation by the Customs authorities.

Chemical Weapons Convention

The Chemicals Weapons Convention is the first multilateral disarmament treaty. The CWC aims to eliminate an entire category of weapons of mass destruction by prohibiting the development, production, acquisition, stockpiling, retention, transfer or use of chemical weapons by signatories (numbering 185) within 10 years of Convention entering into force. All signatories have agreed to disarm chemically by destroying any stockpiles of chemical weapons they may hold and any facilities which produced them, as well as any chemical weapons they abandoned on the territory of other States Parties in the past. It also has a transfer regime that restricts the trade in the Chemicals that could be used in manufacture of Chemical Weapons. A verification regime is created for certain toxic chemicals and their precursors in order to ensure that such chemicals are used only for purposes that are not prohibited. The Convention has enlisted the Chemicals under 3 schedules; i.e., Schedule 1, which is Chemical Weapons; Schedule 2, which is precursors and Schedule 3, which is other Chemicals. Under the Convention, transfer of Parties, and transfer to State Parties is permissible only for research, medical, and pharmaceutical purposes.

The Chemical Weapons Convention Rules, 2005 empower the Customs authorities for getting the chemicals analyzed and tested, verify and endorse the documents, licenses etc. CBEC has issued Notification 121/2003-Customs exempting equipment and samples required by the inspection team of the Organization of Prohibition of Chemical Weapons.

Rotterdam Convention

The Rotterdam Convention is a multilateral environmental agreement designed to promote shared responsibility and co-operative efforts among the parties in the international trade of certain hazardous chemicals, in order to protect human health and the environment from the potential harm and to contribute to their environmentally sound use by facilitating information exchange about their characteristics, providing for a national decision making on their import and export and disseminate these decisions to the parties. The Convention covers pesticides and industrial chemicals that have been banned or severely restricted for health or environmental reasons by parties and which have been notified by parties for inclusion in the PIC procedure. The convention promotes open exchange of information and calls on exporters of hazardous chemicals to use proper labelling, include directions on safe handling, and inform purchasers of any known restrictions or bans. Parties can decide whether to allow or ban the importal of chemicals listed in the treaty, and exporting countries are obliged to make sure that producers within their jurisdiction are complied with.

The Convention entered into force on 24th February 2004 and became legally binding to its parties. As of 2008 73 countries were signatories and 126 were parties. India acceded to the Convention on 24th May 2005. There are 39 chemicals listed in the annexure to the convention and subject to the PIC procedure, including 24 pesticides, 4 severely hazardous pesticide formulations and 11 industrial chemicals.

In India, Customs is empowered under section 3(3) of Foreign Trade (Development and Regulation) Act, 1992 and under section III (d) of the Customs Act, 1962 for controlling and monitoring the imports of such items.

Major Cases of Environmental Crimes Detected by Indian Customs

Following are a few important cases.

1. A large number of cases of smuggling of Red Sanders have been detected. Red Sanders (Pterocarpus Santalinus) or Red Sandalwood is a deciduous tree, considered as endemic in Southern parts of Eastern ghats of India. It is most commonly found in the states of Andhra Pradesh, Karnataka and Tamilnadu.It is a rare and highly valued variety of timber, the export and import of which is banned under CITES. The demand for this endangered exotic wood in South East Asian countries has led to increased attempts to smuggle the item.
2. Rescue and rehabilitation of several thousands of evolutionarily important reptile, i.e., "Star Tortoise" which are covered under CITES, that were being smuggled to South East Asian Countries.
3. Seizure of several consignments of Seahorses (Hippocampus) covered under CITES being smuggled to South East Asian Countries for use in making traditional medicines.
4. Seizure of a huge quantity of Saussurea lappa, a plant root which is an endangered species classified in Appendix - I of CITES smuggled into India by misdescribing it as Inula racemosa and Chinese Ginseng.
5. Cases of smuggling of snake skins have been detected. King cobra and Russel viper are among the most venomous snakes found mainly in South East Asia. They are endangered species and are listed in CITES. They are mainly killed for their skin, which is used to make leather items such as belts, purses and bags. Snakes are caught by poachers and their skin is peeled off when they are alive. Snake skins fetch very high price in European countries and hence they are smuggled out of India.
6. Import of municipal waste in the guise of waste paper—brown mix the contents on inspection after de-stuffing were found to contain pressed bales predominantly of used plastics, including PET bottles, glass waste, sanitary waste, acrylics, metal including scrap, wires, e-waste, food wastes, toner cartridge and other municipal waste and garbage in unsorted condition. Several of the wastes are covered under the Hazardous Waste (Management & Handling) Rules, 1989 and prohibited for import/export.
7. Import of Plastic Waste (import of which is not permitted) in the guise of PET bottle scrap (which is permitted for import).

A consignment consisting of 12 × 20 Containers declared as "PET bottle scrap" was imported which on detailed inspection was found to be pressed bales predominantly of used plastic carry bags, damaged plastic waste materials, used soft drink tins / bottles and other municipal waste and garbage in unsorted condition.

8. Seizure of Ozone Depleting Substances such as dichlorodifluoro methane, chloro difluoro methane, etc.
9. Seizure of hazardous chemicals (lead droze) has also been affected by the Indian Customs.

CITES

The purpose of CITES (Convention on International Trade in Endangered Species of Wild flora and fauna is to ensure that wild flora and fauna in international trade are not exploited unsustainably. The framework and common procedural mechanism are now used by 174 countries that are Parties to the Convention, to regulate and monitor international trade in wild resources and endangered species. CITES regulations are covered under three appendices with about 5185 animal species and 28307 plant species.

Indian Customs implements CITES through the Customs Act 1962, the Foreign Trade (Development and Regulation) Act 1992 and the Wildlife Protection Act 1972 which have provisions for seizure of wild flora and fauna and their products/artifacts, when illegally traded or smuggled in or out of the country.

It is an international agreement between governments, drafted as a result of a resolution adopted in 1973 at a meeting of 80 member countries of the World Conservation Union (IUCN). It aims to ensure that international trade in wild animals and plants does not threaten their survival, and it accords varying degrees of protection to more than 33,000 species of wild flora and fauna. CITES provides a framework to be respected by each party, which has to adopt its own domestic legislation to ensure implementation of CITES at the national level. It has now 174 signatories.

CITES works by subjecting international trade in selected species to varying degrees of control. The species covered by CITES are listed in three appendices, according to the degree of protection they need. Appendix I covers species threatened with extinction and therefore trade in these species is normally illegal but permitted only in exceptional circumstances. Appendix II covers species not necessarily threatened with extinction, but in which trade must be controlled 'in order to avoid utilization incompatible with their survival'. Appendix III includes species that are protected in at least one country, which has requested other CITES parties for assistance in controlling its trade.

A specimen of a CITES listed flora and fauna may be imported into or exported from a country which is a party to the convention only if the appropriate control document is presented for clearance before Customs at the port of entry or exit. Here comes the role of Customs, more so because more often than not the CITES items are smuggled either by concealment or through incorrect declaration. Even where control documents are required to be presented, it is not uncommon that smugglers present forged or fake documents. Customs officers therefore are required to have domain knowledge about control procedures and indicators of suspicious shipments. They are also required to have liaison with the concerned authorities for carrying quick verification. Alongside the implementation of the CITES provisions, the Indian Customs also enforce certain provisions of the Wildlife Protection Act, 1972—particularly those relating to the endangered species mentioned in Schedule I of the Act.

ODS

The Government of India has provided the basic legal support for protection of environment through Environment (Protection) Act, 1986. In exercise of the powers conferred by this Act, rules and regulations have been framed to protect the environment. The Montreal Protocol adopted in December, 1987 deals with protection of environment, and has urged the developing countries for phasing out Ozone Depleting Substances (ODS) by 2010. India signed the Montreal Protocol along with its London Amendment (1990) on 17.9.1992. India has also ratified the Copenhagen Amendment (1992), Montreal Amendment (1997) and Beijing Amendment (1999) to the Montreal Protocol. All these amendments have enhanced the scope of ODS control. Mindful of the precautionary measures needed for the protection of the ozone layer, damage to which has potential consequences for human health, natural organisms and ecosystem, etc., and having regard to the aforesaid amendments which India has ratified, the Government of India has framed the Ozone Depleting Substances (Regulation and Control) Rules, 2000 for regulating ozone depleting substances and their movement across the border. Rule 10 of the aforesaid Rules deals with the regulation of import and export of products made with or containing ODS. Obviously and logically again, it has befallen on Customs to prevent illegal trade of ODS across the border. The illegal ODS trade in India is effected mainly by wrong declaration and false labelling at different import stations. The delinquents amongst the importers have been incorrrect declaring ODS like CFS22, Refrigerant R22, dichlorodifluoro methane of ODS amongst other permissible items in container cargo and of outright smuggling through porous land borders with India's neighbours. Besides, some errant ship-breakers have also been selling ODS recovered out of broken ships locally in India by manipulating documents.

Hazardous Materials and Wastes

The economic and ecological consequences of chemical and waste management, particularly hazardous wastes are now widely recognized as a global problem posing risk to the environment and health. This universal concern has finally led to the development of Multilateral Environmental Agreements (MEAs) that deal specifically with management of hazardous chemicals and their wastes. Some such important MEAs are the Montreal Protocol, Basel Convention, the Rotterdam Convention and the Stockholm Convention.

Article 4 of the Montreal Protocol requires countries to introduce import restrictions in respect of virgin, recovered or recycled ODS. The Rotterdam Convention introduces the Prior Informed Consent (PIC) procedure for certain hazardous chemicals and pesticides in international trade. The Convention enables the world to monitor and control the trade in certain hazardous chemicals. The Stockholm Convention restricts import and exports of ten Persistent Organic Pollutants (POPs) allowing them to be transported only for environmentally sound disposal or for a permitted use. The Convention does not allow recovery, recycling, reclamation, direct reuse or alternative uses of POPs, and it prohibits their improper transport across international borders. The Basel Convention (1989) was principally devoted to setting up a framework for controlling movement of hazardous wastes across international frontiers. It was then left for the ministerial meeting in December, 1999 to set out guidelines for the Convention's activities during the next decade, which included further reduction of the movement of hazardous and other wastes, and prevention and monitoring of illegal traffic. Thus, even in the field of cross border movement of hazardous wastes, Customs has a job to do. Hazardous Waste (Management and Handling) Rules, 1989 provide the framework for control of specified hazardous wastes and the significant role to be played by Indian Customs in international trade of such wastes.

Trans-border Environmental Offences detected by the Customs:

1. Tasked with the mandate as discussed above, Indian Customs has detected a variety of environmental offences and seized many endangered species which would be discussed presently. Of the seizures made recently, the name of Red Sanders (also known as Rakta Chandan) comes to mind first. Red Sanders are grown in a small strip of land) around 100 km. x 60 km.) in Cuddapah, Chittoor districts of Andhra Pradesh. There is no other place in the world growing this plant. It is an Appendix II item of CITES and, it's export from India is banned. But the item has tremendous demand in markets of China and South-

East Asia, where it is used for making musical instruments and high quality furniture. Total seizure of around 1750 MT of Red Sanders by Indian Customs in the past few years indicates the extent of smuggling of this item. If felling of these trees for the ultimate purpose of smuggling goes unabated, we will rightly be accused by our descendents for this species being extinct in future.

2. Smuggling of Star Tortoise, a palm-sized ornamental tortoise, which is also an Appendix II item of CITES has increased recently. Their main markets are in Japan and South-East Asia. In the past two years, Indian Customs have seized about 2600 live Star Tortoises. Other favourite item of smugglers is snake skin and hides of endangered animals like swamp deer, Tibetan antelope, etc. In the recent past, Indian Customs has seized around 54,000 semi processed, processed assorted snake skins, 29 python skins, 40 jackets made of python skin and 576 hides of endangered animals. Such large scale killing of snakes and other endangered animals has huge ecological impact which is not measurable in terms of money alone. Further, peacock feathers continue to be smuggled out of India. In the past few years, there have been seizures of around six lakh pieces of peacock feathers. While the foregoing items were seized while being smuggled out of the country, there has been seizure of endangered species at the point of import too. Recent seizures of organ pipe corals and ornamental fish which are CITES Appendix II items are worth special mention. The illegal import of medicinal herbs is another matter of serious concern. Recently there has been seizures of imported herbs Kuth Root (Saussurea lappa) which is CITES Appendix I item and Salab Panja which is a CITES Appendix II item.

3. In the field of other two environmental affecting substances like ODS and hazardous material and waste, Indian Customs has made quite a few detections. Around 4600 cylinders of ODS like CFC Gas, R-22 refrigerant gas have been seized in the past two years. As for hazardous material and waste, the Indian Customs has made detection of unauthorized importation of around 23,000 MTs of non virgin plastic scrap. The Import Policy allows import of virgin scrap only which is generated during the course of various processing operations where the plastic raw material was not put to any prior use. The idea is that such a virgin scrap can be

recycled into viable commercial products without involving any process of cleaning; whereby effluents are generated, thus adding to the protection of environment.

Thus, Indian Customs is alive to the environment issues facing the mother earth and it continues to do its bit in protecting the environment by keeping a strict vigil on cross border movement of endangered species of flora and fauna, ODS and hazardous materials and wastes. It is important to improve the vigil at the border to protect the environment in the years to come. Greater awareness of relevant issues, improved capacity and enhanced international co-operation is expected to enable Indian Customs to fulfill its environmental mandate as highlighted by the WCO.

Expanding Sunderbans Mangroves

The World Wide Fund for Nature's alarming report on the future of Sunderbans, titled 'Sea Level Rise and Tigers: Predicted Impacts to Bangladesh's Sunderbans Mangroves', has been published in the journal, 'Climatic Change'. Though Indian part of the Sunderbans will not be affected so badly, conservationists wonder how many tigers would be able to survive here with nearly 60 per cent of the habitat gone. Of the total Sunderbans, nearly 60 per cent is in Bangladesh. Tigers do not recognize international borders though and cross from one side to another as and when they choose.

Experts say that every tiger requires a large territory of its own (known as range). An ever-spreading human habitat in the Indian part has already resulted in a drop in the big cats' territory; leading to frequent incidents of straying.

"Tigers have adapted to a life in the mangroves and crabs constitute an important part of their diet. Though tigers are a highly adaptable species, occupying territory from the snowy forests of Russia to the tropics of Indonesia, the projected sea level rise in the Sunderbans may outpace the animal's ability to adapt", a World Wide Fund for Nature source said.

Chapter - 3

Bhopal Gas Tragedy

For most of us, the Bhopal gas tragedy is an industrial accident, in which, 26 years ago to this day, large quantities of poisonous methyl isocyanate escaped from the Union Carbide factory at Bhopal, killing thousands of people and maiming the lives of half a million others. However, that was only the beginning of the tragedy, which continues to unfold as a saga of official callousness, political and administrative ineptitude, legal procrastination, botched medical study of the effects of mass poisoning, large-scale, prolonged human suffering and its cynical exploitation by a few and overall failure to leave the accident behind and move ahead.

Natural degradation of chemicals has cleaned up the factory site. An initiative by Ratan Tata to clean up the toxic site proved to be futile. American chemical giant Dow, which purchased Union Carbide 16 years after the Bhopal accident, continues to encounter public hostility on account of this failure of the syst m to avert such tragedies by taking timely action. Not that Dow is blameless on this count. When it bought Union Carbide, it acquired moral and legal liabilities of the plight of five lakh victims. Dow has chosen not to recognize this, taking an entirely legalistic view of things.

As far as the victims are concerned, no one has played fair – neither the courts that put their seal on a paltry monetary settlement that remains final although the actual number of victims has turned out to be five times as large as the group for whom the compensation was claimed; nor the government that distributed compensation 20 years after the accident and arbitrarily terminated a judicial probe; nor the Indian Council of Medical Research, which discontinued its studies for mysterious reasons; nor industry, which turned its back on the accident. It was easy for Dow to step into this breach and do something tangible to help the victims of the world' worst industrial disaster—as an act of good faith, even if it did not itself play a role in creating it. Instead, Dow has chosen to pretend that its philanthropy with the Jaipur foot would wash away the Bhopal stain. It is still possible for Dow to heed the call of 24 US Congressmen to make amends as also for Indian industry because it is a stakeholder in India and the sufferings of fellow Indians.

In saner societies, the 82-acre compound at Kali Parade, Berasia Road in Bhopal would have been a public monument where you would be compelled to bow down, probably stand a moment in silence, praying for more than 10,000 men, women and children who fell a prey to the toxic fumes that billowed out from here on a midnight 26 years ago. Instead stray dogs, grazing goats and a police contingent greet you at the Union Carbide factory, amid clumsily drawn chalk lines on the ground meant to keep permitted visitors away from touching the rusting carcass of the plant, which was set up in 1969 to produce Sevin, a pesticide, key to India's green revolution.

If nothing else, the mess captures what Bhopal's Balance Sheet looks like after quarter of a century. Victims taken for a ride by their own governments, a criminal justice system that has failed to deliver, and the continuing contamination at the plant site abandoned by the polluter, Union Carbide, now pan of Dow Chemicals as well as the regulator, the state and central governments, these are three Cs - compensation, contamination and criminal justice— that keep the 25-year-old catastrophe alive, posing questions on the moral fiber of the Indian society and the sensitivity of its successive governments. Then there are the mysteries. On February 15, 1989, the Government of India reached a settlement with Union Carbide for $470 million climbing down from its demand of $3.3 billion. Incidentally, just a day before, after a long-drawn out process, the administration in West Virginia, the US, had given its permission to Indian investigators to inspect the 'sister' Union Carbide plant at South Charleston to assess the disparity in safety standards followed at the two units. The plant has since changed hands to Bayer Crop Science; but continues to be America's biggest storage site for the lethal methyl isocyanate.

While the official figures still stand at 1,05,000 victims (including 3,000 dead), the government records show compensation was paid to 5,74,367 (5,207 dead) people. If the number of victims were five times higher than the original estimates, why did the administration slice the paltry sums even thinner instead of adding to the corpus? Going by the rupee-dollar exchange rate of 1989, on which the compensations were meted out even as late as in 2004, the sum that Union Carbide deposited with the government amounts to Rs. 713 crore. That's an average of Rs. 12,410 per victim doled out after almost a decade of the disaster, an abysmally low sum for the affected families, most of them rendered too debilitated to earn a livelihood on their own. Stack it up against the Uphar tragedy in 1997 where a movie theatre went up in flames killing 59 and injuring 104 in the heart of New Delhi. Each of the victims was paid between Rs. 15 and Rs. 18 lakhs, and the injured Rs. 1 lakh. And since the cheques were given out in 2003 – a year before the last Bhopal compensation was paid – the Uphar victims were awarded a 9% interest on their compensations from the date of filing the claims.

Union Carbide's $470 million would be worth some Rs. 2,847 crore, assuming a dollar interest rate of 2% per annum for 15 years and conversion at the 2004 exchange rate of Rs. 45 per dollar. So where is the rest of the money that should still be left in the account since only Rs. 713 crore had been distributed any way? Madhya Pradesh's minister for gas rehabilitation and relief says there is not a single paisa left in the kitty to give out to anyone. "We have done our job," said a former chief minister of the state. In fact, the first nail in the Bhopal coffin was struck by the state government itself. Three days after the tragedy, it set up the Bhopal Poisonous Gas Leakage Inquiry Commission headed by Justice NK Singh, then sitting judge of the Madhya Pradesh High Court. The commission was wound up an year later without any explanation. The ICMR, the country's apex body for formulation, co-ordination and promotion of biomedical research, started its study on the medical effects of Bhopal in 1985. It commissioned 24 projects, but when it closed the Bhopal chapter in 1994, only two of the studies had seen the light of the day. Dr. NR Bhandari was the resident medical officer in the Hamidia Hospital in Bhopal where thousands poured into its emergency wards on the midnight of December 3, 1984. Later, he was drafted into the ICMR team that had started its research on the long-term effects of Bhopal. A pediatrician, Dr. Bhandari says that, 2,500 pregnant women had suffered serious exposure to methyl isocyanate (MIC) on December 3. His team had followed even the last one of them to deliver, on October 1, 1985. "The gas didn't seem to affect newborns to any alarming levels," he says, adding that these kids should have been tracked till the pre-puberty stage to make any concrete observations. Till date, ICMR hasn't given any explanation what happened to those 22 reports, which, according to Dr. Bhandari, could have helped the victims get custom-made care since they would have triggered a wider debate within the global medical community.

From where the ICMR left, Dr. N Banerjee has taken over, with his underpaid understaffed team. He is the chief research officer at the Centre for Rehabilitation Studies, the only body conducting studies on the long-term impacts of Bhopal. A part of the state's ministry of gas relief & rehabilitation, Dr Banerjee and his 46-member team – 25 of them go out to the field to collect data of those who live a hand-to-mouth existence. The entire CRS, an organization that even the most critical NGOs operating in Bhopal admit is doing a commendable job given its constraints, continues to be on the temporary payroll of the state government 15 years after it was set up. A process to automate the set-up and convert the data currently stored in paper folders in dozens of steel cupboards is underway.

The ministry has a network of hospitals that give free care to anyone who has received compensation as a gas victim, but both Dr. Bhandari and Dr. Banerjee say a gas-victim and a non-gas victim diagnosed with, say, pulmonary tuberculosis, cannot be treated in the same way. "The normal person doesn't carry the burden of history, but the gas-victim's lungs would have already been damaged before he contracted TB. So the cure just can't be the same," says Dr. Banerjee. Today, Bhopal is a city ridden with quacks offering steroid injections to those with breathing problems. The low oxygen levels in blood, a fallout of the gas impact, makes the patient constantly fatigued, and quacks often rush in with instant gratification.

Verdict: A mockery of justice

The case registered soon after the December 3, 1984 Bhopal gas tragedy against Union Carbide and other respondents wound up 25 years later with the local magistrate's court hearing it, on June 7, 2010 for pronouncing the final verdict. CBI had chargesheeted Union Carbide Corporation, Union Carbide (India) Ltd, Union Carbide, (Eastern) Hong Kong, UCC chairman Warren Anderson and eight Indian officials for the tragedy on December 1, 1987. Thousands of people were killed in the gas poisoning. Of all the accused, only the Indian officials and Union Carbide (India) Ltd faced trial in the Bhopal court. 'The others, including Anderson, are absconding. Despite repeated demands by the gas victims, the government failed to extradite Anderson from the US. The Bhopal court had last issued a warrant against Anderson on July 22, 2009. Chief judicial magistrate Mohan P Tiwari's verdict comes after the court under several other magistrates had cross examined 178 witnesses and examined 3,008 documents, audio and video tapes during the past 23 years. For the gas victims, the judgment is mostly meaningless as it was not going to bring any of the main accused to book. "We've been betrayed so many times that the verdict fails to interest us," said Bhopal Gas Peedith Mahila Udyog Sangathan convener Abdul Jabbar. He said the government had decided to drop criminal charges without taking the victims into confidence in 1989. "We approached the SC and on October 3, 1991 the apex court directed that the criminal case cannot be dropped." He said the original charge under section 304 (II) was more serious and could have ensured an imprisonment up to 10 years.

"But on September 13, 1996 the Supreme Court reduced the charges against the eight Indian officials to 304 (A) which is death by negligence. The maximum punishment that we can expect for the eight accused "is up to two years imprisonment and Rs 5,000 fine," he said. "What is the excitement about the June 7 verdict?" Jabbar asked. CBI counsel C Sahay told the court that the tragedy at the pesticide plant occurred because of serious design and maintenance flaws which the management had overlooked despite warnings. Sahay argued that a team of experts from UCC, US had visited the Bhopal plant in 1982 and found acute flaws in its maintenance, safety and design. Even after this survey, UC (India) Ltd didn't take the necessary measures to ensure safety. Investigations after the gas tragedy also revealed that the plant was poorly maintained with insufficient safety norms. An experts team that surveyed the plant after the toxic gas leak found the plant was operating under hazardous conditions.

Victims and activists were on 07 June 2010 furious, eight officials of Union Carbide had been convicted for the 1984 Bhopal gas disaster only for criminal negligence, which is punishable with a maximum of two years jail, despite the enormity of the tragedy. "Today's verdict is a disaster... they've made it look like a traffic accident," said Satinath Sarangi of the Bhopal Group for Information and Action, an NGO representing the survivors and an activist who has been involved with the victims since the 1984 disaster. "The charges have been diluted. The victims are disappointed," he said. A quarter of a century after the worst industrial accident in history, a Bhopal district court sentenced seven people, including business leader Keshub Mahindra, for two years in jail under sections of Indian law usually applied to traffic mishaps. The Bhopal Gas Tragedy occurred on December 3, 1984, when leaking fumes of toxic methyl isocyanite from the Union Carbide plant spread to neighbouring slums, killing thousands and impairing a generation for life.

All the sentenced were granted bail in the case, the judgment of which could have an impact on the mooted Civil Nuclear liability bill that will provide for compensation to victims in case of a nuclear disaster. Mr. Mahindra, chairman of car-and-utility vehicle maker Mahindra & Mahindra, was the non-executive chairman of the company during the disaster while the other six were employees of the firm. An eighth accused had died during the course of the trial that lasted 25 years, examined 178 prosecution witnesses and 3,009 documents.

A court at Bhopal held eight former officials of Union Carbide India Ltd (UCIL) guilty of criminal negligence in the world's worst industrial disaster and sentenced them to two years imprisonment. It also imposed a fine of Rs 100,000 on the eight. The eight include Keshub Mahindra, who then headed UCIL, from whose pesticide plant tonnes of lethal gas leaked on December 2-3, 1984 night. Killing thousands instantly and many more later.

The accused were held guilty under Sections 304-A (causing death by negligence), and 336, 337 and 338 (gross negligence) of the Indian Penal Code. A final judicial resolution of the case could take years. Those convicted are sure to appeal, in the first instance, to the sessions court followed by the Madhya Pradesh High Court and the Supreme Court. It's far from clear that any appeal by the state and victims seeking enhancement of the sentence will succeed. In 1996, the Supreme Court ruled that Mr. Mahindra and the others could only be tried for causing death due to negligence. The original charge sheet filed by CBI had charged the Indian employees of UCIL and Mr. Mahindra with culpable homicide not amounting to murder but this section was set aside by the Supreme court. Mr. Mahindra, who had declined a Padma Bhushan award in 2002 on grounds that he was facing trial in the case, and six others were present to hear the judgment, confronted by a throng of television cameras outside the court, Mr. Mahindra declined to comment.

The government says the disaster killed around 3,500. But activists calculate that 8,000 people died in the immediate aftermath and thousands more have died of illnesses related to gas exposure in the years that followed. They say a total of 25,000 people have died since 1984. Activists and health workers say a further 100,000 people who were exposed to the gas continue to suffer chronic health problems today. Sicknesses range from cancer, blindness, respiratory difficulties, immune and neurological disorders, female reproductive disorders as well as birth defects among children born to affected women.

Affected communities say the compensation given was based on government figures from the immediate aftermath that were grossly under-estimated. They say people are still dying due to the ill-effects of the gas. Survivors are demanding that Dow Chemical, which later bought the Union Carbide, pay more equitable relief to the tens of thousands who continue to suffer. Activists and lawyers say the plant site has not been cleaned up and thousands of tonnes of toxic chemical waste have seeped into the soil over the years, contaminating groundwater that is drinking water for around 20,000 people.

A civil case is being fought in the United States against Dow Chemical and lawyers are demanding that the company pays to clean up the site, fix the water supply and give compensation to those suffering the effects of drinking the water. A criminal case is pending against the then CEO of Union. Carbide, Warren Anderson, whom, lawyers say is responsible for the disaster and the contamination of the soil and water around the factory. There is a warrant for Anderson's arrest in India. Dow Chemical says it has no responsibility for Bhopal. It says it acquired its shares of Union Carbide in 2001, more than a decade after Union Carbide settled its liabilities with the Indian government. It says efforts by activists and non-governmental organisations to try to attach responsibility and liability for the site clean-up to Union Carbide and Dow Chemical are misdirected. It adds that it has no first-hand knowledge of what chemicals, if any, may remain at the site and what impact, if any, they may be having on the area's groundwater. The company says that when the Indian government took control of the site in 1998, it assumed all accountability, including clean-up activities.

Bhopal verdict as heuristic tool

The chief judicial magistrate in Bhopal has found seven former employees of Union Carbide India Ltd guilty of criminal negligence in the world's worst industrial disaster, which killed nearly 4,000 people soon after 40 tonnes of poisonous gas leaked out of the plant in the early hours of 3 December 1984, and tens of thousands died slow, disease-ravaged deaths over the years. The ruling throws up three issues. One, the victims of the disaster-those who died, their relations, those who continue to suffer the after - effects of severe poisoning gain little relief from the judgment, not even moral satisfaction that crime has been punished. Two, the Indian judicial system is far too tardy, to the point of being dysfunctional – an eighth accused died of natural causes over the 25-odd years of the trial and the chairman of Union Carbide, Warren Anderson was not tried in absentia. Three, the court ruling establishes the accountability of senior management, executive as well as non-executive, for industrial safety, even as it holds the UCIL officials guilty of criminal negligence, which carries a two-year prison term, rather than of culpable homicide not amounting to murder, an offence for which the penalty can be imprisonment for 10 years. Of course, the ruling will be appealed, and the final verdict will take its own time to materialise. But the last point should not be lost on industry compromising the safety of the workforce and of the community in the neighbourhood is just not acceptable.

There is every reason to believe that the safety systems at the Bhopal plant were under-designed, in comparison to those at the Union Carbide plant at Institute, West Virginia. However, this has not ever been legally established because no Indian investigation agency has ever made a formal visit to the American plant for the purpose. Even the under-designed safety system was not being run according to the prescribed procedure. All this amounts to a cavalier disregard for human life on the part of the company for which there is no excuse. True, the task is to bury the ghosts of Bhopal and move on, incorporating the right lessons from the disaster. But then, the ghosts of those who died for someone else's crimes may not rest till the guilty are punished.

The marathon trial

The trial in the 1984 Bhopal gas tragedy saw 19 judges presiding over it after the chargesheet was filed in December 1987. The CBI filed the chargesheet in the Chief Judicial Magistrate A Sisodia's court on December 1, 1987 here. CJM R.C. Mishra heard the case of the world's worst industrial disaster from September 30, 1988.

After him, Lal Singh Bhati heard the case from July 26, 1989 to November 27, 1991 followed by CJM Gulab Sharma, who referred it to session court on June 22, 1992. Thereafter it was heard by Session Judge S P Khare from July 13, 1992. The case came before two more judges on July 17, 1992 and November 29,1995. Session Judge R G Phapdke heard the case from September 24, 1996 and the matter was sent back to CJM's courts' following the Supreme Court amendments diluting the charges in 1996.

Seven more Judges heard the case before it came to Judicial Magistrate Mohan P Tiwari on February 21, 2009 who pronounced the eight accused guilty on 7th June 2010. The First Information Report (FIR) on the Bhopal Gas Disaster was filed on December 3, 1984 and the case was transferred to CBI on December 6, 1984. The CBI filed the chargesheet after investigation on December 1, 1987. Subsequently, the CJM framed charges against the accused under section 304 Part (II) (culpable homicide not amounting to murder), section 326 (voluntarily causing grievous hurt by dangerous weapons or means) and other relevant sections of IPC. After the accused moved the apex court, it amended the charges on September 13, 1996 to 304 (A) (causing death by negligence), 336 (acts endangering life or personal safety of others, 337 (causing hurt by endangering life or personal safety of others) and other sections of IPC.

The first prosecution witness deposed in the CJM court on September 29, 1997 and the last on August 3, 2005. 178 prosecution witnesses recorded their statement and the prosecution placed 3,009 documents. The first defence witness deposed on June 27, 2009 and the last one of the eight recorded his statement on February 22. Out of the nine accused, B Roy Choudhary, the then former Assistant Works Manager UCIL., Mumbai died during the trial. The eight other accused tried in the case were Keshub Mahindra, the then Chairman, Union Carbide India Ltd (UCIL), Vijay Gokhle, the then Managing Director, UCIL, Kishore Kamdar, the then vice President, UCIL, J Mukund, the then works manager UCIL, S P Choudhary, the then Production Manager, UCIL, K V Shetty, the then Plant Superintendent of UCIL and S I Quershi, the then Production In-charge UCIL and UCIL Calcutta.

Tragedy moulded green laws here

The Bhopal Gas Tragedy has shaped modern environmental jurisprudence in India. First, till Bhopal, industrial risk was understood as something confined to the factory. In 1976, for instance, when the Factories Act (1948) was amended, the focus of the law continued to be on the workforce, and its concern was limited to the factory premises. In a paper called "Communities At Risk: Industrial Risk in Indian Law", Usha Ramanathan, an independent legal researcher, argues that while widening of the scope of industrial risk began with the enactment of laws like the Air (Prevention and Control of Pollution) Act (1981) and Water (Prevention and Control of Pollution) Act (1974) which hold the "first glimmerings of understanding that what happens on the premises of a factory could affect people and communities well beyond its boundaries," it was not till Bhopal that the definition of the community at risk changed drastically. The disaster, she writes, demonstrated the potency of industry to cause mass death, injury and loss well beyond the perimeters where its activities are located, and brought the community living around the project into the calculus of industrial risk. Since then, the response from the Indian state has been twofold. The legislative response took the form of the Environmental (Protection) Act (1986). This Act authorizes the central government to protect and improve environmental quality, control and reduce pollution from all sources, and prohibit or restrict the setting and or operation of any industrial facility on environmental grounds. Since then, it has become an Umbrella Act from which a host of other environmental laws, like the Environmental Impact Assessment notification, the Coastal Regulation Zone, the proposed National Environmental Protection Authority, etc, derive their authority.

The second response came from the Supreme Court where, while ruling on a subsequent Oleum Gas leak in Delhi, Justice PN Bhagwati added the principle of Absolute Liability to India's legal liability regime. Says environmental lawyer Videh Upadhyay, "When the Indian government tried to hold Union Carbide responsible for the disaster, the best legal principle available to it was the strict liability principle. Derived from British Common Law, this says any industry engaged in hazardous activity is liable for adverse consequences even if the industry/enterprise is not directly responsible for them. However, mitigating conditions could be factored in, like acts of god, acts of strangers, etc." While ruling on the Oleum case, Justice Bhagwati went beyond strict liability to create the principle of Absolute Liability. The exemptions were done away with. The Court's order said: "Where an enterprise is engaged in a hazardous or inherently dangerous activity and harm results to anyone on account of an accident in the operation of such hazardous or inherently dangerous activity resulting for example, in escape of toxic gas, the enterprise is strictly and absolutely liable to compensate all those who are affected by the accident and such liability is not subject to any of the exceptions which operate vis-a-vis the tortious principle of strict liability." This was a landmark legal principle developed in the backdrop of Bhopal.

Verdict a lesson for India Inc

Justice delayed also serves, even if it lets down the immediate victims of injustice. So it has been with the victims of the 1984 Bhopal gas tragedy, the world's worst industrial disaster that has, over the years, consumed upwards of 15,000 lives. However, the ruling by the chief judicial magistrate of Bhopal, 25 years on, finding seven senior managers of the erstwhile Union Carbide India Ltd guilty of criminial negligence, establishes a sound principle: there is a price to pay for neglecting industrial safety. Had they been found guilty of culpable homicide, rather than of criminal negligence, there would have been greater clarity on how high the price would be. But industry has been put on notice if you cut corners on safety, of your workers, consumers or the community at large, your highest functionaries, executive and non-executive will personally be held accountable. That is sage advice for sustainable prosperity.

The Bhopal gas tragedy verdict added fuel to the opposition's resistance to the civil nuclear liability bill, asked the government to reconsider the legislation in the light of the Bhopal court judgment, which they described as "too little, too late." They cited the punishment pronounced in the Union Carbide case to drive home the point that in case of a nuclear accident, the reactor suppliers will be absolved of all responsibility under the proposed legislation. "It's painful. After 25 years of hearing, the accused have got only two years of imprisonment," a leader told reporters reacting to the Bhopal gas tragedy judgment. "The nuclear liability bill is under discussion. The government should learn proper lessons from Bhopal gas tragedy...The bill, as envisaged, does not put any criminal liability on the nuclear operator. Any nuclear accident causes long-term damage. In light of bitter experience of Bhopal, the government should reconsider the nuclear bill seriously," he said. Describing the verdict as a "mockery of the justice system", they drew parallels with the nuclear liability bill, which has been referred to a parliamentary standing committee. "The judgment should be an eye opener for UPA government that is trying to push through a nuclear liability legislation that will absolve the nuclear reactor suppliers of all responsibility in case of disaster in nuclear plants". It said the news shocked the conscience of every Indian adding that it appeared that the court had accepted the defence lawyer's plea that there were no lapses in maintenance and safety norms.

Our judicial system cries out for immediate correction. The damage caused to human lives and the environment due to the gas leak was monstrous and continues to have an adverse impact to this day. While a former senior CBI official involved in the Bhopal gas leak case investigations, said that the probe was influenced by the government, former Chief Justice of India Justice A M Ahmadi, who delivered the judgment on September 13, 1996, diluting charges in the Bhopal gas leak tragedy, insulted the dead by likening the disaster to a car accident. "We all own cars. If my driver is involved in a fatal accident I don't become liable under Section 304 (Part II) (culpable homicide not amounting to murder)", Ahmadi told a TV channel while justifying his decision to dilute the charges against Union Carbide officials.

Earlier, a former CBI official, BR Lall, told the media that he was forced by external affairs ministry officials not to follow up the extradition of Warren Anderson. The CBI investigation was influenced and commanded by some officials, as a result justice in the Bhopal Gas leakage case got delayed, hence, denied, said BR Lall. Claiming that CBI was an "under command" organisation, BR Lall said: "We need to make it free from government control to ensure transparency and fair probe. In other countries, all chief investigating agencies have been given autonomy by keeping it out of the control of the judiciary, bureaucracy and executive powers."

On his part, Ahmadi defended his verdict saying that he did not commit any mistake. "I don't think I made any mistake. If I had made a mistake with the judgment there was ample time to get it reviewed, 1996 till now is a lot of time. CBI could have got it reviewed. Why didn't they? The judgment was correct. This was a mass disaster but the law does not provide for such a disaster. There is no scope for vicarious liability in criminal law," he told a private TV channel.

According to US media, Anderson, now 89, lives in seclusion in Long Island, New York, and is unreachable. Activists who have ambushed him in the years since he went into hiding variously report him as being deaf and senile. The US, which promised stern action against those involved in the British Petroleum oil slick in the Gulf of Mexico - President Obama said that he was talking to experts to know whose "ass to kick" - has opted for a different yard stick on Bhopal.

A day after a Bhopal court passed a mockery of a verdict the US said it hoped that it will "bring closure to the families of the victims of the tragedy." In uniform reactions to the sentencing of seven Indian employees to two years in prison each, more than 25 years after the tragedy caused by the American company, US officials said they did not expect the verdict to open any new inquiry. "On the contrary, we hope that this is going to help to bring closure," Robert Blake, the US State department official overseeing South Asia, said of the tragedy which claimed more than 15,000 lives. The statement advertised US insensitivity to Indian concerns as it comes in the backdrop of the US administration's plans to frame criminal charges against BP for the oil spill of the Louisiana coast that claimed 11 lives.

Responding to demands for the extradition of Union Carbide's chairman at the time of the disaster, Warren Anderson, US officials have dismissed the possibility of his extradition now. "The question of extradition - as a matter of policy, we never discuss extradition. So I can't comment on that", Blake said. The US officials also wanted Parliament to pass the nuclear liability legislation in its present form. US state department spokesman P J Crowley said Parliament will have to make a judgment on the matter, "but this criminal case should have no relation" to the liability legislation currently before Parliament. "We just had a strategic dialogue with India. Our countries are closely connected. Our economies are increasingly closely connected. So I certainly would hope that this particular case does not inhibit the continuing expansion of economic, cultural, and political ties between our two countries. We fully expect this will not be the case," Crowley said.

Learn from History

Those who do not learn from history are condemned to repeat it. The verdict, which came 25 years after the world's worst industrial disaster at Union Carbide's India plant at Bhopal is a reminder that we need to improve our judicial system which is responsible for the delay in justice for decades. Secondly, it must never be forgotten that in comparison to the Union Carbide plant at Institute, West Virginia, the safety systems at the Bhopal plant were under-designed. It is true that we must move on in life. However, we must not forget the tragic history of December 2-3, 1984 at Bhopal. History leaves behind obvious lessons regarding our judicial system and the level of safety standards in industry. Let us learn from history so that we are not condemned to repeat it. That Government may find it difficult to wash its hands off the unwholesome twists in the Bhopal gas leak case became more evident when a former bureaucrat in the Madhya Pradesh charged the then governments at the Centre and the state with organising "safe passage" for Warren Anderson.

A day after a former CBI officer claimed he was advised by the external affairs ministry to drop proceedings on Anderson's extradition, the then district collector of Bhopal Moti Singh on 9th June 2010 said the Union Carbide chief got out of India on the government's order. Not just that. Anderson flew out of the city on the official plane of Madhya Pradesh chief minister at that time.

The then chief secretary of Madhya Pradesh Brahm Swaroop called Mr. Singh and the Superintendent of Police (SP) seeking Anderson's release, the ex-collector told a television channel. According to him, the Chief secretary was also asked to arrange a special aircraft to take Anderson to Delhi. Anderson was arrested along with other officials of the company on December 7, 1984, four days after the gas leak and released on bail the same day. He flew out of India from Delhi and never returned.

"At around 2 in the afternoon, the chief secretary summoned me to his chamber in the Secretariat. We went there..." he said "Mr. Anderson was to be released and sent to Delhi by plane which was awaiting him at the airport. We did the legal formalities and Anderson was released on bail. He was put on the plane and he went to Delhi," Singh said.

He also said that he was not told the reasons for Anderson's release. "He was reluctant to leave immediately. He said he wanted to see the affected areas and meet the people. I told him he was not welcome in Bhopal and that there was risk to his life and in no case he could be allowed to go to the affected areas, " he said. Anderson, who was charged with culpable homicide not amounting to murder, had tea with the then President at the Rashtrapati Bhavan after landing in Delhi. Though the government claimed that it has tried to get Anderson extradited from the US, the CBI's investigation chief had said that he had received a letter from the ministry of external affairs asking him to drop proceedings connected to the extradition request for Anderson. However, his claim was refuted by the director of the CBI at that time. "At no stage... neither the MEA nor the CBI... gave up efforts to extradite Anderson. MEA is sharing with us their difficulties which are very simple that is the unwillingness of US to extradite him to India."

Bhopal as environment city

The very site of the factory itself after remediation could also become a location for clean technologies. Ideally, a part of this could be converted into a natural urban forest, a *smriti van* to assert the victory of nature over unwarranted human transgression and the remaining area become a location for enterprises for green and clean technologies. If the central and state governments work together, Bhopal can be repositioned into a global environment city within the period of a decade.

It is time we stopped viewing Bhopal only as a site of pain and of shame. Enough of pusillanimity and looking westward and court-ward. Let us begin to handle Bhopal with a sense of pride in what India can do circa 2011 as against 1984. And what India will, when thrown a challenge. This is not to say that we should not go after the people who erred or correct the decisions that were faulty. By all means these must be a priority and is currently engaging the highest management attention of the government. Experts have commented on what more could be done on rectifying current limitations imposed on the victims through interpretations of law, nature of distribution of compensation, medical care, and remediation of harmful wastes from the site and so on.

Bhopal has considerable global mindshare just as Hiroshima has. It may be negative at present but that opens up the possibility of inversion. This mindshare needs to be leveraged through a big idea. Can we not conceive the transformation of Bhopal where that big idea could be the repositioning of Bhopal as a global environment city? Can it not become a location for clean, green technologies? Can it become a location for research in biosciences? Can it become a symbol of harmonious development in a city that show cases some of India's finest heritage?

Bhopal starts with quite a few inherent advantages. It is a city built on the banks of two lakes and one of them is covered under the Ramsar international convention on wetlands. It is the only city in India within 50 kms of two World Heritage Sites—Sanchi and Bhimbetka—one that represented the high point of Buddhist civilisation and the other the pinnacle of creative expression in prehistoric India. It houses India's finest ethnographic museum called the Museum of Man and its premier knowledge institution focusing on sustainable development, the Indian Institute of Forest Management. In a symbolic but nevertheless important gesture, the ministry of environment and forests has recently chosen Bhopal to locate the National Green Tribunal.

Positioning of Bhopal as a global environment city could begin by making it a location for clean technologies. There are three industrial estates in and around Bhopal of Govindpura, Mandideep and Chainpura all of which provide spaces in their locations and in one case could become an exclusive location for clean technologies. It should become a national effort to promote Bhopal as a location for clean and green technologies to prove a point to the world.

In a world that has already moved into Biology 2.0, Bhopal could be positioned as a location for knowledge institutions in biosciences. The Regional Rural Laboratory of the CSIR system which now has a thematic focus on mineral sciences and which after the bifurcation of Madhya Pradesh, with much of the minerals having gone to Chhattisgarh could perhaps reinvent thematically by focusing on life sciences. The Indian Institute of Science Education and Research opened recently at Bhopal could also have a thematic focus on life sciences. This institutional infrastructure of academic institutions can promote Bhopal as a 'bio valley' of India and complement a new industrial base of clean and green technologies. Bhopal's repositioning as a global environment city could be driven by its inherent advantage as a centre of culture and heritage complemented by the location of clean and green industries and the academic infrastructure of life sciences research.

One way to locate the resources for such a repositioning would be to earmark the proceeds from disinvestment of a public sector industrial enterprise, ideally a petrochemical PSU if its disinvestment is in the front-burner, exclusively to address this along with paying additional compensation to those who have been underpaid. There have been two major failings of Bhopal in addition to many others. One has been the institutional failure of taking away the prime responsibility of the state government from managing the problem by evoking the parent patria provision and locating nodal responsibility for a multifaceted problem with the ministry of petrochemicals. The other has been in permitting the political class to enlarge the area declared as gas affected, thereby leading to thin-spreading of the already meagre compensation amount. Along with the repositioning these issues of the people need to be addressed.

Additional compensation should ideally be targeted to those in the immediate vicinity and more intensely affected and those below the poverty line. It is also time that the government of MP considered pooling its available human resources in the medical profession to provide outreach servicers to complement the hospital infrastructure that has already come up. Kerala made it compulsory in the 1960s and 70s for every medical graduate to do an internship with tuberculosis sanatoriums to ensure that every doctor turned out by the medical college was made sensitive to the scourge of tuberculosis and advice for its cure. Similarly an internship programme could be developed for the Mahatma Gandhi Medical College in Bhopal to have compulsory internships in health outlets in gas-affected localities. New schemes of the government of India like Rajiv Awas Yojana, proposing infrastructure support to slum locations, open up possibilities for improving the physical quality of life in gas-affected slum colonies as Madhya Pradesh is one of the few states that have legislated for property rights to the slum dwellers, a likely conditionality of the scheme.

Chapter - 4

Copenhagen Summit

In 2012 the Kyoto Protocol to prevent climate changes and global warming runs out. To keep the process on the line there was an urgent need for a new climate protocol. At the conference in Copenhagen 2009 the parties of the UNFCCC met for the last time on governmental level before the climate agreement needs to be renewed.

Therefore the Climate Conference in Copenhagen was essential for the world's climate and the Danish government and UNFCCC was making great efforts in making the meeting in Copenhagen a success ending up with a Copenhagen Protocol to prevent global warming and climate changes. The Climate Conference took place in the Bella Center. The conference centre was placed not far from Copenhagen and near Copenhagen Airport, Kastrup.

Governmental representatives from 170 countries participated in Copenhagen in the days of the conference accompanied by other governmental representatives, NGO's journalists and others. In total 8000 people arrived in Copenhagen in the days of the climate meeting.

Challenges for India at the Summit

If some of the popular writings in the western media is to be believed, India's approach to climate change is all that stands between apocalypse and a happy global consensus on the biggest problem being faced by men. Be that as it may, various stratagems have been deployed to make India shun its highly reactive stance. While some try (coquettishly) to get arise out of India by seducing it with its self-image as an emerging global power, the less charitable accuse it of "hiding behind its poor". At one end was the seductive charm of India being assigned a seat at the high table; at the other lied the danger of it being relegated to the role of insensitive party spoiler. As the global community plods on to Copenhagen and beyond, the blame game about who should shoulder the responsibility for failure was already in evidence. The hard facts, however, paint a very different picture from what appeared in popular writing. A recent World Bank study shows that in the 10 years preceding 2006, India was one of the 20 countries in which CO_2 emissions intensity (per unit of GDP on a PPP basis) declined for both halves of this period. Moreover, this decline was more for the latter half than for the first. This happened despite the fact that the share of both industry and services in the GDP rose at the expense of agriculture. Both industry and services actually reduced energy intensity significantly. While traditional biomass consumption remained more or less the same, increase in use of fossil fuels was accompanied by the decreased carbon intensity of such use for both industry and the services sector. Now compare this taking the world at large. Increase in CO_2 emissions globally has been more in the second half of the decade. Of greater concern is the fact that the carbon emissions intensity of fossil fuels which declined in the first half actually rose in the second.

In this background, it seemed that much of the current blame assigned to emerging economies like India stems from the failure of developed nations to square up past responsibilities accepted as part of the United Nations Framework Convention on Climate Change. It also signals the uncomfortable yet inadmissible realization that it is well-nigh impossible for the developed world to meet the stringent and deep emission cuts that would be required if global CO_2 emission levels are to be contained below 400 ppm. As Jim Giles pointed recently in *New Scientist*, any fair allocation of carbon would literally leave the developed nations with no carbon quotas.

Even as international agencies castigate India's energy subsidies for promoting energy inefficiency, these complex cross-subsidies ensure that industrial consumers in India, on a PPP basis, pay the highest power tariffs anywhere in the world. The same holds true for liquid fuel prices where taxes ensure that prices of transport fuels in India are matched by few other countries. While these subsidies may distort the overall energy market, they do create their own pressures for economy of use (it surprises no one that small cars remain the preferred option in India). At the same time, however ham-handedly, they ensure some measure of distributive justice. They may beat fault in the manner in which they square things up for the poorest of the poor, and skew fuel choices irrationally. Should the need to impose greater carbon costs on energy be the result of global consensus, these subsidies will certainly have to be raised and unaffordably so. We have already seen this happen with the runaway oil prices of 2008 and market forces once again point in the same direction. Countries like India, whose per capita emissions are below even the most stringent stabilization targets considered by international bodies, cannot be expected to follow a development path in which their emissions from energy use would decline or even stabilize in the near term. Emissions from such countries will necessarily increase in the foreseeable future even as they decrease the carbon intensity of their growth by greater energy efficiency and by moving towards low-carbon energy sources without inordinately increasing the costs of energy for their poor. Even if hypothetically India with 17 per cent of the world's people were to freeze its 4 per cent share of the planet's emissions at current levels, its contribution in preventing the apocalypse being foretold would continue to remain insignificant. For the global commons to be protected, the world community has to agree to work on a path that eventually leads to a convergence of societies and lifestyles across the world. Targets foisted within any alternative are bound to fail and lead to conflicts. Unless development and action on climate change are addressed simultaneously on common accepted principles of global justice and equity, we will continue to be faced with the current dualism resulting in irresolvable conflicts. The only sustainable consensus remains one that has no room for high and low tables, rather than one that serves to insidiously maintain the status quo.

If a random perusal of various commentaries on the climate change negotiations at Copenhagen is a guide, it is clear that not much is likely to be achieved there. It is unlikely that a mandatory framework of carbon reductions will emerge to guide countries in domestic legislation. One major factor here was the unwillingness of the US to be seriously involved in firm reduction commitments. This was, of course, largely a consequence of President Obama trying to build up a sagging domestic image by concentrating on healthcare reforms. With the passage of the health Bill in the House, his agenda would largely consist of preparing the ground to sign the Bill into an Act by the end of the year. However, if the strength of the environmental lobbies in various countries was an indicator, it was safely assumed that the issue of negotiating climate change was not off the table. Through print, visual and other media, the consequences of ignoring climate change issues – and, in general issues of the clash between environment and development – were likely to be in the forefront in both developed and developing countries. Like no other issue in the past, there is a fair degree of global coordination today between 'green lobbies'. In addition, the EU's commitment to environmental issues is quite apparent. It even dominates many of their present negotiations in trade agreements. All in all, it would be said that 2010 was to test negotiation strength of Indian policymakers not only in trade negotiations but in issues of climate change.

Only mandatory international negotiating forum today is the WTO. The current mood seems to be to set up a similar forum for climate negotiations. While the principles of negotiations are the same, the issues are somewhat different. Most important, while negotiating trade agreements, countries are negotiating an increase in world production and trade of private goods and services. On the other hand, in climate negotiations, the focus would be on increasing the supply of a public good, a clean environment. The difference is important for India. Stalled trade negotiations do not have a major economic impact on India with its share of world trade at fewer than 2 per cent. But stalled climate negotiations would have a major impact as, with 25–30 per cent of world population, India cannot escape the consequences of an adverse climate change. Having said this, it would also be in order to see what India can learn from past WTO negotiations to prepare itself for the future.

The first lesson in negotiations is not to reveal your real preferences. This is where our minister for environment and forests, Jairam Ramesh yet seems to require finer appreciation of what is at stake. As the minister for environment, he is perceived as the final word on environment legislation. In that sense, for him to reveal his preferences defeats the purpose of negotiations, even if that is his private view. In WTO negotiations, it is common for countries to espouse each other's causes after bilateral/multilateral side deals. Thus, while the EU has environment as its main concern, it has used countries like Australia and others to push the issue. Similarly, while opening the Indian market for agricultural goods is more important for countries like Brazil and South Africa, it is the US and the EU that are perceived as pushing this issue. Second, while negotiators need to know the technical consequences of their commitments, it is not necessary for them to be technical experts themselves. Thus, it would be foolish to decide that negotiators on climate change must be bureaucrats from the ministry of environment. This seems to be the presumption in India where the purpose of lobby groups seems to be to ensure that the minister/principal bureaucrat in charge must attend seminars irrespective of who or where the stakeholders are. This is merely a reflection of the feudal mindset in the country. But this fails to understand the dynamics of a democracy where regional interests are beginning to assert themselves politically. India's negotiations in agriculture at the WTO are a perfect case study for this. So, pick your negotiators from the WTO group: they have more than a decade of experience. They know what makes the opposition blink.

Negotiating a mandatory multilateral agreement on climate change—whether under the UNFCC or not—will be very much like negotiating the WTO agreements in 1995. There are similar losses and gains, similar political tradeoffs, but far more severe consequences. But, hopefully, India was not unprepared at that time.

The climate issue has been caught in a deadlock for long with developing and developed countries stubbornly sticking to their stands. Meanwhile, the problem of climate change becomes grimmer by the year. Over the last decade or so, India has made the journey from a large, impoverished and laggard nation to an emerging power almost spoken of in the same vein as China, though still beset with significant developmental problems. As an emerging power, India should also assume the responsibility of leading by example in climate issues. The resulting moral pressure on the rich to clean up their act is sure to have a greater impact than expressions of resolve to not compromise, which have had 'zero success' in mitigating climate change. After all, the impacts of climate change through decreased agricultural yield, floods, droughts and desertification will be felt mostly in the tropical zone, and therefore on India, China and their neighbours. To say that India should not innovate or adjust its negotiating stance is probably sheer folly.

In his attempt to address the logjam, minister was reported to have recommended a new move for India by "not stick(ing) to G-77 alone" as it is now an integral part of G20, taking positive "initiatives to bring the US into the mainstream" and "nuance" from demand for financial and technological support from the, rich countries for climate change mitigation. His proposal had the potential to lead to successful climate change agreement(s) and also endorse India's image as a deal maker, otherwise known as an obstructionist country in every international negotiation. The minister's out-of-the-box thinking was not as impulsive as publicized by the media and politicians. Although supportive of western efforts towards conclusion of climate change negotiations, he had also maintained the essential crucial elements of India's stand: the need to preserve the distinction between the obligations of developed and developing nations, which has been buttressed well by the argument that binding emission reductions would necessarily slow down sustainable economic growth in developing countries, which at their current level of economic well-being is still imperative. The minister was also one of the first international statesmen to recognize the difference between 'rights' and 'responsibilities' – while the South had the right to resist binding emission ceilings it had the responsibility to self-regulate. Should the South not draw a lesson from the naked display of aspirations by the North, which saw the ceaseless use of resources not only in productive activities associated with high emissions but destructive pursuits such as world wars, nuclear bombings and stockpiling of weapons? At the same time, it is true that no climate deals bound the North in its economic march and so it is not difficult to see why the South does not want to restrict its growth prospects by being limited by one. This is especially the case as southern countries have modelled their political economic and resource use structures on the

North. Yet the counterpoint argues that it is time for the South to project a more enlightened stand as the future of the human race is at stake. It cannot afford to be blinded by the prospects of growth at this cost. The South remains wary of the intentions behind this counterpoint as it feels that the northern emphasis on southern 'responsibilities' rather than 'rights', as embodied in the new climate change deal might be another ruse to project northern interests.

But wariness does not justify inertia or the lack of realization of one's responsibilities to the human race. India and China have broken the shackles of global recession ahead of others, and are thus bound to be more hopeful about faster growth. At this point, if these countries are asked to effectively put a cap on such growth, a negative response is understandable. However, they need to shift their motives to a higher plane as the future of the Earth is at stake. Climate change will ultimately drown all of us if none of us take unilateral initiatives. If India takes the initiative of floating a lifeboat others are bound to follow. The double dividend to India: mitigated climate change and elevated status in the global League of Nations. The climate change negotiations are going nowhere with countries entangled in a 'prisoners' dilemma', with each sceptic of the motives of the other and agreeing to take measures only if others do so in equal measure. To prevent a logjam in climate change negotiations, the countries should present unilateral measures in confidence to certain chosen members of the convention. These members would define the guidelines for the new protocol, which would essentially be based on the common measures included in such unilateral reports. This procedure avoids the problem of who goes first and would be acceptable to all, with minor tweaking possible through provisions for country-specific flexibility.

Climate Victims

Just two days into the Copenhagen conference and the fight was out in the open. Two worlds brought together by one climate - uncertain future. But as yet, the climate conference was a dialogue of the deaf. There were many skirmishes and sides in the conference. But the end issue was as follows: The Group-77 and China wanted the world to stick to the commitments made already. They wanted the industrialized countries to cut emissions as agreed under the Kyoto Protocol. In the first commitment period of the protocol, these countries identified as those having to take action first because of their historical and current contribution to global emissions had to cut by a mere 5 per cent over 1990 levels. But instead of reducing, emissions have increased: by 14.6 per cent between 1990 and 2006. The issue on hand was to get these countries to commit to what science and politics say they must do to keep the world below 2 degrees C. The developing countries had demanded at least 40 per cent reduction below 1990 level from the rich world. In addition, this group was demanding that the world agree how it will enhance the implementation of the four issues on the table: mitigation, adaptation, technology transfer and finance. They were reminding the world that at Bali, the developing countries had agreed to take on nationally appropriate actions to cut emissions at home but that these needed to be aided by finance and technology. This was the deal. But it is being reneged upon.

The reason was that the Umbrella group comprising the US, Australia, New Zealand, Japan, Canada and sometimes, Russia, were asking for a completely different deal. They wanted to undermine the UN Framework Convention on Climate Change, which is based on the distinction between the polluters who created the problem and others who need their rights to development. The rich also want to scrap the Kyoto Protocol, which gives them legally binding targets and forces compliance. This group was pushing for a completely new framework: the Copenhagen Accord is what they are calling it. They wanted the conference to issue a political vision to guide action for a new legally binding treaty. But this would be a different kind of multilateral regime—bad for climate change; bad for us.

Their proposal was simple: No country rich or poor will, take on legally binding targets. Instead all countries will agree to 'pledge' what actions they can undertake domestically. These pledges will be the individual reduction targets of each country from Australia's miserly 5–25 per cent emission cut over 2000 levels, to US's meaningless 17 per cent over 2005 levels or India's newly announced carbon intensity reduction target of 20–25 per cent from 2005 levels, all by 2020. All these added together will form the basis of the international agreement with two added components; firstly, which actions will be comparable, though not equal. The countries like India or China must show that their domestic action will be substantial; secondly, all these actions must be monitored, reported and verified. This is the nub of the matter. Because the minute domestic action is internationally monitored or verified it becomes an international legal commitment. The proposal is delicious. (Therefore, India will not as well as takes on legally binding international commitments —interestingly by doing what the environment minister has/has not proposed. So, India sets a domestic target—as it has for 2020 (interesting taking the 2005 base-year, which ends up suiting US). This will be a domestic commitment to its own Parliament. And if we agree that all domestic actions can be internationally verified, then the same domestic target would become elevated to an international commitment.

The cleverest part of this proposition is that it will also change fundamentally, forever, the distinction between the past polluters and the rest of the emerging world. In this proposal all major emitter would be on one page in the same font size or smaller. But no difference: the principle of equity and equal rights of every individual to the atmospheric space would be buried and lost forever. Members quizzed the minister on his statements: will actions supported through international finance or technology transfer only be open for international scrutiny or all actions? On the floor of the house, the minister clarified that unsupported action would not be open for international scrutiny but will be part of an annual or biannual reporting to the UNFCCC (the secretariat of the framework convention on climate change) for "their consideration". Pushed further, he said, that this report would only be for "information". So, he has agreed that we would not, willy-nilly, be part of this second grand coalition of the willing. The problem is this is a coalition of the not-so-willing when it comes to cutting emissions. Their proposal, based on weak and legally non-binding targets will be disastrous for the world's efforts to combat climate change. It will be bad for us. We are climate victims. Let us not forget.

There are two questions: the first is, whether India has a right to expect financial support and technology transfer to enable it to increase the level of its actions; the second is whether our expectations of such assistance would be realistic and what would be the level to which it would be realistic. The answer to the first question is, yes. We certainly have a right and it is a legally recognized right under the convention, which as we know provides that the full incremental costs of mitigation actions taken by developing countries will be reimbursed by developed countries.

The convention specifically stated the extent to which developing countries would implement their commitments under the convention will depend upon the extent to which the developed countries implement their commitments in respect of finance and technology. So it's absolutely clear. The provisions make it clear that we cannot be told to do more than what we are prepared to do in our interests and in our independent national judgment. That does not mean it precludes India from taking actions with incremental costs unless we are compensated. It is up to us to decide whether we want to take such actions or not but we cannot be required to take such actions. That is why these financial provisions of the convention are of vital importance.

While there can be no compromise on these principles, the other question is: is it realistic to expect large flows of finance and technology? It is not so because we are being viewed as potential competitors if not actual competitors in global markets. And, therefore, these countries, regardless of principles of equity and environmental justice, have no intention of passing vast amounts of monies to countries like India and China. So we have to take a call what we can do or not do. But what we must insist on is that what more to do unless you are prepared to back your words with hard money.

Oz Emission Report

Allegedly, Australia had wrongly presented its carbon emissions report by ignoring a massive rise in polluting gases from its agricultural and forestry industries.

This "misrepresentation" by the government had led to severe criticism from all quarters at the summit in Copenhagen. Australia had ignored a massive rise in polluting gases from agricultural and forestry industries, and had managed to make its overall emissions seem much lower than they actually are, the ABC said in the report.

While under the Kyoto Protocol, Australia is allowed to raise carbon emissions by 8 per cent compared to the 1990 level figures supplied to the UN earlier this year say that between 1990 and 2007, the nation's real carbon emissions actually raised by 82 per cent, the report said. This dramatic increase is a result of emissions from rural lands, caused by bushfires and drought. But those are the very same agricultural, grazing plains and grasslands that political parties hope will help offset the country's rising industrial emissions. Australia has led the charge on proposed land use rule changes to the new global climate deal. The changes will open the door to the bonanza of green carbon that can be stored away in the world's rural lands, the report said. But the move was deeply dividing the Copenhagen conference. Christine Milne, climate change spokesperson for Australian political party, the Australian Greens, said in Copenhagen that the country had been trying to "cook the books".

The United States has always wanted to use "Land Use Change and Forestry as a mechanism for not having to do as much in its fossil fuel sector and Australia has always been the fall guy for the US," she said. "So I think what you are seeing is the umbrella group, chaired by Australia, including the US and Canada, trying to really cook the books in some dodgy deals on land use".

The CRU scandal's shadow has stretched all the way from East Anglia to Copenhagen. Climate sceptics have a strong case right now; since the CRU e-mail leaks, any thinking person would have doubts based on the apparent need of the CRU to make up data. However, the UN has ignored these scandalous activities and taken an approach that lacks solid backing. Uncertainty about the consequences of climate change makes it hard to persuade people to spend money on it. It has been observed that developed nations compel the developing nations to cut their emissions without doing enough themselves. And developing nations seem to be more interested in receiving an annual check than making any real changes.

India adheres to UNFCCC guidelines

India has displayed flexibility in its climate change position by offering to adopt the international guidelines under the United Nations Framework Convention on Climate Change (UNFCCC) while reporting to Parliament on its unsupported domestic efforts to deal with climate change. This move can be viewed as a significant step. It conveys to the global audience that India's reporting would be at international standards, at the same time the government would be able to tell the domestic audience that it has not submitted to international review. Environment minister said, "We have agreed to a national communication once in two years for both supported and unsupported actions. For the unsupported efforts the monitoring will be domestic only. The manner in which we do our domestic verification would be on the international guidelines as prepared by UNFCCC but there will be no international verification; only domestic evaluation by our Parliament". India believes in the 'trimurti' of UNFCCC, Kyoto Protocol and Bali

Action Plan. "India is not here to renegotiate agreement. The mandate enables existing two track approach of Kyoto Protocol and the Long term Co-operative action to move ahead. The two tracks must be completed latest by 2010. India has consistently opposed any attempts to dilute the Kyoto protocol. Ramesh said that he had repeatedly stressed that during his meetings. We are there to negotiate the launch of the second commitment period of 2013 to 2017 under the Kyoto Protocol that was what was being discussed. The developed nations have to agree with it. The minister also said that at present there were two draft agreements on the table – the Kyoto Protocol and the Long term Co-operative Action both prepared by the chairs of the respective groups. This is a good starting point for negotiations. The documents are legitimate. There are a lot of problems with the text, the great advantage is that the texts are being driven by all governments and the process is taking place in a transparent manner, which follows the two track approach.

The official text on the Long-term Cooperative Action, that is the Bali track, has 46 paragraphs. India has a problem with six of these. The major problem is with three paragraphs, which do not provide any alternatives, and violate India's redlines. These relate to peaking year, a global emission target without any differentiation between developed and developing countries and a review of 'adequacy of actions'. "We can't accept these as they are," the minister said. "The understanding is that the Alliance of Small Island States has contributed heavily to, the blurring of lines between developed and developing world which is evident in the three paragraphs that India has serious problems with. India is committed to act in a manner that would ensure that global temperatures meet the 20° C threshold by 2050. But we will not accept any other thresholds such as 400 ppm or 350 ppm", he said.

Two of the remaining three provisions relate to monitoring, verification and review of actions taken to combat climate change. It suggests quantification of the domestic efforts and international verification of all measures. The other provision suggests that all countries would contribute funds beginning from 2013. The minister said that this was not acceptable, "however, unlike the provisions on peaking, there is text in square brackets which puts forward our view. So these three provisions can be resolved during negotiations. India had categorically said that the agreed text would be prepared by the night of December 15, 2009. The heads of state/government would be arriving from December 16, 2009 and they had to work on adopting a political statement. It would appear that Australia was taking the lead in proposing that the heads of state should decide on the final text. India, China and Brazil had opposed the proposal.

Climate of Denial at Copenhagen

Climate sceptics, who deny that climate change is caused by human activity and who are admittedly sponsored by Exxon Mobil, the oil corporation, were holding a parallel climate change meeting in Copenhagen. They were just down the street from the Bella Centre, the venue of the UN Framework Convention on Climate Change (UNFCCC) conference whose goal was to come up with an alternative plan to the 1997 Kyoto Protocol that is due to end in 2012. The Protocol made a clear distinction between developed and developing countries in preparing agendas, whether of mandatory emissions targets for the former or clean development mechanisms for the latter. But what might replace the Protocol could bear little resemblance to it, if the Danish draft was taken seriously. Cloaked in secrecy, the host government had been lobbying among developed countries to support its draft that speaks nothing of either monetary help or technology transfer to developing countries. In fact, it recommended that the latter be also subject to targeted emissions cuts. Interestingly, developed countries have only increased their emissions since they signed the Protocol. That they were willing to confer secretly on the Danish proposal belied the spirit of the

UNFCCC that was meant to be an open forum for discussion and debate. There were several opposing camps in the climate change debate, making the issue more complex than it already was. Broadly, there were climate change deniers and climate change activists; the developing world that wanted the rich countries to accept their historic responsibility for industrial emissions and the developed world that wanted emerging economies to promise emissions cuts; sceptists who attribute the current climate crisis to heightened solar activity (or other reasons) and scientists who blamed it on human industrial activity. In the midst of all the crosstalk came 'Climategate' leaked e-mails from East Anglia where scientists chatted about ways to bolster their climate change data. While scientists may not agree on the exact degree of rise in global temperature if current trends in greenhouse gas emissions continue, that a process of global warming is underway is indisputable. This conclusion has been arrived at through numerous independent studies, all of which cannot have been rigged. In any case, scientific projections offer probabilities rather than certainties. While the lower estimates of projected temperature rise may be merely disruptive in future, the higher projections of around 60 °C by the end of this century will have catastrophic consequences. Shouldn't that consideration alone be enough to arrive at a deal that's viable and fair to all the residents of this planet, even as an insurance policy?

On D-Day a Non-Paper-2

The single-agreement would then include all the elements of the now infamous Danish draft, based on a pledge and review. It would remove the differentiation between countries, which have engendered the problem and the rest. And it would include commitments for all countries not based on burden sharing or equity, but on how much they are willing or can be persuaded to be willing to do and by when. So, all that could have happened in Copenhagen will be postponed to another day and another meeting. But this time, it will have the political backing of leaders.

This will be disastrous. Not for us, but for all of us who are already faced with the devastation of a changing climate. It's clear that the world needs an effective agreement to combat climate change. But this agreement cannot work, unless it demands that the rich nations reinvent their growth by substantially reducing emissions. It cannot work until there is clarity that China and India and others need the right to development. But equally it recognizes that we can grow differently without first polluting and then cleaning up. And that this is not possible without the world agreeing to share the economic growth, between nations and between people. In this global deal, equity is a prerequisite for an effective agreement, not a sweet-nothing or the preamble only.

But the game is afoot. Influential western academics like the UK's Nicholas Stern are creating the right conditions for the grand switch to start. They argue that the world cannot have a global deal without the participation of developing countries. The reason is that there is no space in the atmosphere left for the pollution of the emerging world.

But they do not explain that in the apportionment of the carbon budget how much has been filled in the atmosphere and how much space is left is a political decision about how the world will share and allocate ecological space. They don't believe this issue has anything to do with equity or fairness. Instead, it's about cutting a deal: how much without a price. In this scheme of things, the US and the rich countries continue to get disproportionate share of the global atmosphere to fill with pollution. What is curtailed is our right to development. This approach does not explain that countries like India take on the burden of transition, at their cost and their peril.

G-77 to put Kyoto on Top

On the penultimate round of the biggest ever geopolitical game of the decade, played at Copenhagen, went to the developing countries. The attempt by the Danish PM to hijack the negotiations by presenting the West's version of the final reports of the two tracks—Kyoto Protocol for the developed world and a global long-term agreement – was thwarted.

The developing countries, in almost complete unison, demanded that the talks could not be taken out of the hands of negotiators and run behind closed doors through selective consultations. The resistance by the bloc was a far cry from the days when developed world would successfully split the ranks of the developing countries to prevail in multilateral negotiations.

Under fire from the 131-country G-77+China bloc, the Danish host, also president of the UN climate talks, who had the support of other European countries, had to relent, the Danish PM had to finally say that no other text will be used. This means that while, for now, the talks would continue under the two tracks, it is the Kyoto Protocol discussions, which the developed countries want to, shun escaping the emission-cut obligations that will get precedence.

The G-77 was not ready to let the Danes get off easily. They did not mince words as they resisted the ploy of the developed countries to do away with the distinction between the developed and developing countries in respect of emission-reduction obligations. "We would like them to take over the issues. If this is not the case, we do not support you (the Danish PM). The result of this work must be two separate documents (one for developed countries and another for developing ones) and only these documents must be presented to the heads of state", said Sudan, speaking for G-77.

Several members of the G-77 demanded to know who the Danish PM was consulting if all the negotiators were sitting in the meeting and the Danish PM had not talked to any of them even by this late hour. What in diplomatic world would be considered an insult, Tuvalu's representative made a snide remark, suggesting he and others could provide their hotel numbers as well in case the Danish PM finally decided to call them too in the middle of the night to consult. The volley of attacks from them got a statement that made everyone break into sarcastic sniggers. The chair said the Danish PM was at that moment actually consulting about who to consult. The 0.77 kept at it. They had for almost a fortnight demanded that the decisions and joint statement of the heads of states should come only out of formal negotiations and not be parachuted in by select parties from outside.

US offer to Brazil

Negotiators in the G-77 camp saw through the conditionality attached to the US proposal at Copenhagen very easily. The Chinese were quick to react. "We will have legally binding emission cuts nationally. We are also willing to improve the national communication network to have more transparency. But countries should avoid confrontation and being suspicious. We are willing for an exchange dialogue that is not intrusive and does not infringe on China's sovereignty", He Yafei, Chinese vice-minister of foreign affairs, said.

The developing countries have asked for the industrialized countries to compensate for occupying disproportional carbon space with funds transfer using public finance through the UN process and not double count existing development aid as green funds. But the last-minute US offer, it was easy to say, included money it would provide through market routes, existing aid obligations and bilateral and multilateral funds from deals outside the UN. It was also evident from Clinton's statement that most of the money was marked towards deforestation, a deal sweetener for Brazil primarily. The Indian camp though made some contradictory noises on the offer. Environment minister Jairam Ramesh said, "It was a very important step". He also said that India had a 75 per cent agreement with the US on "transparency" while 25 per cent disagreement on "monitoring, reporting and verification". PM Manmohan Singh's absence, even if under circumstances beyond his control, has sent many in the G-77 group into reading more into it than what was obvious.

Re-emergence of the Fantastic Four

Bella Centre, the venue for heated arguments and diplomatic games being played out at Copenhagen climate talks for the last 12 days, had turned into a crucible to observe the emerging contours of new age global geopolitics. The re-emergence of the fantastic four – China, India, Brazil and South Africa —as a united front for the developing world concerns, the waning ability of Europe to dictate terms to the larger developing countries, the unsure position of India as it tried to make a transition in its international position and China's surge and influence in Africa—the elements were all in place.

With thousands of hardnosed negotiators shooting all out to defend national interests in climate talks that were bound to impact the global energy resource sharing regime like no other multilateral talks ever had before, Copenhagen had become a two-week time-lapse snapshot of the global power balance, a primer for the novice to flip through. The influence of the industrialized world over the small island states and the least developed countries became evident when one watched the economically dependent Tuvalu—a tiny island country close to Australia and New Zealand—asking the emerging economies to cut emissions (read energy consumption), something that helps contain their increasing growth.

When tiny and fractured Sudan gets up before 192 countries and its representative delivers speeches against the industrialized world for not paying its dues to write off the weight of historical injustice, one is quick to connect the influence China has over in Africa today. When Ethiopia cut a deal with France that other African countries slam, the old divisions of the African countries along lines of colonial division were easy to map. The fractures in Latin America along lines of Left rebellion and FTA linked US friendly economies came out as their negotiators take contrary positions.

Participants at the UN climate talks were starting to hunt for scapegoats. But, it was not as if awareness did not exist. Most countries planned to reduce emission intensity; it was just that no one wanted it to be legally binding.

China

6.8 bn tons annually, 5.5 tons per capita

What it's giving?

China said it will cut its carbon intensity by 40–45 per cent by 2020, compared with 2005.

What it wanted?

Developed nation's targets to reduce GHG emissions was not deep enough. It expected average cuts of a least from 1990 levels by 2020 and wanted a promise of more aid and technology.

The US

6.4 bn tons annually, 21 tons per capita

What it's giving

The US had promised to cut 2005 emissions by 17 by 2020. It would extend cuts to 30 per cent below 2005 levels by 2025, and 83 per cent by 2050. The US would work toward a goal of jointly mobilizing $100 bn a year by 2020. It also pledged $1 bn towards slowing deforestation.

EU

5.03 bn tons annually, 5.5 tons per capita

What it's giving?

EU leaders agreed in December 2008 to cut emissions by 20 per cent below 1990 levels by 2020 and by 30 per cent if other developed nations follow suit. EU leaders had agreed that developing nations would need about $147 bn a year by 2020 to adapt to climate change.

What it wanted?

EU wanted developing nations to curb the rise of emissions by 15–30 per cent by 2020.

India

1.4 bn tons annually, 1.2 tons per capita

What it's giving?

Aims to cut carbon intensity between 20–25 per cent by 2020, from 05 levels

What it wanted?

Like China, India wanted rich nations to cut emissions by at least 40 per cent by 2020.

Japan

1.4 bn tons annually, 11 tons per capita

What it's giving?

Japan would cut emissions by 25 per cent below 1990 levels by 2020. PM Hatoyama said Tokyo would also step up aid.

Africa

Negligible emissions

Where they're willing to compromise?

African group scaled back demands for aid from rich countries, meeting offers made by developed nations.

What it's giving?

Wanted developed nations to cut emissions by 45 per cent below 1990 levels by 2020.

Green Activist may Move the UN Court

Hinting at a possible failure to arrive at a consensus to move to a more sustainable path of development as the rich tried to backtrack on their commitments made in Rio and Kyoto noted environmentalist Vandana Shiva said she would move the International Court of Justice as a member of World Future Council with like-minded individuals and government bodies. Just back from the Copenhagen summit, Shiva expressed her disappointment at the divide between rich and poor nations and the consequences people would have to bear because of that. The World Bank may now be brought in to push the developing nations and smaller units and farmers will be completely marginalized", she feared.

"The carbon emissions that happened 200 years ago in the UK is ensuring the melting of our glaciers in the Himalayas today", said Shiva. "Worse was the emission of greenhouse gases like nitrogen oxide and methane that is 300 and 200 times more dangerous than carbon emission. This was climate reality and developed countries, with the US at the helm, were only compounding the situation by being adamant about cutting down on emissions," Shiva felt.

Eco-school Churns out Future Climate Warriors

Today's young students, not the world leaders at UN climate talked in Copenhagen, would be the ones battling to save the planet if predictions of catastrophic temperature rises came true. And few may be better equipped to deal with that nightmare than graduates of a unique eco-school on the Indonesian island of Bali, where an innovative curriculum has been designed to produce future "stewards of the environment". Founded last year by Canadian John Hardy and his American wife, Cynthia, the Green School is nestled in a tropical grove near Ubud, in the centre of an island better known for its luxury beachside resorts. From the main road through Badung village, visitors follow a stone path to the banks of the Ayung River that runs through the 20 acre campus. The only man-made structure visible at what amounts to the school gate is a 140-foot bamboo bridge with a sweeping roof made of traditional grass slats known locally as alang-alang.

Small crops of rice and vegetables grow on each side of the river. Living class projects meant to connect the children to the food they eat. Following the path on the other side of the bridge, the hypnotic humming of cicadas and the gurgling of the Ayung is suddenly broken by children's laughter, the first reminder that this is actually a schoolyard. Opened in September 2008, the school has around 150 students from 23 countries, ranging from grades one to nine.

In Global Discourse, only Loud Gets Heard

The leader of the Maldives, an Indian Ocean island nation, whose very existence is threatened by global warming, was emphatic. "In all political agreements, you have to be prepared to negotiate," he said in Copenhagen. "But physics isn't politics". Passionate, emotional and desperate, President Mohammed Nashid was also wrong. These days, everything is politics. Everyone who's talking insists at high volume that they're right. And now, amplified by the Internet, anyone, knowledgeable or oblivious, can talk to the entire world. Once, not so long ago, the planet's prevailing voices were those of the experts—the people who, right or wrong, had years of training to back up what they said. Then came the Internet, and everything changed.

Consider the global warming debate: The sceptics shout. The sceptics' opponents shout back. The scientists insist they have research in their corner. And public debate shifts from the provable and the empirical toward the spectacle of argument. Democracy in action? That's one way of seeing it. But is something deeper afoot? As the amplification of human opinion becomes more democratic, is the suspicion of the expert and the intellectual-along-held trope in American society going globally viral?

Because whatever side you're on, to sample the worldwide conversation in the age of the broadband connection and the constant, instantaneous comment is to be confronted with one recurring thread: Knowing what you're talking about isn't what it used to be. "What you have is the (presumption) of expertise by ordinary people who feel their opinions are as valuable as anybody else's. And at the same time, you have experts behaving like gods beyond what they know", says Frank Foredi, a sociologist at the University of Kent and author of *Where Have All the Intellectuals Gone?* "Society," he says, "has authorized everybody's opinions". As an ideal, direct democracy has great appeal. Everyone has their say, and truth and justice prevail. It doesn't work quite that way in the real world. That's why most operating democracies are representative democracies, where the people choose the men and women who will speak and act on their behalf.

Nevertheless, the notion that everyman's wisdom can trump formal training is a powerful one. The climate conference in Copenhagen has underscored and crystallized the wariness of expertise. As a polarizing force, climate change is both preposterously intricate and relevant to billions of people and unfolding just as social media use is exploding.

Disagreement at the Summit

Tension was palpable at the Bella centre. There was mayhem outside. People had been waiting for hours in the freezing cold to get in. But there was even greater chaos. The African nations walked out, protesting against the industrialized world's eagerness to renege on the Kyoto Protocol. They wanted real numbers on the table: how much would the rich world cut its emissions and by when.

Nobody knew what heads of state would sign when they arrive at Copenhagen. There was no paper ready, at least, as yet, for them to sign. All negotiated text on the table was still full of brackets (UN parlance for disagreements). And there was no breakthrough on the big issues, from the continuation of Kyoto Protocol to finance and technology transfer. It was rumoured that a paper would miraculously emerge, just in time. But given the logjam, this paper, which powerful leaders of powerful countries would fly long distances to endorse, would not meet the expectations of people who wanted effective action against climate change. It's planned as a non-paper, a mandate to continue to talk. It would not have any numbers of how much the industrialized countries would cut. It would not have the framework for technology or financial assistance to the rest of the world so that it leapfrogs to a low carbon economy. It would not have any real money for adaptation.

But this non-paper could still be enough for the rich world to dismantle the current climate framework. It could include some innocuous lines on the need for the world to begin discussions on a single-legally binding agreement on climate change and it could give a date by when this agreement will be ready. This would then signal that the world will junk the Kyoto Protocol, not today but by the next meeting.

World leaders insisted that the climate deal clinched in desperation at the UN summit was the best that could have been drawn as they returned home to a lashing from critics. Newspapers widely called the summit accord a failure and experts such as the head of a Nobel Peace prize winning climate panel said "urgent" action was now needed. US President Barack Obama acknowledged that all of the world's polluters would quickly have to do more, but German chancellor Angela Merkel said the critics would only hold up the battle against rising temperatures that threaten devastating floods, storms and drought. Obama returned to the White House and said "extremely difficult and complex negotiations" had been needed in Copenhagen. "This breakthrough lays the foundation for international action in the years to come. But even the US leader said "we will have to build on the momentum" and get the US Congress to pass mandatory cuts in greenhouse gases blamed for global warming. Merkel hit back at the critics: "It is a first step toward a new world climate order, nothing more but also nothing less," she told *Bildam Sonntag* newspaper. "Those who are only putting Copenhagen down are helping those who want to blockade rather than move forward". "We now need to build on Copenhagen," she said. The Copenhagen Accord, only passed by a procedural motion after two weeks of tense negotiations, has been widely condemned as a back-door deal that excluded the poor and doomed the world to disastrous climate change. The agreement was assembled by the leaders of the United States, China, India, Brazil, South Africa and major European nations, after it became clear that the 194 - nation summit was in danger of failure. China, the world's top polluter, has given the warmest welcome to a summit that experts say it has benefitted by making fewest concessions. "With the efforts of all parties, the summit yielded significant and positive results," foreign minister Yang Jiechi said in a statement. The summit set a commitment to limit global warming to two degrees Celsius, but did not spell out the important global emissions targets for 2020 or 2050 that are the key to holding down temperatures. The summit promised 100 billion dollars for poor nations that risk bearing the brunt of the global warming fallout, but has not given a fixed payout plan.

So far, the United States has promised to contribute $3.6 billion to climate funds for 2010-2012 period, with Japan contributing a total of $11 billion over the same period, and the European Union $10.6 billion. Even the UN chief Ban Ki-moon admitted the agreement had failed to win global consensus and would disappoint many who demanded stronger action against climate change.

"Many will say that it lacks ambition," Ban told at the end of the summit. "Nonetheless, you have achieved much". Rajendra Pachauri, chairman of the Nobel-winning Intergovernmental Panel on Climate Change (IPCC), said: "Developing countries, certainly Africa, are very concerned and very suspicious of the developed countries on whether they are really genuine in making these offers. We will have built on it, we will have to make sure it moves quickly towards the status of a legally binding agreement and therefore I think the task for the global community is cut out. In the next few weeks and months we will have to work very hard to see that we get a binding agreement that really moves action in the direction we need," he told a news channel. "We really have to move on rather quickly to reduce the emissions of greenhouse gases. There is growing evidence of the impacts of climate change and if we delay action these impacts are going to become much worse, far more serious," he warned.

Earlier that morning, the lounge at the Bella Center saw four men - PM Manmohan Singh, premier Wen Jiabao,

Brazilian president Luis Ignacio Lula da Silva and South African president Jacob Zuma, all sitting together to iron out the last issues of the climate change deal, particularly on the verification procedures and reducing, temperature rise to 2 degrees. The buzz in the room grew, and soon the four men found themselves surrounded by other heads of state and government who had gathered there. By this time, the four countries had, thanks to their accumulated clout and a unified front, grown to become a formidable bloc. When the PM landed in Copenhagen, it had become clear that the western officials were preventing any cutting of a deal, leaving it to the heads of government. This was not how India, or China, wanted it, but Indian officials going in realized soon enough that the whole game was going to be that the heads of government would use their personal charm or force to push through a deal—the amazing spectacle of principals poring over texts and battling over phrases. In a pre-emptive move, Wen held what could only be described as a heart- to-heart with Singh. Holding hands, Wen told Singh, "I admire you very much. They will try to split us, but India-China unity should hold".

The PM reassured Wen, "Mr. Premier, India will certainly stand by you". The conversation went on in this vein for a while, said sources. "Many difficulties in the bilateral relationship were patched up," said an official with satisfaction. The China-India bonhomie may not last, certainly on other issues where the two countries are at odds, but this time it worked. China was the one country everybody hit most during the summit. In retaliation, Wen even refused to show up for a meeting with Obama, saying he was meeting Singh instead. After the meeting, Obama walked across the hall to brief the Europeans (who had been left out of the crucial meeting). Walking back, he ran into chief Indian negotiator Shyam Saran. Putting his arms around his shoulders, Obama said, "Thank you for being so constructive and positive. It will work out well, I promise"

The Copenhagen Accord, for all its hype was little more than a "meaningful deal", in the words of the US president Barack Obama and the UK PM Gordon Brown, who addressed the media after the summit. The words had been chosen carefully—not a historic deal, just a meaningful one.

All it did was to bring countries together in "recognizing" that global temperature rise should be kept below 2 degrees Celsius. It was far more than had seemed possible just a few hours before but far less than what had been hoped for when the meeting began.

So what have these talks achieved? Almost from the start they had become little more than the backdrop to a series of much wider disputes - disagreements between the rich and poor nations, the rivalry between the United States and Europe, and between West and East, and the interest of the oil states. The biggest problems of all lay with the Chinese. They firmly refused to accept any notion of legally binding limits on their emissions. The opposition of Sudan, Cuba, Venezuela and a handful of others meant the accord could not be formally approved so instead it was simply "noted". For some, the battles between China and the US signal far more than a battle about how to tackle climate change. A UN official said: "What we are seeing here is China flexing its muscles. They are the new emerging super power and are determined that the US should respect them for that. That's the real agenda, not climate".

Inept and dubious are the only words that come to mind in describing the negotiations that have led to India endorsing the Copenhagen Accord. India chose to identify itself with the US, China, Brazil, South Africa—all well above India in every socio-economic parameter, all with much higher emission levels, and all with much lower levels of vulnerability to Climate Change. If there is any real concern for the bottom 80 per cent of Indians living below the two-dollar poverty threshold—largest such concentration of vulnerable humanity anywhere in the world—then now is the time to rise above party politics and thoroughly reject the deal made with the US at Copenhagen. India can't claim to be the world's largest democracy while ignoring the interest of 80 per cent of her people.

Historically American emissions have already usurped 30 per cent of the available global environmental space to support consumption of less than 5 per cent of the world population. Despite this, the US remained the world's largest emitter till 2007 when it was overtaken by China. If one accounts for the embedded emissions in the net imports guzzled by American consumers, the US remains the largest emitter; by far, even today.

China, the country most similar to India in the group supporting the US-driven Copenhagen Accord, has an economy and current emissions that are three times that of India. China's emissions in recent years have risen at an annualized rate that is three times that of India and China's share of available global environment space is almost 2.5 times that of India. In succumbing to the pressure and legitimizing the Copenhagen Accord that benefits the world's two largest polluters, India has also legitimized a weak 20 per cent emission cut over 1990 levels by the European Union. The real casualty of India's acquiescence has been a binding international response to climate change. Even President Obama, who crafted the Copenhagen Accord, while calling it an "unprecedented breakthrough" acknowledged that it fell well short of combating global warming.

The burial of the Framework Convention, the Kyoto Protocol and the Bali Action Plan has begun. By accepting the accord and abandoning commitments made under the Bali Action Plan, India has blessed a global warming of at least 3 degree Celsius at no or little cost to the rich. India's poor will be the fodder for such a warming driven by the unsustainable consumption of the developed world. Historical responsibility, the touchstone of the Framework Convention, doesn't find any mention in the Copenhagen Accord. While rejecting any notion of a "climate debt", funds offered place an unacceptably low price on the lives and livelihoods of the world's poor. The source and hence the predictability of such funding remains unclear. The accord "recognizes" the 2 degree Celsius goal but doesn't endorse it. The accord opens up nationally appropriate actions to "international consultations and analysis". And to top it all, there is no clarity on the way forward other than an "assessment" of the accord's implementation by 2015. In short, the entire international consensus built up since Rio has been set aside to the dictate of a new world order dominated by the US and China. India has played a supporting role to make all this possible!

The coup d'etat that the Copenhagen Accord delivers belies all the official pronouncements and grand standing by Indian government and the only saving grace is that India has escaped any binding commitments—for the time being. Reference to peaking was dropped for both developed and developing countries, thereby legitimizing global warming. Most importantly, the democratic multilateral process of the UNFCCC has been replaced by the will of the powerful. And if to believe Mat Mcgrath of BBC, the countries that supported the coup against this democratic process will be honoured on the front of the final document—a final threat to the weak-kneed among the 194 member countries to fall in line or forego even the financial crumbs put on the table. Commend those from Latin America and Africa that stood up to the pressure and ensured an outcome whereby COP 15 was forced to merely "take note" of the Copenhagen Accord without adopting or endorsing it. The way forward remains a mystery.

There is no doubt that a positive spin will be put on the outcome of Copenhagen by team India. The ball is now in the court of our political leaders, our institutions, our civil society and indeed our media to explore and understand the reasoning behind the change in India's stance as enunciated at the highest levels of government. Why did India acquiesce in an accord that has been questioned worldwide? A report in a British newspaper has accused IPCC Chief Rajendra K Pachauri of making a fortune from his links with "carbon trading" companies.

Apart from listing the number of companies, banks and institutes with which the IPCC chairman is associated, the report in *The Telegraph* of London alleges that Pachauri's The Energy Research Institute (TERI) continues to have "close links" with the Tata Group (which set up the institute) and that this relationship has helped the latter in its green and carbon trading businesses. Reacting to the report Pachauri told *TOI*; "These are a pack of lies from people who are getting desperate. They want to go after the guy whose voice is being heard. I haven't pocketed a single penny from my association with companies and institutes. All honoraria that I get go to TERI and to its Light a Billion Lives campaign for reaching solar power to people without electricity. All my dealings are totally above board".

Pachauri pointed out that the previous IPCC chairman was in the World Bank and the one before that was a professor. "Can you then say the university benefited from his association with IPCC? The people who have flung these charges are part of the same vested interest group which hacked the server of UK's East Anglia University. They are getting desperate because the world is now serious about moving away from fossil fuels. I want to ask them how much money they spent in the operation. Hacking a server is a costly exercise," he said. On TERI's links with the Tata group, Pachauri said, "Our ties ended when Darbari Seth, who was on our board, died in 1999. We haven't received a single penny from Tatas for years and have no ties with them". He added that TERI submits its yearly accounts to the government under Section 12 of the income tax law. "We fully comply with all government laws," he said.

Pachauri, who recently took up the post of the head of the Climate and Energy Institute at Yale University, said the appointment was held up for a while because he had insisted that his salary be credited to TERI. "My conscience is clear and that is why I am cool towards these allegations. On whether he intends to take legal action against the report, Pachauri said he hadn't made up his mind. "Action against these people only gives dignity to these guys," he added.

At 'Hagen, hunt on for excuses

The developing countries would emerge victorious, if they do, only because they saved the Kyoto Protocol from immediate death. They would walk out relieved but really, if science of climate change is a failure, they shall know they lost the battle to hold the industrialized countries accountable. But they shall hope the world knows (and writes) they tried. The African countries, with a fiery Sudanese representative as its face, will redefine the failure as its inability to forge a consensus with all G-77 countries to demand more from the rich countries funds, technologies and deeper emission cuts keeping global temperatures from rising beyond 1.5 degrees over pre-industrialization levels. Smaller country representatives would leave as much in a daze as they came in ten days ago draped in. The size of the geopolitical gamble they participated in as much evident in their being left out of the talks on crucial moment as in their daily routines – ministers, hot shots in their lands, mingling with ordinary citizens out of context.

Negotiators worked hard to prevent UN climate summit from ending in catastrophic failure after developing nations staged a five-hour walkout and China accused the West of trickery. As the White House said Barack Obama wants a deal that imposes "meaningful steps" to combat global warming, ministers admitted they had to start making giant strides. But their hopes were hit when Africa led a boycott by developing nations of working groups; only returning after securing guarantees the summit would not sideline talks about the future concerning the Kyoto Protocol.

That core emissions-curbing treaty ties rich countries that have ratified it to binding emissions curbs, but not developing nations. The reader may refer to the article: *African frustration erupts at UN climate talks.* It does not include the US, which says the protocol is unfair as the binding targets do not apply to developing giants that are already huge emitters of greenhouse gases.

The walkout delivered another blow to the summit, which has already been marred by spats between China and the United States. The White House said President Obama was "committed to pursuing an accord that requires countries to take meaningful steps", but acknowledged there was a great deal of work to be done. "There's no doubt that there are issues that will remain outstanding for quite sometime", said the spokesman.

The Copenhagen climate talks will generate more carbon emissions than any previous climate conference, equivalent to the annual output of over half a million Ethiopians, figures commissioned by hosts Denmark show. Delegates, journalists, activists and observers from almost 200 countries had gathered at the December 7–18 summit and their travel and work created 46,200 tons of carbon dioxide, most of it from their flights. This would fill nearly 10,000 Olympic swimming pools, and is the same amount produced each year by 2,300 Americans or 660,000 Ethiopians— the vast difference is due to the huge gap in consumption patterns in the two countries—according to the US government statistics about per person emissions in 2006.

Despite efforts by the Danish government to reduce the conference's carbon footprint, around 5,700 tons of carbon dioxide was created by the summit and a further 40,500 tons created by attendees' flights to Copenhagen.

The figure for the flights was calculated by the United Nations Framework Convention on Climate Change (UNFCCC), while the domestic carbon footprint from the summit was calculated by accountants of Deloitte, said Deloitte consultant Stine Balslev. "This is much bigger than the last talks because there are many more people here," she said, adding that 18,000 people were expected to pass through the conference centre every day. "These are preliminary figures but we expect that when we do the final calculations after the conference is over, the carbon footprint will be about the same". Deloitte included in their calculations emissions caused by accommodation, local transport, electricity and heating of the conference centre, paper, security, transport of goods and services as well as energy used by computers, kitchens, photocopiers and printers inside the conference centre.

While deadlock persisted in the climate change negotiations at Copenhagen, California governor Arnold Schwarzenegger has lauded the efforts of people in India for initiating the 'Lighting a Billion' lives project. The project, initiated by The Energy Research Institute (TERI), plans to provide solar lanterns to millions of Indians. Pleased with the project, Schwarzenegger, while talking to NGOs and media persons at the UN climate conference, urged others to take a cue from the project and work for taking voluntary actions for mitigating climate change, without waiting for government action.

"Movements have always begun with the people and not with the government. So whether it is US civil rights movement or any other, the governments have always reacted after people have stood up," Schwarzenegger said.

He was invited to address the conference to highlight the efforts of states and other local governments. He said, "Countries are trying to do their best to work on climate change. But the governments alone cannot solve the issue of climate change without the help of states, provinces, activists, scientists, universities and individuals".

Arnold committed California to cutting greenhouse gas emissions three years ago. "California will reduce carbon emission by nearly 30 per cent by 2020 to 1990 levels. I urge other governments to take up the challenge and have sub national goals for themselves".

Despite being the fourth largest economy, India's per capita emission levels are 70 per cent below world average and 93 per cent lower than those in the US, says a latest climate report. Jointly prepared by business chamber Assocham and consultancy firm Ernst and Young, the report highlighted that carbon emissions in India increased by 65 per cent between 1990 and now and are projected to grow by close to 70 per cent in the next decade or so. But it remained low as compared to other major economies, accounting for only 2 per cent of cumulative energy emissions since many decades.

India's declaration of a cut on emission intensity by 20 per cent to 25 per cent has invited a lot of criticism. But some measures at home front can actually make India's path less difficult. Like India's own energy efficiency trading mechanism, very much like the clean development mechanism, except that here super efficient industries can sell their energy saving certificates to not-so-efficient industries. This is part of Bureau of Energy Efficiency's new regulation that sets mandatory efficiency targets for 714 designated industries, failing which penalties will be imposed. The mechanism finalized after consulting industry bodies like FICCI will kick start from 2011 and can lead to a savings of around 10 million tons of oil equivalent of fuel, according to BEE. Thermal power stations, aluminium, steel, fertilizer, iron and steel, chlor-alkali, pulp and paper, textile and many others are included among the 714 most energy intensive industries. Asked what action BEE was taking to make India's growth path less energy intensive, director general Ajay Mathur said "The most energy-intensive industries have been shortlisted. They are called our designated consumers. We're formulating targets for them according to how efficient they are. The industries that do more than their targets will get energy saving certificates which they can sell". The implementation of this measure, also part of the national energy efficiency action plan, started from April 1, 2010, when BEE sat with each industry group and prepared baselines and targets. All those inefficient industries will be shaken out of their slumber through this.

Climate Fund

As we seek to better our energy efficiency profile and further cut down on the emission intensity (per unit of output), we need to call for the Climate Fund to be headquartered here. It would make sense to have mechanisms in place to leverage the moneys and parts invest in technology and venture capital funds. It requires a thriving ecosystem of innovative clusters for research and development. We do need to engage the US and other mature markets to be upfront on emission reduction commitments. But we need to stop seeing global climate parleys as merely zero-sum games, with dear winning and losing parties. The policy focus surely ought to be on joint R&D and other collaborative efforts. Instead of seeking just aid, Indian policymakers need to be much more subtle.

Suggested Measures

Horst Rechelbacher is often described as the 'green guru'. This ecopreneur is the founder of Aveda and believes chemicals will soon be replaced by nutraceuticals in the cosmetic industry.

Every entrepreneur should think about the ecological impact of his decisions. The future beckons to be environment friendly entrepreneurs. Horst Rechelbacher an activist for an organic environment developed a personal-care product line, made from food-based ingredients. So, from shampoo to lip balm to body lotion, the products are, literally, good enough to eat. He believes that being an ecopreneur is about 'redesigning the system'. Everything we put in our bodies must be nutritious and safe. So, he tried to set the example by living a green lifestyle. He became an organic farmer to understand the interconnection between soil, seed, water, sun and air. He also reduced his carbon footprint through the use of solar, wind and geothermal energy. He urges entrepreneurs not to use fake environmental issues and rename petrochemicals as natural.

In today's age, ecopreneurs have to be about show and tell. You have to tell the world, how you're bringing about a difference. You've got to show people how to change the world and make profits in ways that benefit the planet. We really need to bring more consciousness and information. Right now, even nature is telling us to work towards greening the planet. Green capitalists need to create a new economy, which purifies it. We need new technology, which is engineered to protect the environment, and not toxicate it. India has quite a few low-hanging fruits, when it comes to making its contribution to arresting climate change. The voluntary commitment that India has made, that emission intensity—emissions per unit of output—would be brought down 25 per cent over the 2005 base year level is only a fraction of what is achievable, at little cost.

Take the easiest thing to be done. This is in lighting which accounts for about 15 per cent of all electricity consumption. The scope for raising energy efficiency in lighting is huge. The conventional incandescent lamp yields 15 lumens of light per watt. The compact fluorescent lamp (CFL) is five times more efficient, and produces 65 lumens per watt. Modem light emitting diodes (LEDs) are capable of producing as much as 125-150 lumens of light per watt (most traffic lights these days consist of circular arrays of these pin-points of light).

If we replace all conventional lamps with LEDs, total electricity consumption can come down by at least 10 percentage points. But that would cost a pile. Just as CFLs are more expensive than conventional lamps, LEDs are more expensive than CFLs. But there's a way out: economies of scale.

Can the government place a massive order to replace all existing lamps in all government buildings across the country with LEDs? Can it call upon all information technology companies, automobile manufacturers, all public enterprises, etc. to join in and enhance the size of the order? Such a massive order would force the world's LED manufacturers to set up huge capacities in India, and LED prices would come crashing down to a fraction of the current cost. The saving in lighting costs would then persuade households to switch voluntarily to LEDs. All newly electrified rural homes could be supplied with LEDs, which have a long life, as an additional benefit.

Another low-hanging fruit is coal beneficiation. Indian coal is low in sulphur but high in ash. About 40–45 per cent of what is sold as coal is non-combustible material which turns into fly ash. Removing/reducing the ash content is called beneficiation. Coal mining being a government monopoly, there is extraneous matter other than ash that spoils the coal—corruption and inefficiency.

India's un-beneficiated, high-ash coal wastes energy in multiple ways. The Railways earn about 40 per cent of its revenue hauling coal. Passenger loads and high-value parcels weigh less than bulk cargo like coal. So the energy spent on earning one rupee of coal-hauling revenue would be higher than the energy spent on one rupee of other revenue. It would be safe to assume that at least 50 per cent of the Railways' fuel bill would come from transporting coal. But 40 per cent of that so-called coal is rock shale, etc. that will finally turn into fly ash. In other words, 20 per cent of the Railways' fuel cost is spent on transporting worthless proto-fly ash over long distances. If the coal were beneficiated to bring down the ash content by half before being loaded on to railway rakes, the Railways could save 10 per cent of their fuel. The fly ash, once generated at the power plant, has to be then transported somewhere else, consuming yet more energy. Ash is an insulator and, inside the boiler, reduces the heat being transferred from the burnt coal to the boiler tubes, reducing the overall thermal efficiency of the system. Fly ash hastens climate change in yet another fashion. Once its fine particles form a haze in the air around the power-plant, it interferes with the radiation of heat (we are discounting the energy consumed in patients' to and fro movements to doctors to treat pulmonary infections created by the fly ash in the air). Concerning Coal India, the state-owned monopoly, to beneficiate coal before it sells there's a choice between conventional wet beneficiation and newer technologies of dry beneficiation. In wet beneficiation, a large quantity of water is spoilt and pollutes the ground, and also adds to the moisture content of the coal. When wet coal is burnt, it produces water vapour, a greenhouse gas, and also wastes some heat on boiling off the water in the coal. So, for all non-coking coal dry beneficiation is clearly what the climate doctor has ordered. There are similar other low-hanging fruits in multiple sectors.

Ten steps to success in Copenhagen

According to the WWF, these are the top ten ingredients for a fair, ambitious and binding Copenhagen deal.

The Secret Recipe

What is necessary to turn the Copenhagen Climate Summit into a satisfying success?

1. Governments at Copenhagen need to create a legally binding framework with an amended Kyoto Protocol and a new Copenhagen Protocol, which secures the survival of countries, cultures and ecosystems and clears the way to the low carbon economy.
2. Global emissions peak before 2017 keeping overall warming well below the 20C danger threshold, going down to below 1.50C as soon as possible.
3. Industrialized countries commit to reduce their emissions by 40 per cent by 2020, compared to 1990 levels.
4. Developing countries agree to undertake significant action making emissions at least 30 per cent lower than Business-As-Usual by 2020.
5. Zero net greenhouse gas emissions from deforestation and degradation by 2020, taking into account indigenous peoples and local communities rights.
6. A framework for immediate adaptation action is set in place, especially for vulnerable countries and ecosystems, including the provision of insurance and compensation.
7. Public finance in the order of US $160 billion per year is provided to developing countries for adaptation and mitigation through innovative sources of finance.
8. Mechanisms are set up to strengthen technology transfer and technology cooperation on research, development and dissemination of low-carbon and climate-resilient technologies.
9. A new institutional set-up under the UNFCCC allows for coordination, implementation and funding allocation, in a transparent and democratic way, and incentivizes compliance.
10. Parties agree transparent and comparable standards for carbon markets, forests and land use, mitigation efforts and

inventories, and ways to limit international aviation and shipping emissions.

Flexible Stand Required

Making a virtue out of the inevitable would appear to be the way forward in climate change negotiations. After the US agreed to reduce aggregate emissions 17 per cent over 2005 levels by 2025, and China agreed to reduce the carbon intensity of its growth (emissions per unit of output) by 40 per cent on a voluntary basis, there is pressure on India to place its own emission reduction targets. India should oblige. It can, happily. The fact was that emission intensity had been coming down steadily over the years, thanks to technological changes. Even if the same level of incremental gains in energy efficiency are maintained, India can safely reduce its carbon intensity by some 25 per cent by 2025. And this was the level of cuts that environment minister had suggested as viable. If additional measures are taken, which India can and should, intensity can be brought down even further. So, it makes sense for India to accept measurable, verifiable cuts in energy intensity, in return for finance and technology to make those cuts happen.

The Chinese 'sacrifice' was something that will happen as a by-product of their ongoing efforts to bring down visible levels of pollution. If the Chinese were to switch to a market economy where capital comes at its true cost, Chinese growth would become more resource-efficient. India's growth already enjoys low carbon intensity on this count. We need to do much more, particularly for the poor. India's poor are the worst sufferers of high-carbon progress: they can protect themselves least from the ill-effects of pollution. They would also suffer the most if and when climate change really bites. So, there is no case for making the poor of India an excuse for continuing with business as usual. There are any number of things that India needs to do for its own efficiency and welfare gains, which will bring down carbon intensity drastically: shifting to higher thermal efficiency technologies in power generation even with coal, more widespread use of compressed natural gas in public transport, creation of efficient public transport and taxation to induce a generalized shift away from private transport, building new towns designed to eliminate/reduce the need for commuting to work, green buildings, etc. If we add up the carbon gains from such moves, they will be more than anything we commit ourselves to.

Accountability

The statement by Prime Minister Manmohan Singh, in a way, assures that India is willing to work for ambitious global emission cuts and, perhaps, sign on to some sort of binding commitments, provided there is sharing of the technological and fiscal burdens. However, along with this, there is also the news that India is even considering the drastic step of walking out of the conference along with Brazil, South Africa and China (BASIC bloc). Apparently, according to the minister for environment and forests, China will play the lead in developing a BASIC 'draft', which 'fully meets India's goals and aspirations'. The walkout, however, may not happen given the prime minister's optimistic reminder that the Bali Action Plan adopted in December 2007 had, indeed, laid cut the goal of an 'agreed outcome' for Copenhagen. All this seems to present a certain lack of coherence and dear sense of purpose in India's approach. It will be a welcome change if the country is to play a bold and assertive role in pushing for deep emission cuts while keeping options open for appropriate mechanisms to achieve this. India's position, perhaps, has veered around to accepting deep cuts in the emission intensity, which does mark a welcome departure from the traditional adherence to the per capita emission (PCE, tons CO_2) entitlements approach. In the absence of a nuanced and more substantive, rendering, the approach based on PCE has tended to become something of a dogma and has lost its capacity to push for substantive forward steps to cut emissions. Its application has tended to become more as a negative instrument to oppose certain positions than advance any positive proposals. Irrespective of the approach used, negotiations must lead to imposing serious obligations domestically and multilaterally on the nations to address the twin challenges of poverty and global climate change.

The global financial crisis has definitely dimmed the possibilities of a 'strong' treaty emerging from climate talks in Copenhagen. Yet, it underscores and brings the need to move beyond the tall talks of voluntary commitments to the fore. In fact, experience clearly points to the limits of excessive reliance on self-regulation and underscores the need for strong binding mechanisms. It is clearly time to put an end to voluntary commitments and the dreams of self-regulation. There are two sides to this.

The first is the fundamental nature of the global climate change crisis with deep roots in market failure. There is no mechanism that appears to allow the effects of economic activity to be transferred into the realm of markets within sufficiently-reasonable time to make a self-regulating effect. The time lags over which that could happen, if it ever does, is too long and uncertain to work as a self-correcting feedback on the market economy. Besides this, there is also the near-complete impossibility of arriving at any reasonable causal connection between climate change effects in one geographical location with the economic activities in another. The only way open at this stage is to put in place a sufficiently-dynamic regulatory regime that can bring accountability in the response to global climate change concerns.

Copenhagen is certainly an opportunity to recognize the importance of a larger regulatory framework based on a system of binding commitments within which nations could both negotiate and trade. Between Kyoto and Copenhagen, all countries had the time to prepare for a transition into a tighter accountability system.

If anything, even with a 'weak' treaty, Copenhagen must begin to put in a place appropriate regulatory approach with binding provisions on all nations and reduce reliance on self-regulating assumptions. Without this, no real progress can be made towards deep emission cuts. The agreement could comprise binding commitments besides extending the market-based approaches institutionalized by the Kyoto protocol.

Secondly, the PCE entitlements cannot be taken as absolute and extended in perpetuity. This just principle requires a more sophisticated application. Demographically, while several developed countries are faced with negative population growth or its stabilization, most developing countries continue to register high growth rates. In some of the developed countries, high human development index (HDI) is coupled with low PCE (e.g., Switzerland 5 tons). While the high PCE of developed nations such as the US (20 tC) must certainly serve as the reference point, the process itself cannot be based on attaining parity with the historically attained high PCE values. The poor in poor countries are the worst victims of both pollution and climate change. The negotiations could leverage the skewed PCE distribution to adopt low carbon-intensive growth by seeking concessions to make use of new economic opportunities. It may also make sense to link PCE with indices like HDI to tightly integrate the steps in both directions: (a) controlling emissions and (b) reducing poverty. This is, perhaps, a more nuanced way to work for a new agreement. Willingness to adopt binding commitments will help countries like India to bargain for economic opportunities that can ameliorate poverty and sustain the current high growth rates with significantly lower emission intensity. This will call for action on both fronts to be measurable and accountable. This is the paradigm shift that must be attempted in negotiations so that such commitments could co-exist with certain degree of continuity of the Kyoto protocol. The position must become one based on binding commitments, as that' will also open the doors for substantive quid pro quo in 'burden-sharing'. The binding commitments must not only be verifiable but also subject to some form of accountability framework. Nations must follow up the international treaties with corresponding national laws to make them accountable within the country on both obligations. The onus is on democratic countries like India to show leadership and leverage the position of a growing economy with the new economic opportunities of cleaner growth. It can use that to help ameliorate poverty as well, instead of hiding behind the veil of voluntary commitments sans international and domestic accountability.

Tougher Stand at Home

There is needless controversy over India's position on climate change. We need to negotiate hard for green technologies and finance at Copenhagen. But domestically, we surely need to be more proactive and climate-friendly, to rev up energy efficiency, supply and induce better allocation of resources economy-wide. This is why climate change talks are similar to global trade negotiations. Just as our bound tariff levels are much higher than the actual applied rates, there's really no contradiction between chalking out an ambitious green agenda at home while refusing to take on binding reductions of greenhouse gas emissions in multilateral talks. India's current per capita energy consumption levels remain no more than those in the least developed countries; hence the need for stepped-up investment to boost energy supply. But concurrently, our utilities, corporate and even households do need to function energy-efficiently, to reap huge benefits.

There would be other benefits as well in going green. For instance, developments in solar photovoltaic could spur innovation in related fields. So alternative-energy technologies could yield competitive advantages in more ways than one; hence the need to be proactive, green and environment-friendly even as we remain firmly energy-deficient. New domestic legislation would be in order, say, to mandate stricter emission norms, to bring about more efficient combustion of global warming-causing fossil fuels. Yet there's no reason why India's climate-change negotiators abroad need to be on the back foot when questioned about domestic policy. Actually, a forward-looking policy on climate change at home can rightly be emphasized in talks abroad to keep up the pressure for climate action in the mature economies. The fact remains that emission-reduction targets for the developed countries, as per the Kyoto Protocol, have simply not been met, reason enough to seek significant emission reductions in the North by 2020 and beyond. India must do its share, for its own sake.

Danish Draft

Realizing that the draft political statement proposed by the Danish government has a Trojan horse embedded in it—a clause that would indirectly impose emission caps on developing countries—India has moved to block the move at the Copenhagen climate meet.

Environment minister Jairam Ramesh took the lead in Beijing along with Brazil and South Africa accepted that they would not allow imposition of a 'peaking year' on their emissions. Sources said the draft prepared by the Danish government, also the chair for the UN negotiations at Copenhagen, contained a clause demanding that India and other emerging economies 'peak' their emissions by 2025. This draft, shared with just a few countries by the Danish government, was shown for a small while to the Indian and Chinese delegations at the recently concluded preparatory meeting of ministers in Copenhagen. The Danish draft was shared with India and others in a preparatory meet at Copenhagen. But the 'peaking year' issue has now become one of the four non-negotiable the four emerging economies will go to Copenhagen with.

After the key emerging economies steadfastly opposed being shackled by emission caps, the industrialized countries introduced the concept of 'peaking'. Simply put, they demanded that the emerging economies not let their emissions rise beyond a particular date. This, without saying as much, requires India and other leading developing countries to begin reducing the growth of their emissions immediately and finally cap them within a few years. Thereafter, they would be required to keep their emissions at the peak level in perpetuity or reduce them further. The deadline for the cap being suggested was 2020 or 2025. With India at an extremely low level of per capita emissions in comparison to the industrialized world, its economy would have got force-locked into a relatively lower level of access to reasonably priced energy than other countries. This, experts within the government and outside had warned, stunt the country's growth process by making energy sources expensive. The move now led by India, along with the three emerging economies, blocked the attempt by industrialized countries to smuggle emission caps into the political statement was finalized at Copenhagen. With expectations of a detailed, legally-binding agreement fading at Copenhagen, the industrialized countries' had a month back begun lobbying for a political agreement. As in all multilateral negotiations, sources said, the advantage always lies with the bloc of countries or group that can set the agenda for discussions based on their draft documents. China's move to' take leadership and host a meeting with Brazil, India and South Africa has now helped craft a document that could compete for acceptance from the 194 gathered countries.

Suggested Key Terms

If the Copenhagen climate change negotiations are a key battle for economic dominance, PM Manmohan Singh did some chest thumping while attending the Commonwealth heads of government meeting. India is willing to sign on to an ambitious global target for emission reduction or limiting temperature increase if it is accompanied by an equitable burden-sharing paradigm.

1. Internationally Binding Quantified Emission Reduction Targets or Commitments: Say, today a country right generates Rs. 1,000 per annum national income by economic activity and emits 100 tons of carbon every year for this. But way back in 1990, when it was still building its infrastructure, economically it emitted merely 50 tons of carbon every year. If it takes on an internationally binding

quantified emission reduction target it will set a date by which to do so. Say 2010. Then, by 2010 it will commit to the international community under the UN treaty that it will bring down its emissions to 30 per cent below what they were in 1990. So by the end of the decade, it would be emitting merely 35 tons per annum. These are absolute reductions achieved in terms of tons of carbon per annum regardless of whether a country's economy is getting bigger or smaller in terms of GDP. Because it has set an absolute target, it will have to bring its emissions to 35 tons per annum even if it generates Rs. 2,000 national income. Right now, only the industrialized countries are obliged to do so under the Kyoto Protocol. Nobody has even asked India or China to undertake such targets in near future. So you are really not hearing anything earth shattering.

2. Reducing carbon intensity voluntarily: This is what China has announced it will do and India has proposed to follow suit. India and China are slowly moving towards becoming economically developed. They have to build more power plants, more roads and improve poor peoples' lives in order to generate a greater GDP and maintain a high economic growth rate. This means these countries will have to use more energy—much of it coal and oil as these are the cheapest. Therefore, in coming years, they would be emitting more and more gases annually than they do in 2009. By taking a carbon intensity target, they intend to make sure they squeeze each drop of oil and each handful of coal to generate more value and income for the nation. Right now, China has offered cuts while India is thinking of taking such targets domestically, and voluntarily. This means, they will not put up their achievements against the set targets for international review. Not unless the rich countries are paying China and India to achieve the target and some other countries want such targets to be put as a pledge by the two large economies as their commitments within a new UN treaty and for the world to review them in performance against the targets. India and China have refused to do so.

3. Deviating below business as usual and peaking at acertain year it is quite complicated now. And this is what some rich countries want India and other emerging economies to do.

> Say India's economy is growing by 8 per cent every year, now, its annual national income is Rs. 1,000 against 100 tons of carbon emissions to generate such income. As expected, if the economy becomes bigger, the country would earn a larger national income but also spew more emissions. By past records, experts draw a trajectory of next 10 years of its growing national income on one hand and greenhouse gases it emits to reach that level of income. This is called a business as usual scenario. Say in 2010, it will be earning Rs. 2,000 and emitting 150 tons. In 2011, will earn Rs. 3,000 and burn 200 tons of carbon annually and so on. If it takes a commitment to de-viate from this business as usual scenario by 10 per cent by 2011 it will be bound to limit its emissions to 180 tons only (10 per cent less than 200) in 2011 even as it generates Rs. 3,000.

Now, this one is a tough cookie to achieve because it is not simple to draw BAU trajectory for an emerging economy. It might generate Rs. 100 next year by increasing its software industry sales. But software industry obviously consumes less fossil fuel and is cleaner compared to producing steel. It is hard for anyone to predict what the economy would look like in coming years: would India produce more steel or more software or both to generate the extra Rs. 100 next year? This product mix would decide what emissions one would produce against that Rs. 100. And to take a commitment to push its emissions below BAU even as the economy grows would be like rolling out a chapati with one hand tied behind the back. India and China have refused to do so.

The carbon tax proposed by French President Nicolas Sarkozy and backed by EU is meant to be a punitive option for countries which show no concern for climate change issue, said a highly-placed official in the French government, who is also associated with functioning of the French mission in Brussels. Sarkozy has been insisting domestically that countries have to respect the "rules of carbon emission reduction to be able to export to France", the driving force behind EU. He has found powerful supporters in Germany and Italy.

Britain, however, has described as "protectionism" the move which could result in Indian exporter having to buy pollution permits to trade with EU. Sarkozy is in process of formulating a plan for imposing a carbon tax even on domestic industries to deal with climate change and believes that an import tax on goods on EU's borders would complement the domestic initiative. Admitting that India looked upon this tax as detrimental to international trade, the French official said the tax, as and when it comes into force, wouldn't be an across-the board phenomenon but used just as an incentive for countries which took interest in cutting down carbon emissions. A top official of French government in Paris said France was aware of the constraints India was working under, including recent outrage in the country over the money ($1.4 trillion as per estimates) stashed away in tax havens.

Rich Vs Poor at Copenhagen

The climate change draft prepared by Denmark that removed the distinction between developed and developing countries is threatening to split the participating nations with G-77 members threatening to stall the negotiations. The Danish proposal will work against the interests of the developing countries as it contradicts their position that the primary cause of global warming is the emissions from the developed countries. The developing countries want to keep the framework of the 1997 Kyoto Protocol which required 37 wealthy nations to cut greenhouse gas emissions by 2012.

What angered the G-77 nations was the way Denmark trying to force its draft on the summit. The Danes selectively shared their text with member countries. India and China were not given copies of the proposal though they were allowed to go through the document before the pre-COP meeting in Copenhagen. The Africans were spearheading the move to halt negotiations. While India was not in the frame yet, the Chinese were learnt to be giving tacit backing to the Africans. Obviously, the Chinese did not want to take the blame for any possible collapse in talks. There was also bad news for the efforts of the developing countries with two of the signatories of the "Basic" draft South Africa and Brazil—expressing strong doubts about the efficacy of the exercise. The absence of substantive issues in the draft appeared to be the chief reason for the lukewarm response.

But the "Basic" text had not been abandoned officially. The G-77 and China are working on it and inputs are being taken from the group members. For the "Basic" draft to be a workable proposition there is a need to address issues such as the quantum of financing architecture of the carbon market technology transfer and deep emission targets for Annexed I countries. Experts say the other issues that need to be dealt with include compliance issues, while Annexed I countries have enforceable targets, developing countries need to ensure that their targets which they have announced for domestic action are part of the facilitating track. In other words, they are not reprimanded for failure to meet targets.

Stark reality: 'The Survival of the Fattest' a sculpture in Denmark, represents an overweight Lady Justice figure, symbolizing the rich industrialized world, sitting on the back of a thin worn-out African man. Europe's leaders attempted to agree to a €2-billion annual endowment to the world's poorer countries in order to jolt the Copenhagen climate negotiations into a new gear. But with many getting uneasy about dipping into sorely depleted national budgets in post-recessionary times scarred by high unemployment, their success or otherwise would say much about Europe's role and its credibility on the international stage. The 27 leaders of the European Union had a battle on their hands if they were to reach this target contribution, amounting to $3 billion dollars per year between 2010 and 2012, not least because the sums were to be raised voluntarily. Raised targets for cutting emissions within a decade down the line were already problematic, but as one European source underlined, here "it is a question of instant money, within the context of an economic crisis and squeezed budgets". Opposition during negotiations on the issue in late October proved intense, gathering France, Germany, Italy and eastern EU powerhouse Poland behind an argument which said there should be no commitment to set figures. Why reveal all before discovering the intentions of the world's other great historical polluters, its advocates maintained. "Nobody wants to pay for Copenhagen," Poland's European affairs minister, Mikolaj Dowgielewicz, said then.

Rift in G-77

In what signalled a major setback for the unity of G-77 countries at the Copenhagen negotiating table, the Alliance of Small Island States (AOSIS) sought a new legally binding protocol alongside the existing Kyoto Protocol that would force India and China to take emission commitments. This will dilute India's efforts to keep the focus on the Kyoto Protocol. The proposal put forward by Tuvalu, which has the backing of the AOSIS and several vulnerable African countries, is for two legally binding protocols—one for the signatories of the Kyoto Protocol and the other for the Bali or Long-Term Co-operation Action track. The move is also part of a bid to bring the United States into a legally binding obligation though the US has made it clear that it will not accept Kyoto by another name. The European Union has not objected to this move. For long, the EU has chaffed at the idea of the US not being legally bound in taking emission targets. The AOSIS proposal, like a similar one by Costa Rica, doesn't suggest quantified emission cuts from developing countries. Big developing countries fear that their unilateral action would become subject to international monitoring if a legal outcome is agreed upon.

A section of experts said that these apprehensions were premature as what was under discussion is not the content of a legal outcome but the need for one. "The question was of the nature of the outcome and the text had not yet been finalized. India can ensure that its interests are protected. India will be asked to take commitments like

Annexed I countries as it cannot be qualified as one under any parameter," a senior official close to the developments said. Speaking on behalf of the AOSIS, Tuvalu demanded, and got a suspension of negotiations of the Conference of Parties—the full gathering of all countries—until the issue could be resolved. Tuvalu's negotiator, Ian Fry, made it clear that his country could accept nothing less than full discussion of its proposal for a new legal protocol which was submitted to the UN climate convention six months ago. "My prime minister and many other heads of state have the clear intention of coming to Copenhagen to sign a legally binding deal. Tuvalu is one of the most vulnerable countries in the world to climate change, and our future rests on the outcome of this meeting," Mr. Fry said. China, India and Saudi Arabia opposed the move for a full discussion on the proposal and maintained that the Kyoto protocol is a "valid system". "The main task of this (conference) is to adapt an agreed outcome from the Bali Action Plan (agreed in 2007) and we should very much focus on that," said China's lead negotiator Su Wei. Even as they objected to Tuvalu's proposal, India, China and other developing countries reiterated their demand for bigger cuts in greenhouse gas emissions by developed countries.

The G - 77 plus China group had so far; put its resources and negotiators on full gear to prevent any dilution of the agenda of enhanced commitments of the rich countries under Kyoto Protocol and inclusion of the US, set by the Bali Action Plan in 2007. But Tuvalu, speaking on behalf of the Association of Small Island States (AOSIS) group, demanded that a contact group – a set of negotiators getting into a smaller huddle—be formed to discuss the creation of a new protocol that would help prevent global temperatures from rising more than 1.5 degree above pre-industrialized levels.

While the AOSIS group has been vocal in its criticism of the large economies within G-77 in closed door meetings, this was the first time the convention saw divisions within the developing country bloc spill out in the open. India was the first to notice a concerted attempt being made by the AOSIS countries to set a different course for the negotiations. It pointed that the talks had to focus on the two decided tracks and that Kyoto could not be weakened. But the chair, held by Danish climate and energy minister Connie Hedegaard, supported the formation of a contact group.

Insfficient Efforts Made by the Developing Nations

The United States blamed China's "inability to commit" for the absence of a legally binding agreement. Though India wasn't named, it was clear that the recent flurry of domestic measures announced by India and other developing countries are not seen as sufficient by the largest emitter. Instead, US demanded that these domestic commitments be "wrapped into an international deal, an international commitment". Making the announcement of a 20-25 per cent cut in emission intensity by 2020, the Indian government had assured Parliament that this commitment would not be legally binding. At Copenhagen, US special envoy for climate change Todd Stem made it clear that these efforts from the big developing countries were not good enough. "If you look around, many countries are doing a lot. China has put down a number, though it was not as high as expected. Brazil and India have put figures as well. But what is important for an international agreement is that they announce things domestically and put it in an international agreement so that the country will stand behind those commitments. There needs to be transparency to ensure that everybody does what they say they are doing. Transparency can't be just trust, there has to be some consultative process", Mr. Stem said. Making a push for getting countries like China to sign an internationally binding agreement, Mr. Stem said: "It is true that our emissions have gone up since 1990, but the country whose emissions are really going up is China, we can't ignore that. It will go up by 60 per cent by 2020 and 80 per cent by 2030; they will be emitting 28 per cent of the global emissions. Math is math, you can't ignore it. The significant emissions of China and their inability to commit are the reason why there can't be an agreement".

There has been criticism that the $10-billion fast track fund is not enough, or probably just enough "to buy coffins". Developing countries have demanded a larger sum, as much as 1 per cent of the GDP of developed countries for financial assistance to developing countries. This is part of the reparation that developed countries need to make for their historical emissions. Stem clearly rejected the notion of a "climate debt", the basis on which the developing world has been demanding financial commitments from developed countries. "I reject the notion of debt. For most of the 200 years, people were blissfully ignorant about emissions. It's a wrong way to look at it. There is no sense of guilt or reparations, I completely reject it". The US official also confirmed that the major developing countries would not receive public funds. "I don't envision public funds going from America to China. There is only limited money. That is reality. It's just life in the real world. "Pushing for an agreement, Stem said this is not about "capping emissions" but about development". We recognize our historical responsibility and must help those who are in the early stages of development to do so in a sustainable manner". Taken together, this could be seen as part of the effort to divide the developing world into the less developed and the more advanced, a move that would undermine the UNFCCC and the Kyoto Protocol.

European Union under Pressure

With the 'Danish text' the draft climate change agreement circulated at the Copenhagen summit, divided the wealthy and developing countries on the issue of emission control. Europeans were under pressure to refrain from cutting deals on the side before the ministerial negotiations. G-77 countries had blasted the circulation of the text —worked on by a handful of countries, which include the US, the UK and Denmark—as it proposed to give more power to the developed countries and significantly reduced the role for the UN process. There were clear signs of the British contingent backing off from its participation of the drafting of the text. The draft had proposed unequal caps on developing and wealthy countries and sought to reverse a key Kyoto Protocol mandate that requires rich countries to take the lead in curbing carbon emissions. According to the text, by 2050 poor countries would have to limit per capita emissions at 1.44 tons while rich countries would be given extra leeway at 2.67 tons per person.

The developing countries argue that this would result in setting unequal limits on carbon emissions, enabling developed countries to emit more than developing countries. India and other developing countries had opposed the peaking year for developing countries when they were shown the draft in November. The reworked Danish draft has retained the peaking year requirement. What has also angered G-77 was the proposal in the Danish text to give the control of climate change finance to the World Bank. G-77 countries created a ruckus here with its negotiators calling it an unfair practice by the host country. Lumumba Stanislaus Di-Aping, who heads the Group of 77 developing countries, attacked the Danish Prime Minister Lars Lokke Rasmussen, saying he wasn't a neutral host. The Danish side got into damage-limitation mode by clarifying that it did not represent the official position and that it was one among the many texts for the summit's consideration.

Power Savers to be Rewarded

India was quietly raising its stake in the global green game, even as leaders haggle over global warming in Copenhagen. The government was expected to clear a proposal to put in place a market-based mechanism to force industry and commercial establishment to improve energy use, a move that will lower emissions automatically and narrow the power supply gap. The proposal was to introduce tradable 'Energy Savings Certificates' for energy-intensive industries such as steel plants and other major commercial consumers like hotels, malls and theatres etc. Before the certificates come about, the government will prescribe how much energy an industry can use for each unit of production—say, a ton of steel, manufacture a car or refrigerator.

Energy consumption is measured in 'units' in terms of MTOE (per metric tonne of oil equivalent). Those who meet the norm or consume even less energy than is prescribed will earn the certificates in proportion to the saving. Those who fail will have to buy such certificates in proportion to the excess power or energy they consume. "This will lead to a revolution and transform the manner in which we use energy, particularly electricity. India wastes 20 per cent of energy due to inefficient usage. About half of this can be saved through rightful ways of electricity use in the next few years. That means availability of 10 per cent more power at no extra cost and will automatically lead to an enormous reduction in emissions", said RV Shahi, former power secretary who had drawn the blueprint for star rating for electrical appliances. The amendments also suggested bringing existing commercial buildings such as office complexes or hotels and malls etc within the ambit of energy efficiency norms. Any existing building with a consumption of 500 kW (kilowatt) or a contract for supply of 600 kVa (kilo volt ampere) will be included for energy rating. So far, the rating norms applied to only new buildings. The amendment will also give the government powers to ban manufacturing or import of equipment and appliances that do not meet energy efficiency norms. The proposals have been suggested by the Bureau of Energy Efficiency under the ministry as part of amendments to the Energy Efficiency Act of 2001. The amendments have become necessary to start the PAT (Perform, Achieve and Trade) scheme for industry suggested in the National Mission for Enhanced Energy.

Transparency in Tops Urged

The deal to save the planet from catastrophic climate change must be made in full public glare with transparency and not in corridors with select access, the developing countries have warned. With the host country being slammed all around for playing a deceitful game, developing countries have now got wary of green rooms being opened quite early in the fortnight to cut deals on the side—green room meetings were held at the ministerial level usually with access to the most influential countries and was used to thrash decisions among the major players at the negotiations. Fearing that such green rooms and informal discussions among select players could alter the turf against the developing countries, the G-77 had demanded that the talks be held in an open and transparent fashion. "The level of mistrust is already too high. To hold discussions on the side and to leave out countries that have less influence out of the discussions merely to get a deal at any cost is patently unfair;" an Indian negotiator told. The G-77 chair, Sudan, also warned that games of divide and rule were already being played by the industrialized countries and transparency had been given short shrift. Di-Aping Lumumba from Sudan and spokesperson for G-77 took the unprecedented step of even accusing UN secretary general Ban Ki-moon of siding with the interests of the industrialized countries to the detriment of African and other poor countries. Also, experience of Bali meeting, where green rooms led to a weaker accord than developing countries wanted and the UN convention secretariat being accused of being partisan, are still fresh in the minds of negotiators.

Emission Intensity Target

A World Bank study, done on India's request, has contradicted the UPA government's claims while pledging a voluntary emission intensity target of 20-25 per cent below 2005 levels by 2020. Contrary to the government's claims, the WB study has estimated that the country would have to make substantial financial investments in order to reduce its emissions. It has estimated that just the capital costs in setting up cleaner grid power could rise by 15–25 per cent. Capital cost is just one of the several cost factors. The government has claimed, based on homework done by the Planning Commission, that meeting the 20–25 per cent emission intensity cut target would be easy and that the country could, in fact, look at a more ambitious target.

The report also indicated that even if the government was to undertake no new targets and just implement the existing plans, its emission intensity would continue to drop regardless and remain well below that of most developed and developing countries. This is what the study states.

A synopsis of the report also points out that several of the major proposals that India has now suggested it would undertake under the 12th and 13th Five-Year Plan to meet its target would cost massive amounts. The study calculated the cost of each type of action at the current state of technology and found that moving towards cleaner coal technologies itself would be the most expensive proposition. Several critics had raised questions whether the government had assessed the costs different sectors and segments of the economy would have to bear and others that would gain from the moves before it suddenly unveiled the 20-25 per cent emission intensity cut target.

India has already undertaken a roughly Rs. 75,000 crore solar mission target, the decision triggering a controversy about the diversion of limited resources to a renewable energy source that is right now prohibitively costly in relation to traditional sources such as coal. The report warns such subsidies (required to promote costly renewable power) run counter to the general prescription for economically efficient energy pricing and compete with other priorities for scarce resources, including expanding the availability of modern energy services for the poor. The report concludes that by adoption of various measures, India can lower its GHG emission trajectory compared to business-as-usual, but cannot, under any scenario of increasing living standards to their poorest, stabilize by 2030 with current available technologies, and institutions. The report also indicates that overall emissions of the country would have to increase substantially if the poorest two-thirds population has to be provided a reasonable level of assured electricity and yet

India would have a much lower level of access to energy than the industrialized world.

The cat is out of the bag. However, the leaked political draft agreement crafted by the Danes holds few surprises. There is nothing in the draft that was not known before. Indeed the direction has been obvious since the G-8 meeting in L' Aquila. The desire for a new agreement that negates historical responsibility, diluting obligations to provide finance and technology, dividing the developing world into new categories, requiring peaking of emissions by the more developed-developing countries, and the review of domestic actions by international standards – all these have been on the table for some time.

The truth is that in our laudable effort to remain engaged, we have been afraid to call a spade a spade. China, India, Brazil and South Africa (the BASIC bloc of four) can't claim not to have seen the Danish draft earlier. In fact, the BASIC draft version of the political outcome of Copenhagen was crafted in Beijing by them in late November as a response to the Danish draft. The agility of the BASIC group in coming up with an alternative must be commended. India's proactive stance is in line with our Prime Minister's direction to be part of a solution. Indeed, India must not just be seen to be part of a solution, but should take the lead in crafting such a solution because there is no other country or region in the world that will suffer as much as India because of climate changes. However, India's position is unique even within the BASIC group. India must give full expression to this difference within the bloc as failure to do so might alienate a wider constituency within the G-77 grouping. But before we get into that, it must be pointed out that India is already a part of the solution to climate change.

Between 1990 and 2007 the developed world with a population of the same order as that of India has grown its annual emissions by over 2.2 gigatons despite an obligation under Kyoto Protocol to reduce emissions. India's absolute annual emissions during the period have grown by less than half that while delivering a GDP growth rate that's twice as high! It can be said that India is on a sustainable development path while the rich countries have still not managed to peak their emissions. Coming to our differences within the BASIC, India is bang in the middle of a group of 81 countries that had a 2005 PPP-GDP (GDP calculated not at the official exchange rate but based on purchasing power parity) of $4000 or less. This group accounted for almost half of the then global population but was responsible for less that 9 per cent of the global energy related rise in CO_2 concentrations from 1990 to 2005!

Importantly, most of India's socio-economic comparators and its Human Development Index lie within this group. So do India's vulnerabilities to climate change – only on a much larger scale! China, Brazil and South Africa are not part of this group. Their PPP-GDP in 2005 was 2.1 to 3.6 times that of India. Brazilian and South African per capita emission levels are already close to European levels and China will reach those levels well before 2020. India's likely per capita emissions in 2020 will be about 30 per cent of current European levels. So, India is the natural leader of the bottom 50 per cent of the world. This is the coalition of the low emitters who will suffer the most due to climate change. Indeed, India has the moral authority and hence the moral responsibility to deliver an equitable solution to this bottom 50 per cent of the world. India is uniquely endowed with the capacity to craft an equitable solution within this group. India's solution must protect every provision of the Framework Convention, the Kyoto Protocol and the Bali Action Plan. India's solution must also protect the right to development that is enshrined in these legally binding agreements and it must ensure that rapid development of the bottom 50 per cent of the world is accepted as the best form of adaptation that the rich can deliver against the consequences of climate change. India deserves a place at the high table; but India will never win the argument by donning a tie on a torn shirt and trying to gatecrash the party of "haves" with Savile Row suits. India must never forget her great son who got us on the high table clad in his dhoti and a walking staff. A 21st century variant of that approach is our only hope to avoid a bad deal. Copenhagen should be seen as a process and not as an event that is an end in itself because a bad deal is worse than no deal. With the African countries, Bangladesh and other developing countries hiking their demand for the share of the climate fund, it is becoming increasingly clear that countries like India and China will have to depend mostly on funding from private sources. Bangladesh minister Hasan Mahmud has said that it will demand at least 15 per cent of the climate change adaptation fund since the country is the most vulnerable. UNFCCC executive secretary Yvo de Boer said the market-based mechanism for financing has worked well for the big countries. "In CDM, 80 per cent of the resources has gone to eight countries, and these are the countries that also get foreign direct investment". Though de Boer did not categorically suggest that the bigger developing countries would be left outside of public financing, the indications were clear. The UNFCCC boss said India and Brazil would be able to access public funds for deforestation and forestation. Brazil, whose central concern is funding to prevent deforestation, would lay claim on a major share of this funding. For India, market mechanism like the CDM (clean development mechanism) will be an important mainstay for finances. Experts say India needs to make sure it can derive maximum benefit from the carbon market. A high emission target for Annexed-I countries would work to India's advantage. As the CDM projects are offset against emission by Annexed- I countries, a higher target would mean more projects. More importantly India will need to make sure that CDM projects taken up by the private sector in developed countries involve high cost technology. It is argued that the low cost opportunities should be taken up by India ownself. This would count towards India's domestic effort at bringing down emission intensity. Meanwhile, the head of the UN Environment programme Achim Steiner has said the biggest polluters like the US should invest heavily in the global fund to help developing countries cut their emissions. The global fund for the purpose is expected to be around $10 billion from next year, rising to $100 billion per annum by 2020.

Copenhagen Lessons for Doha

Copenhagen was not supposed to be the be all and end all on environmental matters. It was part of a process and, even if it disappointed many, it remains a significant second best milestone, which will determine the future of climate change negotiations. The debate has certainly shifted from 'poverty is the biggest polluter' to 'justice for the poor victims of pollution by others'. The drama will resume at the future summits and all the global powwows before that. Our political leaders may again sing in chorus as they have been doing on the Doha Round of negotiations by the World Trade Organization (WTO) members: let's do something. And in this high voltage drama, we often forget that economic, social and political challenges are powerful enough to take care of many environmental concerns that the world is facing today. Countries will not have much choice but to take unilateral mitigation and adaptation measures rather than wait for action through global consensus. Our farmers and other common folk have been doing this in their own indigenous ways for centuries and will continue to refine and innovate.

We can discuss whether Copenhagen was an utter failure or a muted success till the cows come home. Writing obituaries of legally-binding multilateral treaties serves no purpose. Instead, we should think seriously about the process of arriving at such treaties. A process involving 194 countries to arrive at a consensus at the highest level through negotiations over two weeks has little chance of success. This is especially so when our political leaders lack capability as well as intention to reconcile global challenges while, at the same time, satisfying their domestic constituencies.

Negotiations have to be a continuous process with a clear roadmap in mind along with ready and implementable alternative plans in order to address its ups and downs. In this respect, it is good to note that a proposal was made in Copenhagen to hold permanent negotiations on climate change in Geneva. This idea received support from many developing countries, as it would allow them to access the negotiating resources of their permanent missions in that city.

Unfortunately, the other big multilateral negotiation, the Doha Round on trade, is suffering from the Copenhagen syndrome and the root cause is the same. WTO's 153 members are trying to thrash out a legally binding, multilateral treaty through 'consensus' when their interests are as different as chalk is from cheese.

One may argue that if the Uruguay Round, the round that launched the WTO, could be successfully concluded through consensus in early 1990s, why not now. The world has changed. The days of forced consensus are over. It is no longer possible for the US and the EU to arrive at a deal among them and sell it to others. There is a new political equation that includes the big emerging economies as equal partners and, sometimes, formidable opponents to the traditional powers. Giving the devil its due, let us take lessons from the positive developments in Copenhagen. Without compromising their basic positions and those of others who were looking at them for leadership, the BASIC group comprising Brazil, South Africa, India and China of emerging economies was able to get the US back to the high table of serious negotiations. Both should be complimented as they have shown the world that they are politically mature to make deals. This initiative should be nurtured as a future model to get interests of others on board and balance them properly while addressing the challenges of making the benefits of global public goods such as climate and international trade accessible to people at large, bearing in mind the principle of common but differentiate responsibilities. Consensus should be developed brick by brick rather than through a sudden act of imposition of will.

This is the most important lesson that Doha should draw from Copenhagen. Fortunately, this lesson is there in the

Doha process but is yet to be clearly understood. From the vicissitudes of Doha, a New Quad of Brazil EU, India and the US have emerged. In late 1980s, it was Arthur Dunkel who saved the Uruguay Round from demise by preparing a draft negotiating text (famously, or infamously, known as the Dunkel Draft) and weaving (largely Transatlantic) interests around it. Given the current geopolitical scenario, it is not possible for the present incumbent at the WTO, Pascal Lamy, to do so. It is up to the New Quad, or G-4, to take up this mantle. Earlier this year a leading development agency predicted a scenario that the global community may face the disaster of de-globalization unless global and national institutions channel their energy towards more policy coherence involving multiple stakeholders, including the civil society. The new leadership can do it by drawing inspiration from the post-World War-II leadership, we have to revisit Potsdam. Through a recent Unctad-initiated negotiation on South-South trade, Brazil and India have shown that they can make politically-saleable deals. The EU has shown its willingness to take a leadership role. Now, it is up to the US administration to show the world that it can take a leadership role as a deal-maker; not a deal-breaker. The time is ripe for them, for a public survey in the US has shown that today the public at large in that country is less sceptical about trade than it was a year ago.

Whether it is climate change or global trade, while countries have accepted multilateralism of sovereignty, it will be difficult for them to satisfy domestic constituencies if their sources of competitiveness are compromised. Pascal Lamy has aptly stated this in his response to Copenhagen: "The more we move towards a multilateral framework on climate change, the more unilateral trade measures will be difficult to explain".

Earth Hour

Word celebrates earth hour. The white-shelled roof of the Sydney Opera House fell dark on March 27, 2010 one of the first landmarks to turn out the lights in an hour-long gesture to be repeated by millions of people around the world who are calling for a binding pact to cut greenhouse gas emissions. Asian cities followed Australia and New Zealand as the fourth annual Earth Hour cranked up. Buildings in some 4,000 cities in more than 120 countries were expected to unplug to reduce energy consumption and draw attention to dangers of climate change, according to organizers.

The event started across the world, with participants turning off the lights when the clock strikes 8:30 p.m. local time. From a shopping mall in Manila to the Eiffel Tower in Paris and the Empire State Building in New York, landmarks and skylines will dim. "We have everyone from Casablanca to the safari camps of Namibia and Tanzania taking part", said Greg Bourne, CEO of World Wildlife Fund in Australia, the environmental group that came up with the idea that started in Sydney in 2007. The shutdown is completely voluntary and street lights, traffic lights and other safety measures are unaffected. Andy Ridley, a WWF worker in Sydney who cooked up the idea of Earth Hour in a pub with friends, said he hoped this year's event would inspire world leaders to strive for a much stronger climate agreement than that struck at December's Copenhagen climate change summit. Some 88 cities participated in last year's Earth Hour, which has the backing of the United Nations as well as global corporations, nonprofit groups, schools, scientists and celebrities. Earth Hour organizers say there's no uniform way to measure how much energy is saved worldwide, but that the simple fact that so many places have signed up to take part should send a message to leaders that global warming is a topic of great concern to people worldwide.

Earth hour is also celebrated in India. The lawns of India Gate turned bright with enthusiasm and hope as hundreds of Delhites holding candles made a pledge to fight against climate change. As part of the Earth Hour campaign, India Gate for the first time slipped into darkness between 8.30 p.m. and 9.30 p.m. on March 27, 2010 still standing tall without its eye-catching illumination. It was left to only candles and solar lanterns to spread light during the one-hour switch-off at the lawns. Even the Indian Ocean band had to bank on LCD lights for its live performance as part of the green celebration. CM Sheila Dikshit was brimming with hope. She said: "Last year when Delhi experimented with Earth Hour for the first time, the power demand dropped by 700MW to 800 MW. It is important to send a message to the world that we are now much more conscious about climate issue," she said.

As the clock slowly edged towards the 8:30 p.m. mark, Dikshit chose to spend the last minute-and-a-half talking about birds. "Birds have started coming back to Delhi because we have successfully re-energized a lot of lakes. Around 80 to 90 species of birds visit Delhi every year," she said. As Dikshit's speech ended, the audience all got up, each person holding a candle, and the CM and WWF India CEO Ravi Singh both walked to the 'big switch' and pressed the button dimming all lights. There was a huge cheer from the audience as the lights started fading away and within seconds India Gate was in complete darkness.

The event started with a performance by noted dancer Shovana Narayan and her troupe and then popular band Indian Ocean took the stage. Actor Tom Alter was the host for the event. The Indian Ocean band members acknowledged that this performance was doubly special because they usually require up to 100 lights on stage when they play. The Amateur Astronomers Association of Delhi also set up four telescopes at the India Gate lawns to spread awareness about climate change and the importance of night sky and pollution.

As well-intentioned gestures go, Earth Hour is hard to beat. At the stroke of 8:30 p.m. on Saturday, March 27, nearly a billion people in more than 120 countries demonstrated their desire to do something about global warming by switching off their lights for an hour. In a show of official solidarity, the lights also went out at many of the planet's most iconic landmarks, from the Opera House in Sydney to the Great Pyramid at Giza, not to mention Beijing's Forbidden City, New York's Empire State Building, London's Big Ben, Paris's Eiffel Tower, and the skylines of both Hong Kong and Las Vegas.

Whatever else it may be, Earth Hour is surely one of the most successful publicity stunts ever dreamed up. First organized in Sydney, Australia, in 2007 by the local chapter of the World Wildlife Fund, its popularity and the level of participation (both individual and official) that generates has exploded in recent years to the point that there is barely a corner of the earth that the campaign hasn't touched. As Greg Bourne, CEO of World Wildlife Fund in Australia put it: "We have everyone from Casablanca to the safari camps of Namibia and Tanzania taking part".

But has Earth Hour actually done anything to halt or even slow the global warming? Not so much. The event's popularity is not hard to fathom. Who but the most diehard global-warming denier could resist the notion, as Earth Hour's American website phrased it this year, that merely "by flipping off your lights on March 27 at 8:30 p.m. local time you will be making the switch to a cleaner, more secure nation?"

Needless to say, this was not quite the case. The main thing was to make it harder to see. The environmental impact was negligible. Indeed even if everyone in the world had participated the requisite hour, the result would have been the equivalent of turning off China's carbon emissions for roughly 45 seconds.

Of course, this wildly optimistic calculation assumes that nobody used more power afterwards. Recent research by two Canadian psychologists found that people who spent money on green products were, immediately afterwards, less likely to be generous and more likely to steal than those who bought non-green stuff. Apparently doing something virtuous, like turning off the lights, makes us feel entitled to act badly afterwards. The Earth Hour organizers acknowledged the symbolic nature of the exercise. Turning off the lights is just a "call to action," they noted. As WWF Director-General James Leape explained, it provides "a global platform for millions of people to - voice their concern about the devastating effects of climate change". Added another WWF official, "It is saying to our politicians, you can't give up on climate change".

But according to Andy Ridley, Earth Hour actually has a more specific agenda than that in addition to being the guy who first came up with the idea for the event over drinks with friends in a Sydney pub several years ago, Ridley is also the executive director of Earth Hour Global, so he presumably speaks with some authority on the subject. "What we're still looking for in this coming year," he told Associated press, "is a global deal that encourages all countries to lower their emissions".

Therein lays the big problem with Earth Hour. As much as we would like to believe otherwise, the fact is that carbon emissions won't be lowered by a deal. If that were politically possible, it would have been done a long time ago, if not at the 1992 "Earth Summit" in Rio de Janeiro, then in Kyoto 12 years later; and if not in Kyoto, then in Copenhagen last December. But it wasn't.

Indeed, after nearly two decades of trying, the best climate deal that countries have been able to agree on is one that imposes no real obligations, sets no binding emissions targets, and requires no specific actions by anyone. Surely, there is a lesson here.

Alas, the organizers of Earth Hour prefer to ignore this inconvenient reality. But there is no getting around it: if we are serious about wanting to solve global warming, we need to take action that actually does good as opposed to wasting valuable resources on empty agreements and moral posturing that merely make us feel good. Switching off our lights and promising to cut carbon emissions may make us feel momentarily virtuous, but that's all it does.

A meaningful solution to global warming is to focus on clean-energy research and development rather than reductions in carbon emissions. For just 0.2 per cent of global GDP, or $100 billion a year, we could bring about the game-changing technological breakthroughs that will be required to make green energy cheap enough to fuel a carbon-free future. So let's stop stumbling around in the dark and do something meaningful for a brighter future.

India's Arid Waterscape

The government has informed Parliament that groundwater in more than a third of the districts is unfit for drinking due to high levels of iron, fluoride and arsenic. The era of seemingly endless reliance on groundwater for both drinking water and irrigation is well high over as an increasing number of aquifers reach unsustainable levels of exploitation. Fortunately, community-led management of groundwater resources, such as the Andhra Pradesh farmer-managed groundwater systems project (Fams), is emerging as a dependable institutional tool for participatory hydrological monitoring and crop water budgeting. This merits the close attention of the Centre and the states. Hard-rock aquifers, such as those in peninsular India, have low storage; theys fill quickly during the monsoon and also deplete quickly with use. But Farms, implemented in seven drought-prone districts in Andhra has led to rationalization of water use by a combination of crop diversification and water-saving irrigation methods. Follow-up surveys reveal reduction in the area under high-water-use crops, with 50 per cent reduction from baseline figures over two years, in some instances. It's important to note that farmers have not "sacrificed profitability" to reduce water use. The results show that farmers, in fact, have consistently improved profitability, with the net value of output nearly doubling during the project period.

India is by far the largest groundwater user in the world with more than 60 per cent of irrigated farming and 85 per cent drinking water supplies dependent on the resource. And the key objective of Fams, a UN Food and Agriculture Organization project, is to enable groundwater-using farmers with the necessary data, skills and knowledge to manage groundwater resources sustainably. The objective is to figure out the state of the aquifer and the gap between what is available and what is desired in the aquifer community. Given that two-thirds of our aquifers are of the hard-rock variety, each generally confined to 5–10 habitations, it would make eminent sense to scale up Fams pan-India.

Managing Climate Change

The world works to a global climate deal in Cancun, advanced developing countries like India will come under increasing pressure to commit to higher targets to reduce greenhouse gas emissions than these countries have put on the table. While the industrialized countries are understood to be responsible for the stock of greenhouse gas (GHG) emissions created during the first 200 years of industrialization the developing countries with fast-growing economies are expected to increasingly contribute to the flow or current emissions. The pressure on these economies would be to limit their emissions in the imminent future, in a bid to keep global emissions at safe levels. This would require working out an effort or burden sharing formula, which would decide the steps taken by different contries to know as to how much finance and technology is provided to developing countries.

Pressures are likely to increase, as the Copenhagen Accord acknowledges the need to limit global average temperature to 20 degrees Celsius above pre-industrial temperature.

In accepting the temperature threshold as a guiding principle, the world has also accepted that a limit has been set on the total global carbon emission. Experts say that carbon budget between 1990 and 2100 is at 1800 gigatons (GT) of carbon dioxide equivalent. With global emissions on the rise since 1990, the net cumulative carbon budget between 2009 and 2100 is limited to 870 GT of carbon dioxide equivalent.

Emission between 2000 and 2006 was at around 234 GT, and assuming constant rate of 36.3 GT per year, the existing carbon budget could be exhausted anywhere between 2024 and 2039. To ensure that the world does not have to contend with the adverse impacts of climate change, it is important that GHG emissions are limited to this budget. The developing countries, whose primary goal is development, have to operate within the constraints of a limited carbon budget. Given that unlike the West, the developing world has to operate in this constrained scenario, the model of development that is adopted will be critical to the occupation of the carbon space.

The debate over which model should India choose while deciding on burden sharing gives India two pathways. First is the low carbon development pathway where development is decoupled from emissions. Using renewable, developing countries are able to occupy negligible carbon space and yet develop. In this scenario as low carbon development technology is expensive, the developed world provides technology and finance to move to a low carbon development model. This would mean that the developing world would ask for a small share of the carbon space, allowing the rich countries to occupy it.

The second is the per capita convergence model where carbon space is let off by developed countries and then developing countries occupy this space. In the meantime, developed countries would go on a zero carbon emission pathway where they will use renewable energy and energy efficiency measures which will lead to reduction in the price of green technology.

Prices for green technology will reduce as developing countries will take it up, leading to the eminent convergence of emissions. The per capita emission approach does present some problems. It helps countries to leverage on their large populations, as is the case with India and China, but it doesn't necessarily push forward the inclusive development agenda. It allows for the rich in these countries can hide behind its poor. China, which is the world's top emitter, can leverage its population to arrive at a relatively low per capita emission figure. This approach also has a single convergence date, i.e., when the per capita emissions from the poor and rich nations will match.

How that can be implemented in a manner that the less developed countries too have a fair shake at pulling its people out of poverty is difficult to establish. A model that New Delhi would consider is put forward by US-based economist Arvind Subramanian. Breaking away from the traditional per capita emission approach, it borrows from Amartya Sen's capabilities approach by taking energy as an input that is a key contributing factor to development. This burden sharing model fits in with the inclusive growth agenda of the government.

In a departure from the "per capita emission" model the Subramanian model focuses on energy consumption, Subramanian argues that the basis of equitable burden sharing should not be the "right to pollute" or equity in the allocation of future rights to emission but equity in access to energy. In making energy and not emissions the basis for an equitable framework, development once again becomes central to the debate. However, the Subramanian model doesn't co-relate its energy-based approach to the temperature threshold. The model though best suited to the requirements of developing countries, will need to be adapted to climate terms. It also needs to be co-related to the carbon budget. The other issue with this model is that it does not look at distributing responsibility—the world is divided into rich and poor people, this makes it difficult to work out a compensation framework, whether it is in the form of technology or finance.

Flop Copenhagen

There was total mismanagement of COP 15 and the untold daily misery and shoddy treatment that visitors, including certain Parties (UN parlance for participating governments), had to put up with in gaining entry to the conference. The brutal stifling of the people's democratic right to demonstrate peacefully and be heard, not because these concerns are not important, because the chaos and confusion that ruled within the guarded precincts of COP 15 outshone the chaos and confusion outside, because the political outcome that was likely to sugarcoat the failure of COP 15 could well be the proverbial last straw for 80 per cent of Indians who live below two dollars a day.

Notwithstanding the sudden shift of the COP /CMP presidency from Danish minister, Connie Hedegaard, to Prime Minister Rasmussen by the Danish hosts COP 15 may go down in history as the first COP wherein the well established bottom-up multilateral process driven by the Parties was given up. The inclusive, one-country-one-vote democratic process of the UNFCCC had been thrown to the winds. And when countries like Brazil, China and Sudan took the lead in denouncing the secret goings-on among select groups that might foist a political declaration that hasn't been debated and crafted by the Parties, the Secretariat and the Presidency fumbled. Finally, caught in his own web of words, an exasperated Rasmussen invoked the people outside the precincts of the conference and their demand for a solution, not a process! Whose solution and a solution for whom? The Indian delegation would not forget the father of our nation, for whom the process was as important as the goal. And to the Secretariat and the Danish hosts is indeed the process that will ensure a transparent and legally binding agreement, not a political declaration.

The hard truth was that just a day and a half before the heads of states meet in Copenhagen to adapt the said political declaration, there's no closure on any of the key issues. No commitments under Kyoto for post-2012 period; no agreement on the level of support or the institutional framework for providing such support for adaptation, financing and technology transfer; no agreement on the international oversight or the lack thereof for domestic voluntary actions. In short, there was no agreement on upholding what was agreed to under the Bali Action Plan or on preserving the sanctity of the Framework convention and the Kyoto protocol. While past undertakings in these legally binding agreements were being reneged, new promises under a new agreement that includes all nations were being held out as the reward for compliance. China, Brazil and the Africa group had saved the day for the developing world thus far. India lost the most from climate change in comparison to any other country in the world. Although, individually revered as an intellectual powerhouse,

Team India (which has fielded its largest delegation ever), in the words of a very senior negotiator, appeared confused on what it wanted. This was understandable because the team Captain had been absent from the field ever since the real hard negotiations started. Team India appeared to commit itself to continue negotiating and give the bitter flop show at Copenhagen a coat of artificial sugar through a political declaration that might shackle future negotiations.

As Indian minister mentioned at his press conference, he did not go to Copenhagen with the mandate to save the world or humanity. His mandate was to defend India's right to develop at a faster rate. India's approach to COP 15 at Copenhagen was anchored in the sanctity of the troika – UNFCCC, the Kyoto protocol and the Bali action plan.

It was also India's stand that the widely accepted principles of (a) historical responsibilities and (b) common but differentiated responsibilities are sacrosanct. On the basis of the above, what had been the outcome of the Copenhagen meet? Globally, COP 15 was a great disappointment essentially because there were no legally binding emission cuts. The Indian concern was that some countries wanted legally binding emission commitments not only from the developed world but also from emerging markets like China and India. The US insisted on our accepting the concept of a peaking year and that even unsupported mitigation actions by non Annex I countries should be subject to international monitoring and verification. In return, the US offered almost nothing at all. In this scenario what could India do? India wanted to be a deal maker and not a deal breaker. India was fortunate in being pan of the BASIC group of countries. This group could resist the pressures from the US, in a meeting between President Obama and BASIC countries, a final agreement was hammered out. This accord however inadequate was better than no accord at all. BASIC countries succeeded in getting the US on board and formed a strong group which will help them in future negotiations.

There were doubts about the Accord from the Indian point of view – the sanctity of the Kyoto protocol. It continued to exist but the language of the Accord allowed the developed world to move out of their obligations. The Accord speaks of achieving peaking of global and national emissions as soon as possible. However, the Accord recognizes that the time frame for peaking will be longer in developing countries. Mitigation actions, even if unsupported, will be reported to the Secretariat for international consultation and analysis rather than for information. This naturally raises doubts even though the guidelines for such consultation and analysis will ensure that national sovereignty is respected. As a responsible nation, we had agreed to cut our emission intensity to GDP by 20–25 per cent by 2020 on 2005 levels. To the extent this will be unsupported it will be a cost to the nation and to the Indian corporate, but even though the developed world is behaving in a highly irresponsible manner, we should be proactive to help reduce the adverse effects of climate change. Of course, with our per capita emissions about 7 per cent of the US and a third of China and with a per capita income of less than $1000 against more than $40,000 in the US, we cannot ignore growth and development. India should work towards sustainable development while ensuring that it does not succumb to the unreasonable and inequitable demands of the developed world. A grouping like G-20, including BASIC countries, may need to work together to reach a satisfactory accord by the next COP.

Need for a Durable and Binding Agreement

The world lost an opportunity in Copenhagen of saving the planet through a planned landing with a clear roadmap of reducing greenhouse gas (GHG) load than a certain ecological crash in the absence of one.

In the run up to Copenhagen, it was clear that we will not get a deal to extend Kyoto Protocol in 2009 owing to a lack of agreement on some basic issues. But, it was hardly expected that the Accord would be worse than the no deal that we were all reconciling to. India should be a leader demanding capping of emissions by developed nations as well as by countries such as China that have higher emissions than the US, rather than being defensive, that we were, and now jubilant of having escaped of binding commitments.

There was no logic for us to do so, though it seems we took these threats rather seriously and made some strategic errors in positioning ourselves. Despite being the fifth largest GHG emitter, India has the most number of poor in the world and thus cannot be equated with China, which has more than twice of our GDP as their foreign exchange reserves and four times of our wealth. It was a good tactic for China to be clubbed with us, to hide behind equity issue and escape any logical and inevitable binding targets. We had no conclusive scientific evidence of man-made climate change when Kyoto happened. This is available now through Intergovernmental Panel on Climate Change (IPCC).

India is the most vulnerable country to vagaries of climate change, resulting in crisis in water and agriculture. Agriculture minister claims that the more 20 per cent rise in food inflation is due to climate change. Our coasts and fisheries are under threat. Cost of adaptation for India could be easily 4 per cent of GDP. Therefore, we needed a deal which would limit the global emission load to 350 parts per million (PPM) as scientists demanded or at least the one to restrict temperature rise to 20°C as politicians agreed. We also needed access to finance for adaptation. India needs a legally binding commitment deal, not only for our own but also in humanity's interest to achieve these. We seem to be proud that we got an accord at last, which is non-binding, optional, abstract, non-specific, ambiguous and intrusive in our national action. It doesn't talk of the necessary ingredients of a treaty but in a way replaces a legally binding, principled, hard-bargained Protocol.

We must work hard till Bonn and Mexico get a real, durable and a principled deal. While we work on it using diplomatic means, we must also strategize to take advantage of this once-in-a-lifetime opportunity to make India a global hub of clean technologies. World has to embrace climate-proof technologies once we have a sound regime to combat climate change. We have the information technology, scientific technology, human capital, reverse engineering capabilities and domestic market to reap the benefits of the paradigm shift that the world is required to make. Could India also remind the world that we have a Parliament like some of them and thus could also use parliamentary approval as a strategy to get a better deal for ourselves?

Opposition Slams the Accord

The Government came under attack from the Opposition for being part of the Copenhagen Accord that allows US to undermine the Kyoto Protocol. "The US will no longer be bound to its pledges on emission cuts," said the Opposition on the eve of a statement from the prime minister in the Rajya Sabha on the Copenhagen summit.

In a statement, the CPM Politburo blamed the government's pre-summit concessions for the new development. "The CPM had warned the government that unilateral concessions before the negotiations, and without conditional linkages to deep cuts by developed countries, would not yield results. This is indeed what has happened," the Politburo said.

CPM said that the summit's failure to meet its goal of a legally binding agreement for the second commitment period of the Kyoto Protocol will hurt the interests of the developing world. Without a treaty committing the rich and industrialized countries to deep emission cuts, the lives and well-being of hundreds of millions of people, especially in the developing world, have been put at risk. This will most adversely affect people in South Asia, large parts of Africa, least developed countries and island nations that could be entirely submerged under rising sea-levels.

CPM said that the political leaders who gathered in Copenhagen have failed their people by not delivering an effective and equitable climate change agreement. Such an agreement in Copenhagen was made impossible by the positions and tactics of the US and other developed countries. From the first day to the last at Copenhagen, the US and its allies tried their utmost to kill the Kyoto Protocol itself, negate the cornerstone principle of differentiation between the industrialized and developing countries, and pressurize the developing countries to take on the major burden of reducing global emissions. Their inability to achieve these aims was due to the stiff and united resistance put up by the developing countries, it said.

It recalled that major developing economies such as the BASIC bloc as well as Mexico and Indonesia voluntarily announced reductions in emission growth rates. However, the US, EU and other developed countries did not budge an inch from the low emission cuts they had declared before Copenhagen. A leaked draft of UN Report has revealed that pledges made by large developing countries will contribute more to emission reductions than the low commitments of the US and other developed nations.

CPM said since the "Copenhagen Accord is expected to become the reference point for future negotiations, there was possibility of varied interpretations of the text on emission cuts by developing countries, fund and technology transfers. India should therefore ensure that in future negotiations, the red lines as committed by the government in Parliament are adhered to. India must also press for deep and immediate emission cuts by the US and other developed countries and work with other developing countries to ensure sustainable development and equitable terms in any final Treaty.

Copenhagen Fails but transparency becomes a Gain for India

It would be easy to dismiss the 15th Conference of Parties at Copenhagen (Cop 15) as a cop-out on climate change. Measured against the conference objective of coming up with a successor to the Kyoto Protocol, which committed developed countries to measurable emission cuts by 2012, the conference failed. What an agreement brokered by US President Barack Obama with the BASIC group of China, India, Brazil and South Africa has done is to commit countries to keep negotiating to reach an agreement, hopefully, at

Cop16 in Mexico. This agreement was 'recognized' rather than adopted by Cop 15. Unless all 193 members of the UN agree to this, it will have no legal sanctity. But this has to be seen in the context that the Kyoto Protocol, which had legal sanctity, has not made developed countries cut their emissions as promised. In the absence of mechanisms to either effectively penalize or resolve disputes, international obligations are hard to enforce. Government commitments to their own national expectations will have far more force. The US-BASIC agreement envisages $30 billion will be made available to developing countries for fighting climate change by 2012, and larger sums thereafter. More significantly, the agreement says that both developed and developing countries will list their climate change actions, and, crucially, provide information on these actions through national communications and international consultations and analysis 'under clearly-defined guidelines'. This is likely to get the goat of many high-minded nationalists in India, who will fault the government for submitting to 'imperialist' pressure. This Pavlovian reflex completely misses the advantage it bestows on India.

While the Chinese make grand commitments to fight climate change but insist on remaining stereotypically inscrutable on vital questions of how and how much, even as parliamentary democracy keeps such information transparently in the public domain in India, India's international competitiveness would suffer should the Chinese choose to fudge their figures. That the Chinese have agreed to international consultation under defined guidelines offers some insurance against this risk. India must refine its position to become an even more aggressive climate negotiator. Let us put more 'no regrets' commitments unilaterally on the table and then demand reciprocal action by developed and competing developing countries.

Basic Difference at Copenhagen Summit

When the dust settles down on the Copenhagen Accord, the summit will be best remembered for the emergence of the

BASIC group consisting of Brazil, India, South Africa and China as a powerful negotiating bloc. By breaking ranks with the G-77 countries in the climate change negotiations, India and the members of BASIC have signalled a new role in an evolving world order. And many see this evolution as necessary given the unwieldy nature of G-77 as a group. "Today countries like India, China, Brazil and South Africa are making a transition from developing to the developed. They are in both camps and they are working out a compromise," said former foreign secretary Lalit Mansingh. Analysts further pointed out that the evolution of the BASIC grouping is almost similar to the way G-8 has now become G20 and shows the new alignments at play. "While remaining in the NAM and G-77, it is inevitable that India would have a calibrated engagement along with like-minded select developing countries with the developed countries. An example of this is the way G 20 has evolved," said former secretary in the external affairs ministry KC Singh.

India and other BASIC countries had little choice but to break ranks with the G-77 in an effort to save the Copenhagen talks from breaking down completely. Finally, they (BASIC) had to change their position," said one official pointing out that the G-77 grouping was too diverse and their differences too many to be carried forward together. Analysts also concurred that given the diverse nature of the grouping there was no way the entire grouping could have moved forward. "We can't take a rigid position and say take it or leave it. There had to be a compromise. And India and others protected interests of developing countries to a certain extent," said Mansingh. The accord, which was accepted by 26 countries, holds the promised of $100 billion in annual aid from 2020 for developing nations and pledges $30 billion by 2012. The accord sets a target limiting temperature increases to up to two degrees Celsius, but does not quantify greenhouse gas emission cuts. Even though New Delhi has moved away from the G-77 reference point, it is also trying to walk a tightly balanced line. Prime

Minister's special envoy for climate change Shyam Saran was careful to state that there was no split in the G-77. He pointed out that at least 15 developing countries were part of the group that hammered out the accord.

But many believe that Copenhagen has changed the nature of G-77 grouping. "First of all the whole concept of G-77 has undergone a big change. It is no longer the only platform for developing countries which have broken up into different groups including LDC and emerging markets and whole lot of other coteries in between," said Mansingh.

Gains from Copenhagen Agreement

Though an acrimonious and anarchic Copenhagen Summit, it appears that there has been a method in the madness. Just run through the ensuing version of Copenhagen Climate Copenhagen witnesses the expected. G-77, India and China bargained hard on issues close to their heart common and differentiated responsibilities and demands for fair, non-commercial flows of finances and low carbon technologies. The North, barring a few countries from Europe, was clear that it would not unduly pain itself by accepting tough mitigation targets. The Danish Drafts and the BASIC drafts collide against each other in mid-air and fall to the ground is played out as cracks surfaced in the main coalition formation of the nations of South. Pressure mounts on India and China to contribute to carbon reduction. The denouement happens in with the grand entry of the 'Nobel' President of the US who charms and reasons with the BASIC countries to stick to their pre-Summit carbon intensity reduction commitments without any legally binding targets. The gentle caveat is that these pledges would be watched in a matter that does not infringe national sovereignty. Thus, Barrack Obama has regained his pride to some extent.

Though Copenhagen Accord is not a legally binding instrument with concrete targets on emission reduction commitments, it has the following implications: First, the 'audacity' of moral suasion and political leadership that has triumphed over procedural complexity and philosophical objections. This is what was witnessed at Copenhagen in India's sensitivity about the Measurable, Reportable and Verifiable (MRV) mechanism when it originally emanated from the OECD countries. The policing like provisos of the MRV had no chance of being accepted by an emerging country even if it had to accept mitigation targets. Under the Copenhagen Accord, BASIC countries are required to commit themselves to voluntary but internationally pledged mitigation targets something we would not have allowed given that our targets are voluntary. Obama's suasion has changed all this.

The second and more serious implication of the Accord is that it inadvertently draws the BASIC countries to the fold of developed countries, an 'identity makeover' in the new scheme of things. Graduating clauses (explicit or implicit) in a new Climate Protocol can produce great uncertainties to emerging economies like India that have very low per capita CO_2 emissions. In the face of it, the Copenhagen Accord pushes into the back-burner the per capita emission principle. India has been in the G-77 bracket on account of its low per capita emissions (the other way our demographic dividend has helped us). This raises further implications about the continuing relevance of the principles of common and differentiated treatment to BASIC countries. The third implication relates to finances. The Accord talks of a modest annual aid of $ 100 billion to help poor countries during 2012–2020. Given the nature of the Accord and its implicit graduation clauses, BASIC countries will not be entitled to any share in the pie.

The Accord also talks of a Green Climate Fund which promises to be another Global Environment Facility within the UNFCCC system. This is good news to us, but given the implicit graduation clauses in the Accord and the real problems that the GEF has been having with leveraging privately held and IP (Intellectual Property) protected low carbon technologies, it may not be advisable to transplant a GEF type governance system to the proposed Green Climate Fund which appears to be the critical issue insofar as climate change is concerned. Given that the world has changed for the BASIC countries after December 19 do we flog the dying horse—the Protocol of Kyoto? We are now made to see the world of climate change differently. We can no longer assume that international public financing will flow to us given our new elevated status. Post-Copenhagen, given the diminishing prospects we are likely to encounter in accessing international public funding for mitigation activities in the long run and our partial stakes in the carbon markets from the Clean Development Mechanism (CDM) projects, it is time that we are proactive in working on a equitable carbon market, to ensure that we generate greater revenues (by correcting under-pricing associated with our carbon avoidance permits). Also given that India's public funded labs and companies have nascent R&D capabilities in the areas of renewable and Carbon Capture and Storage (CCS) techniques, the chances of co-development of low carbon technologies are high. We have a stake in multilateral technology transfer mechanisms and need to have a global structure that advances our national interests in the changed policy environment.

Copenhagen Accord: A Strategic Gain

The Copenhagen Accord is a deal. At Copenhagen, unity amongst the developing countries appeared, for the first time. Once the heat and dust settles, this achievement will be seen as a 'game changer' in eliminating a remediable injustice. Clearly, the United States was very desperate to secure a deal.

By moving the multilateral discourse on climate change away from emissions to equitable access to atmospheric space, governments persistence is as important as it's initiative, at the Stockholm Conference on the Environment in 1972, in pointing to poverty as the greatest polluter, with the potential to shape future negotiations.

Of course, perceptions will differ. Many see climate change in terms of environmental damage, and the most popular image is one of polar bears floating on ice flowes. Hence, any agreement, despite the consensus that world temperatures must not rise above two degrees, that does not focus on global emissions reduction is considered flawed. For others, the human impacts are more important, whether it is recurrent drought in Darfur or one billion citizens lacking access to modern energy and, for them actions must be taken in context of sustainable development.

According to the accord, reducing global emissions by 50 per cent in 2050 below 1990 levels will take into account the right to equitable access to atmospheric space. A sustainable approach requires the atmospheric resource to be allocated fairly. Nicholas Stern has pointed out, "If the allocation of rights to emit in any given year took greater account both of history and of equity in stocks rather than flows, then rich countries would have rights to emit which were lower than two tons per capita (probably even negative). The negotiations of such rights involve substantial financial allocations: at $40 per ton of CO_2 equivalent a total world allocation of rights of, say, 30 Gt (roughly the required flows in 2030) would be worth $1.2 trillion per annum".

There is no reason why these rights should be considered differently from property rights, even if it entails large-scale transfers from developed to developing countries. The emerging market mechanisms, on the other hand, provide for developed countries allocating emissions allowances to themselves. They also earn emission credits from emission reductions of developing countries, moving towards a commoditization of carbon, based on an inequitable occupation of atmospheric space and allocation based on annual flows, thereby disregarding historical emissions.

A closer look at the facts reveals the significance of a new framework that is not based on national emissions. According to analysis done by Ecofys, a think tank in Germany, to limit warming to two degrees reductions of around 13 Gt of CO_2

equivalents would be needed. Current developed country emission reduction proposals as a whole are estimated to be around 11–19 per cent below the 1990 levels, amounting to only about 2–2.5 Gt. Moreover, the total amount of surplus emissions credits is large enough to allow these countries to follow a business-as-usual pathway until after 2020, while still complying with the currently announced emissions targets. An agreement that cemented such a deal would have led to developing countries meeting a large part of the shortfall, after having agreed to limit warming.

Shifting the focus of the negotiations to defining the criteria for burden sharing establishes a new agenda that will lead to greater fairness, and transparency. The Accord recognizes that long-term cooperative action to deal with climate change will be on the basis of equity and in the context of sustainable development. The developed countries had, in the earlier negotiations, wanted the focus to be solely on emissions reduction.

TheAccord brings other benefits as well. The principle of common but differentiated responsibilities and respective capabilities has never been defined, and the focus has so far been on transfer of financial resources, which has been provided as development assistance rather than as an entitlement. The amount of less than $4 billion that has been made available to the financial mechanism of the Convention is insignificant. A high-level panel will now study potential sources of revenue to provide $100 billion, a year by 2020.

Developing countries have gained what they had been fighting to achieve over the last 15 years. For the first time transfers of financial resources are treated as substantive commitments and subject to verification. The majority of new funding will go for adaptation in the least developed countries, and will be provided over the long term. A new fund has been established under the Convention as well as a new mechanism for technology transfer. Developed countries had wanted to review national development strategies of developing countries. This was strongly resisted, and is now limited to international consultation and analysis of the national communications detailing with identified mitigation and adaptation measures, a technical review. As all actions are referenced to the principles and provisions of the Convention, and with no agreement to kill the Kyoto Protocol, the differentiation between developed and developing countries, which was sought to be erased, will remain as the essential safeguard for future economic growth.

An assessment of the implementation of the Accord has to be completed by 2015. This is also a euphemism for developing countries taking on similar commitments as developed countries. Here again, the timing secures the second commitment period under the Kyoto Protocol, which begins after 2012, and further cements the differentiation. With the equitable sharing of atmospheric space on the agenda, this provision may well turn out to be a pyrrhic victory for the developed countries. We now have the opportunity to set the agenda to determine the criteria for burden sharing, or sharing of the atmospheric space, which has been and remains, the key issue of the negotiations. Preparations for these negotiations, to develop guidelines and flesh out details, are best done through wide participation of the states, business and other stakeholders.

Kyoto Protocol vis-a-vis Copenhagen

The arrogant language and ostentatious self confidence that fill the Bella Center present a similar scene: Kyoto, 1997. There, world leaders actually signed a legally binding deal to cut carbon emissions, something that will elude the Copenhagen summit goers. But what did the Kyoto Protocol accomplish? Virtually nothing so far. To be sure, Europe has made some progress towards reducing its carbon dioxide emissions. But, of the 15 European Union countries represented at the Kyoto summit, 10 have still not met the targets agreed there. Neither will Japan nor Canada. And the US never ratified the agreement. In all we are likely to achieve barely 5 per cent of the promised Kyoto reduction.

Let's say we index 1990 global emissions at 100. If there were no Kyoto at all the 2010 level would have been 142.7. With full Kyoto implementation, it would have been 133. In fact, the actual outcome of Kyoto is likely to be a 2010 level of 142.2 virtually the same as if we had done nothing at all. Given 12 years of continuous talks and praise for Kyoto, this is not much of an accomplishment. The Kyoto Protocol did not fail because anyone nation let the rest of the world down. It failed because making quick, drastic cuts in carbon emissions is extremely expensive. Whether or not Copenhagen is declared a political victory, that inescapable fact of economic life will once again prevail, and grand promises will once again go unfulfilled. This is why abandoning the pointless strategy of trying to make governments promise to cut carbon emissions is advised. Instead, the world should be focusing its efforts on making non-polluting energy sources cheaper than, fossil fuels. We should be negotiating an agreement to increase radically spending on green energy research and development to a total of 0.2 per cent of global GDP, or $100 billion a year. Without this kind of concerted effort, alternative technologies simply will not be ready to take up the slack from fossil fuels. Unfortunately, the COP 15 delegates seem to have little appetite for such realism. At the conference, United Nations climate change chief Yvo de Boer declared his optimism about continuing the Kyoto approach, "Almost every day, countries announce new targets or plans of action to cut emissions," he said.

Such statements ignore the fact that most of these promises are almost entirely empty. Either the targets are unachievable or the numbers are fudged. For example, Japan's pledge of a 25 per cent reduction in carbon emissions by 2020 sounds incredible. China, meanwhile, drew plaudits just before the Copenhagen summit by promising to cut its carbon intensity—the amount of CO_2 emitted for each dollar of GDP—over the next 10 years to just 40-45 per cent of its level in 2005. Based on figures from the International Energy Agency, China was already expected to reduce its carbon intensity by 40 per cent without new policies. As its economy develops, China will shift to less carbon-intensive industries. Then again, spin always trumps substance at such gatherings. Consider how quick these delegates were to dismiss the scandal now known as Climategate—the outcry over the release of thousands of disturbing emails and other documents hacked from the computers of a prestigious British climate research centre.

What the stolen emails revealed was a group of the world's most influential climatologists arguing, brainstorming and plotting together to enforce what amounts to a party line on climate change. Data that didn't support their assumptions about global warming were fudged. Experts who disagreed with their conclusions were denigrated as idiots and garbage. Peer-reviewed journals that dared to publish contrarian articles were threatened with boycotts. Dissent was stifled, facts were suppressed, scrutiny was blocked, and the free flow of information was choked off. Predictably, the text of more than 3,000 purloined emails have been seized on by sceptics of man-made climate change as 'proof' that global warming is nothing more than a hoax cooked up by a bunch of pointy-headed intellectuals. And this is the real tragedy of Climategate. Global warming is not a hoax but at a time when opinion polls reveal rising public scepticism about climate change, this unsavoury glimpse of scientists trying to cook the data could be just the excuse too many people are waiting for to tune it all out. Instead of papering over the flaws in the Kyoto approach and pretending that grand, promises translate into real action we need to acknowledge that saving the world requires a smarter strategy than the one being pursued so dogmatically in Copenhagen.

Climate change has long been considered a pollution problem caused by industrialization. With the services sector emerging as the engine of growth worldwide, the individual citizen is now being recognized as the driver of environmental change. This shift in structure and activities has implications for both the multilateral negotiations and national policy development.

The nature and scope of the problem of global sustainability has long been recognized, but not acted upon because of political considerations. The report, US priority interests in the environmental activities of international organizations, prepared by the Committee on International Environmental Affairs of the State Department, in the run-up to the first United Conference on the Environment in 1970, noted that long-range policy planning to cope with global environmental problems must take account of the total ecological burden. Since controlling that burden by systematic reduction in per capita production of goods and services would be politically unacceptable, the report concluded that a concerted effort is needed to orient technology towards making human demands upon the environment less severe.

The paradox is that while global energy intensity – final energy use per unit of GDP, largely driven by technology – fell by 26 per cent during 1990-2005, energy use per capita – largely driven by increase in wealth – increased more than 6 per cent in developed countries and less than 1 per cent in developing countries. Consequently, even though carbon dioxide emissions from manufacturing have not increased, overall emissions increased 15 per cent in developed countries during the period. What is more significant is that since 1990, the reduction in energy intensity has been double in India and triple in China when compared with Europe. Even in the electricity generation sector, the potential for improving efficiency is greater in developed than in developing countries. In developed countries, the rate of energy efficiency improvement has been half that in previous decades as climate policies have had little impact.

These conclusions from an analysis by the International Energy Agency show that developing countries have done better than developed ones in improving energy efficiency. As developing countries need to build their infrastructure, the global leaders should recognize this effort and the negotiations should really be an opportunity to discuss options for making societal transformation to achieve sustainable development. The global community would then ask a different set of questions and frame the issue differently. They would for example, need to identify which longer-term trends should be modified and the best way of doing so at national level. At the global level they would need to lay out a time table for joint research and development of new technologies as well as mechanisms for their transfer to meet the scale and speed of the response. In each of these areas, developing countries should also agree to take actions as part of their common but differentiated responsibilities. There are three reasons why we need a new approach.

First, global energy consumption has grown most quickly in the transport, services and household sectors, and these sectors already account for more than two-thirds of global energy use. The global dialogue provides an opportunity to identify sectors and activities where energy efficiency can support both the environment and economic growth. In developed countries, the transport sector accounts for nearly a third of final energy use. In India, just 10 per cent of emissions are from the transport and residential sectors. This situation is going to change rapidly. As India's commitment that its per capita emissions will not exceed the per capita emissions of developed countries is a national average, a sharper focus must be given to activities that generate emissions.

The main driver of energy demand up to the year 2050 will be the movement of some 300 million people into towns. The strategic policy issue for decoupling energy use from economic growth will be a modal shift in transport pattern to railways and modifying the nature of the urbanization process itself, in particular new land-use patterns that minimize personal transportation and maximize natural resource use.

We should not shy away from the development of methodologies that measure energy consumption and deviation from business as usual emissions, for example, in the household and transportation sectors in the metros. This would be contingent on developed countries taking on commitments to modify their lifestyles or consumption patterns to a level where patterns of resource use are common for all countries.

Second, as the main determinant of a country's adaptive capacity is economic wealth, such unprecedented adverse impacts of climate change will severely constrain development and lock the poor in long-term poverty traps. A large share of this burden will inevitably fall on the national budget, and we have to accept this responsibility. However, such an international understanding should be contingent on the developed countries providing funding for natural disaster insurance, a provision that exists in the Climate Convention, and joint research for the development of drought-resistant seeds etc on the lines of the green revolution.

Third, there is a global consensus that a technological shift, unprecedented in the scale and speed of deployment, will be critical in determining environmentally sustainable patterns of resource use to meet the challenge of climate change. Global policy needs to focus directly on jointly developing new energy technologies and drought-resistant seed varieties, rather than leave it to the market.

The response at the multilateral level to the seismic shift in economic power and demand from Asia, particularly from China and India, has largely been of a scarcity mentality seen as a zero-sum game, rather than developing a shared vision where patterns of resource use are common for all countries, and we must take the leadership in changing this perception.

FCCC is the only existing tool that imposes emission reduction targets on industrialized countries. The US, even though a member of the convention, has never signed on to the protocol and has refused to do so even under the Obama regime. The opposition of the rich countries to Kyoto Protocol, besides a wide rift on other key issues, had earlier scuppered all hopes of any comprehensive deal emerging at

Copenhagen and had made world leaders resign themselves to a mere political statement as the only possible outcome. Non-industrialized countries, at present, are required only to undertake greenhouse gas reducing actions if they are fully compensated by the rich nations. The single legal instrument would blur the distinction between the rich countries and the energy-hungry developing countries. The latter have warned the proposed single legal instrument was a ruse to lower the obligations of the rich nations while piling on commitments on the poor countries. The current impasse, triggered by the fresh demand from rich countries for a "new legal instrument" to be imposed through the political statement, has left the fate of the Copenhagen meeting hanging by a very thin thread of hope.

Sources from the G-77 countries told that if the industrialized countries stick to this stand at Copenhagen, even a political statement would become difficult. Or else, the statement would become a shallow shell of niceties. India and other developing countries have long demanded that the parties to the Kyoto Protocol take deeper cuts in its second phase, starting 2013, while the US undertake similar cuts under a new tool since it is not a signatory. This is referred to commonly as the two-track formula, which is mandated under the Bali Action Plan signed by all countries in 2008. The two-year mandate of the Bali Action Plan ends at Copenhagen and the "political statement", in the absence of a comprehensive deal, was expected to set the ground for another year of negotiations along two tracks: Kyoto Protocol and "a long-term agreement" that finally leads to a full scale deal by the end of 2010. Sources said that while US tried to show how it was undertaking ambitious greenhouse gas emission reduction targets in the long run, the developing world leaders remained unconvinced of the intentions of the rich countries to come up with ambitious midterm targets as demanded by the UN's Intergovernmental Panel on Climate Change. Earlier, African countries had even boycotted negotiations, demanding rich countries table such targets. The Kyoto Protocol is dead; long live the Climate

Convention. Developed countries have stated in the ongoing negotiations that they will not take legally binding commitments to reduce their emissions of greenhouse gases. They do not want to impose any economic burden on their citizens, even if this amounts to a violation of international law. They also want to rewrite the Convention, something that we must prevent in the interest of the global environment and the poor. The spin is that new rules to secure action by China and India are needed to save the planet. It suits the European Union as their emissions of greenhouse gases continue to rise. The United States has not ratified the Kyoto Protocol, and is averse to taking on internationally mandated commitments.

Collectively these countries have so far specified a reduction in their emissions of 11–18 per cent by the year 2020, with respect to 1990 levels, against the scientific consensus of a reduction of at least 40 per cent. Clearly their concern is not the global environment, but burden sharing. There is an impasse in the ongoing negotiations because, as this is the first time since 1992 that developing country actions are being considered, the key issue for developed countries is the extent of responsibility that developing countries' accept, now and in the future. Developing countries focus on the close link between energy use and economic growth, and the policy issue for them is deep cuts in developed country emissions so that atmospheric space is available for their economic growth to industrialized country levels.

According to Stiglitz, Nobel laureate for economics, the key problem is how to allocate emission rights, currently valued at about $2 trillion annually, which is 5 per cent of global GDP. The only defensible principle is equal emission rights per capita, adjusted for past emissions. Even if this entails large redistribution, it is not clear why this should be treated differently than any other property right. Stiglitz argues that climate change will need a new economic model focusing on changed patterns of consumption and innovation, to ensure that the burden is not shifted onto developing countries.

On the other hand, since developed countries have commitments to take measures to reduce emissions, the policy issue for them is the cost effectiveness of these actions. Recent analyses by the OECD show that the costs for them can be minimized through policy instruments, with a focus on carbon pricing, applied across all countries. This has led to country, schedules identifying the most cost-effective interventions for bringing emissions down to sustainable levels. Not surprisingly, developed countries are pushing for inclusion of common actions, inscribed in schedules, in the negotiations.

It is virtually impossible to base any policy decision on estimates of global costs and benefits, because of the uncertainty and highly subjective judgements involved. The current framework also avoids the ethical question of developed countries emitting greenhouse gases above their fair share of safe global emissions, and the immediate duty to reduce their national emissions without regard to global cost-benefit analyses and international agreements. So, what could be the contours of a political statement at Copenhagen? It is time for us to shape the agenda, to end the impasse.

First, we should suggest that we agree to disagree or the implications of the historical responsibility of developed countries in causing the problem and role of the carbon market in finding solutions. The debate would then shift to developing rules that focus on demand-side management and new forms of international cooperation.

Second, it is essential to maintain the balance of rights and obligations under the Climate Convention; otherwise existing inequities will be perpetuated. Therefore, the global community should reaffirm the provisions of the Climate Conventions that developed countries are to take the lead in modifying longer-term trends, and developing country actions are in the context of sustainable development. This differentiation would shape the shared vision, where all countries would cooperate to support transformation of the global economy and human activities in ways to ensure that patterns of resource use are common for all countries.

Third, with the growing importance of the service sector, and consumer demand worldwide, this approach points to the need for all countries to focus on demand side management, and for the developed countries to immediately reduce their emissions from the services, household and transportation sectors down to the global average. These sectors are projected to account for more than half of all global emissions in 2050.

Fourth, there is a global consensus that a technological shift, unprecedented in the scale and speed of deployment, will be critical in meeting the challenge of climate change and its adverse effects. Global policy, therefore, needs to focus directly on jointly developing new energy technologies and drought resistant seed varieties, and their transfer to developing countries, rather than leave it to the market. Aggregate global efforts must also be continually assessed by matching international cooperation in joint research, development and transfer of technology in the industry, electricity generation and agriculture sectors with mitigation and adaptation results in all countries.

Fifth, we should suggest that the major share of financial resources should be earmarked for the least developed countries.

Sixth, the global goal of countries at different levels of development—per capita GDP as well as emissions—must have environmentally sustainable growth as the central objective, with carbon management as a result and not the other way round.

Just changing the narrative may lead us into a trap as developed countries are rewriting the rules, and we really need to set the agenda. Rather than responding to demands that in subsequent reviews and commitment periods would shift the burden on to us, we should adopt a leadership role by proposing a new paradigm for long-term cooperative action.

CS-A

It matters a lot, especially if we want to tackle global warming rather than just talking and arguing about it. Global warming is global problem requiring global solutions. The atmosphere doesn't stay within federal or provincial boundaries. It is a globally common to all. Greenhouse gases emitted in Canadian provinces mix with those from every other part of the world and affect everyone. A molecule of carbon is a molecule of carbon. It has the same impact on the environment whether it came from a smokestack in Toronto or a taxi's tailpipe in Kuala Lumpur. Every nation must do its part. And each country needs reassurance that others are also acting. We need a global agreement that is legally binding with rules clearly outlined. The science of climate change is evolving rapidly. The Intergovernmental Panel on Climate Change's last report is now two years old, and the research in that report is more than four years old. Recent scientific information shows that the impacts of climate change are happening much more quickly than expected. The polar Ice cap is melting at an astonishing rate. Ocean levels are rising more rapidly than predicted. And weather-related disasters are mounting.

Leading scientific institutions such as the US National Academy of Sciences, the UK Royal Society, and the Royal Society of Canada have declared that current scientific information points to a need for immediate action.

We have no time to waste. Copenhagen is our moment. In fact, two years ago the world agreed that the Copenhagen summit would be the deadline for forging the next global agreement to strengthen and build on the Kyoto Protocol.

Kyoto was always considered to be the first step by industrialized countries, whose fossil-fuel-powered growth created the problem. Establishing the legal framework was an important part of that first step, as were very modest emission reductions. But Copenhagen has to be more than just another small step. Science suggests the issue is urgent, so this step needs to be much bigger if we want our actions to keep pace with increasing climatic changes.

Industrialized countries need to accept binding commitments to reduce their global warming pollution much more dramatically in the next phase of the Kyoto Protocol, after 2012. But we also need to craft a companion treaty to Kyoto, one that lays the kinds of actions that major developing countries like India and Indonesia, will take to curb their emissions.

A recent study commissioned by Global Humanitarian Forum president and the former UN secretary-general Kofi Annan indicates that 50 of the world's poorest countries collectively produce less than one per cent of the global greenhouse gas emissions that cause global warming. Yet, these very same countries have been disproportionally affected by climate change. Thus, an essential part of any fair climate agreement must include support from industrialized countries to poorer nations, support in the form of financing and clean technologies so that poorer nations can wean themselves off fossil fuels and better adapt to the impacts of climate change.

This principle—that rich countries like ours have filled up the atmosphere with pollution in the course of our development, and that it's now our responsibility to assist less-developed countries to follow a clean path to prosperity—is one that goes back to 1992. It was enshrined in the Rio Convention and reiterated in Kyoto, and again two years ago in Bali. But we have yet to meet that promise, and it is time we did.

It is now up to our global leaders—presidents and prime ministers, ministers of finance and environment—to be visionary, to look beyond shorter-term political timelines and imagine a future world of security and prosperity, where our homes and workplaces are fed by clean energy. And it is up to global citizens to ensure that they do.

Visionary leadership requires active and engaged citizens to keep the politicians feet to the fire. Your efforts have never been needed more to help make this happen the UK Royal Society, and the Royal Society of Canada have declared that current scientific information points to a need for immediate action.

Chapter - 5

Glacier Theory: A Himalayan Blunder

For the first time in its history, the UN's Inter Governmental Panel on Climate Change (IPCC) admitted that proper "procedures" were not followed while reaching this sensational conclusion that the Himalayan glaciers ran the risk of being wiped out by 2035.

For one, the report is said to have borrowed from a 1996 Russian study by VM Kotlyakov and bungled on the glacier melt deadline predicted by it—the study set the deadline at 2350, while the IPCC made it 2035, perhaps due to a small typographical error, but which in effect advanced the deadline by over 300 years

What's remarkable is that this deadline was hotly contested by the Indian government. The IPCC team, led by TERI chief RK Pachauri, brushed aside these objections and didn't even care to double-check its facts, even though the conclusion of its findings meant as dramatic a development as the disappearance of Himalayan glaciers in the next 25 years.

IPCC's lack of rigour also becomes clear from the fact that it shunned peer-reviewed science reports published in well-known journals, and instead lifted references from a report by WWF, an NGO that supports strong action on climate change. It now transpires that WWF had picked up this alarmist view from a pop-science magazine, the *New Scientist*. In turn, the magazine had quoted an Indian scientist, Syed Hasnain, then with the Jawaharlal Nehru University; but currently working for TERI.

Pachauri clarified about the reference to Himalayan glaciers melting by 2035 was wrong. He further said that in this case there has been an error, but the overall findings, the problems of the melting glaciers, we stand by it. In fact, this was a thousand page report, and this one statement was the result of an error. They had placed series of procedures and processes, and very particular about choosing individuals (for IPCC positions) but where you have got 4,000 people, undoubted there would be one or two are likely to falter, so oversight functions have to function. They have very good procedures but where we may falter is when someone fails to adhere to them.

They won't take any action but this is something they will keep in mind because this will certainly be something reflecting on the performance of individuals. And, they are in the process of selecting authors for the new report and we will keep in mind.

He is keeping the options open but he does not want to stoop to the level of muck that some people are unnecessarily trying to create. They want him to lose his cool but he is not going to do that. He has been scrupulous from the day he joined this institute. This is dirty stuff (the accusations). IPCC only funds his travel for the meetings and nothing else.

He cannot undertake the extensive travels as chairman. The government of India supports him in part for staff he has dedicated to IPCC at The Energy and Resources Institute (Teri) but it doesn't bear other costs which are very high.

Hasnain has been with Teri for two years and this has come to light only now. He took him on because he amongst the glaciologists has done such sustained work in India over 30-odd years. He does not see any conflict of interest. There are others who are authors of the IPCC report in Teri. They do the best they can, he is sure that Hasnain did. If during an interview he ventured an opinion, he is entitled to do that.

IPCC's admission of getting its facts on Himalayan glaciers completely wrong has again brought out concerns about the use of science, and pseudoscience, to put pressure on India to take stronger action on climate change or to put greater responsibility for the climate crisis on it.

The '2035 demise' date drawn by IPCC in its fourth assessment report for Himalayan glaciers was used very often to demand that India should take greater action to reduce its emissions in order to protect people from catastrophes like glacial melts and floods. Similarly, a 'premature' release of information on the so-called Asian Brown Cloud was used by several western NGOs and governments to pin the blame on the melting of glaciers and other climate change impacts on pollution from burning firewood and cow dung in India.

While the UN released a preliminary report suggesting that India's poor were adding to climate change by using firewood and cow dung for heating, it later retracted, admitting that the results were partial and preliminary in nature and clear evidence linking the haze to changes in Indian monsoon and other factors had not been established with certainty. The release of the report, timed closely to crucial climate negotiations where the industrialized countries were keen to get India to take international commitments for reducing its emissions, did not go unnoticed.

The discussions on the ABC - a thick layer of seasonal smog that forms over parts of the world continues to surface periodically even today and unnervingly, timed close to ongoing climate negotiations. One of the key authors of the work on ABC was V Ramanathan of the US-based Scripps Institute of Oceanography, who is now going to be funded by the Indian government to carry out further studies on the issue at Teri.

One of the earliest cases of scientific manipulation that caused furore was when the US Environment Protection Agency tried to pass the blame of climate change to poorer countries like India. It had claimed that wet paddy fields in India were emitting very high levels of methane, an extremely high potential climate warming gas, but with very short life in the atmosphere. It had suggested that India had to check its survival emissions.

It was later found, through research done independently in India, that emissions from wet paddy fields and animal husbandry in India were less than one-tenth of those of the US. EPA had claimed and that their impact was highly insignificant than the large volumes of historical and existing emissions by the industrialized countries.

Glacier Melts: Credibility of Climate Science

Barely recovering from Climategate, IPCC's credibility has come under a cloud yet again in the wake of Glaciergate. After vociferously dismissing a report by India's senior-most glaciologist VK Raina that questioned IPCG's claim as voodoo science, the RK Pachauri led panel went into damage control mode. The UN panel was forced to acknowledge that it had erred on the Himalayan glaciers and not Dr Raina.

Fearing that a delay would only further undermine its standing, after days of prevarication, IPCC issued a statement expressing regret. The panel acknowledged that its 'finding' was based on poorly substantiated estimates of rate of recession and date for the disappearance of Himalayan glaciers. The fourth assessment report of IPCC had stated that the Himalayan glaciers would disappear altogether by 2035 if sooner. For the UN panel which has been scathingly dismissive of alternative views on the subject, it was an embarrassing climb down.

Together with Climategate, it is a blow to its credibility as the reliable authority on global climate science. IPCC is the world's premier outfit on climate change science and its assessments form the basis of government policy.

The shadow of doubt cast by Climategate and Glaciergate is likely to boost the stand of climate sceptics. Given the serious nature of the climate challenge, this close succession of credibility calls could not have been more ill-timed for the panel.

That is a cause of real concern was evident from reactions by IPCC vice-chair Jean-Pascal van Ypersele. In damage control mode, Drvan Ypersele told BBC, some people will attempt to use it to damage the credibility of IPCC, but if we can uncover it, and explain it and change it, it should strengthen IPCC's credibility, showing that we are ready to learn from our mistakes".

The panel bosses expressed regret about the poor application of well-established IPCC procedures in this instance. This episode demonstrates that the quality of the assessment depends on absolute adherence to IPCC standards.

This vindicated his support of Dr Raina's report. Environment minister too stressed to ensure that the controversy doesn't become grist to the climate sceptics' mill. "The clarification is long overdue. I am glad IPCC have issued the regret but the fact remains that the Himalayan glaciers are in very poor health and we need to take immediate remedial measures. We need to ensure that this should not give a handle to climate sceptics," the minister said.

At the time of the release of Dr Raina's report, IPCC chief RK Pachauri had accused Ramesh of arrogance and of "strengthening the claims of climate change deniers". It would now seem that Pachauri's steadfast unwillingness to consider an alternate position could well have given climate sceptics a stronger footing.

Interestingly, Dr Syed Hasnain, whose comments to the New Scientist led to IPCC's claim, has now said that he had never given "any date or year on the likely disappearance of Himalayan glaciers neither in any interview nor in any of my publications in various journals". Dr Hasnain who has for the last two years maintained silence on the issue, now insists that the year for disappearance was a "journalistic assumption interpolated by the interviewer, over which I had no control".

IPCC controversy

Differences over India's climate negotiations that contributed to prime minister's special envoy Shyam Saran opting out of PMO seems to centre on differing appreciations of what constitutes the quid pro quo for India to consider altering its stance on binding commitments. As chief negotiator, Saran was clear that in the absence of any preparedness on part of the developed world to support technology transfer and adaptation or a meaningful fiscal plan India could not dilute its opposition to legally binding emission cuts. A global deal could not retard India's growth but had to be an "addition" that helped it grows. The former foreign secretary saw himself working within the confines of a brief approved by Prime Minister Manmohan Singh and the cabinet. Any conditionality that slows growth was simply not acceptable politically as it would hurt not the upper crust of India but those who are economically and socially most at risk.

While India had not crossed any redline at Copenhagen, the post-summit pressure of developed nations to further blur existing legal commitments while nudging countries like India to accept cuts was bound to increase. Beyond a point, negotiations could not be "popularity contests" and India would have to mark out its territory. While Saran's discomfort with environment minister Jairam Ramesh's "flexibility" mantra was evident, the decision to move on was his own. Saran conveyed this to the Prime Minister who suggested he reconsider. There would be no "embarrassment" over Shiv Shankar Menon becoming national security adviser. Saran would be elevated to MoS rank, Saran explained he felt it was time to get on. "One should know when to walk away," said sources.

India's climate negotiations in the next few years would be crucial in terms of wider implications for the economy. Developed nations, reeling under an economic slowdown and viewing emerging economies as likely rivals, were not willing to pass up sale of new technology. They felt nations like China and India could now pay for these while trying to wriggle out of what was agreed at Kyoto and earlier at Rio de Janeiro. With Ramesh having accepted his differences with Saran and stressing the "final say" of the political executive, a replacement for the special envoy is not expected. With the climate negotiating team being recast, it needed to be seen whether it will move to the environment ministry from the PMO. So far, the negotiating team had adopted an intensely debated, but collaborative approach. Ahead of the Copenhagen summit, aware that the meet is part of a process that will settle a new global pecking order; the Indian team had worked to ensure it would not be seen as a hold-out.

Reiterating New Delhi's unequivocal support for IPCC chairman RK Pachauri, the Centre made it clear that it would fight any attempt to unseat him. In the meantime, Pachauri has ruled out any possibility of resigning as the boss of the Nobel Prize winning climate change panel. Responding to questions on the Himalayan glaciers in the Rajya Sabha, Environment Minister Jairam Ramesh, who had been accused by the IPCC boss of indulging in 'voodoo science', came to Mr Pachauri's defence. "We have full confidence in the chairman of IPCC. The prime minister and I have, time and again, publicly and categorically backed the IPCC chairman. We will fight any attempt to unseat him", Ramesh said. The minister said that what the government had objected to was the 'panic and alarm' created by IPCC's fourth assessment report which said that the Himalayan glaciers would disappear by 2035. The report was based on poorly substantiated estimates of recession. "In drafting the paragraph on the subject in question, the clear and well-established standards of evidence, required by IPCC procedures, were not applied properly," Ramesh said.

He made it clear that he had no objections about the IPCC chairman. Ramesh added that that India's objection was to the language and the "political use of the IPCC report" to pressure India to make concessions in negotiations and take on emission commitments. "India's objections to the report were upheld and we were vindicated," the minister said. There has been intense pressure on Pachauri to resign. Sources said that there is no provision for the removal of the IPCC chair, which is why there has been pressure on Pachauri to resign. However, there has been some relief for the embattled climate change panel chief as heads of states and governments rallied around him and offered support. UN Secretary General Ban Ki-moon, who recently announced that the Amsterdam based Inter Academy Council would review the working of the IPCC, too gave Pachauri his full backing.

Reiterating his faith in Pachauri's stewardship of IPCC, Ban Ki-moon stressed that despite "a very small number of errors" in the IPCC's; fourth assessment report, he has seen no credible evidence that challenges the main conclusions of that report. Taking comfort in the support he has got, Pachauri said, "The IPCC has already instituted an inquiry. It will reveal the entire thing once the probe is completed"

Post Saran, new climate team will reveal PM's tilt with the PM's special envoy on climate change Shyam Saran's exit, the government could now be looking at a change in the core climate negotiating team, which guides India's stance in international talks. The move, which has been pending at the level of the PMO for months now, could become the first clear signal after the Copenhagen talks where PM stands on the climate tussle between the 'flexibility' brigade and those wary of the elasticity of policy Union Environment Minister Jairam Ramesh has come to represent.

While the shake-up in core team, formed in March 2008 by orders of the cabinet secretary when institutional structure to respond domestically and internationally to the emerging issue was set up by PMO, was initially proposed to expand and include officials from key ministries like finance, policy circles are keen to see if the critics will be shunted in the process.

The PMO has not shown willingness to move on the issue despite different groups pushing for a radical change in core team, which includes serving and retired government officials. But the minister's continued strained relations with negotiators and the 'retirement' of PM's special envoy has, after they were first voiced before the Copenhagen meet in 2008, again raised head—will the PM, the minister and Congress party take the same stand when it comes to altering stance at the climate talks?

While the issue may not influence domestic politics, the party is seen to understand the link of negotiations to future prices of electricity—an aam admi concern. Reacting to the latest controversy over minister bid to discount the per capita principle, Congress spokesperson said, "Providing commercial energy to 550 million Indians identified in Integrated Energy Policy as well as fuelling an economy that is expected to grow at 8–10 per cent over the next decades must be juxtaposed against the need to preserve planet Earth. That minimalist imperative may be doctrinal."

Inaction is disadvantageous

With a concerted effort to question the intensity of climate impact, Intergovernmental Panel on Climate Change (IPCC) chairman RK Pachauri talks about the high cost of undermining the findings of science.

He said, "Status of accord is not clear. There is some sense of intent, particularly the intent of some countries. There are elements for building on what was agreed to by some countries. Of course, to extend this understanding to all the countries presents a daunting challenge."

Regarding 2 degrees Celsius temperature threshold, he clarified that, "For the first time the UNFCCC community accepted the principle of 2 degrees Celsius. This flows out of the IPCC fourth assessment report, and is an acknowledgement of the impact of climate change and the attractiveness of mitigation action. However, there is total disregard for the emission reduction required to ensure that the temperature threshold is met. As I pointed out at the recent Delhi Sustainable Development Summit, if we don't bring about this reduction then we will reach overshoot scenario. If we continue to increase emission, it will lead to a temperature increase of beyond the 2 degrees threshold. At that time, we will have to take more stringent action, which will be more expensive and the impact of climate change will be even more drastic. This would be undesirable. I have consistently said it is better to take a long-term view and take measures now to stabilize temperature."

He said further, "I have been speaking to the developed world about the plight of the developing world. This is what forms the ethical basis for developed countries to give assistance to developing countries. Between now and Mexico, I plan to draw attention to the fact that it is important to realize the disadvantages of inaction and the attractiveness of action. This is not mere rhetoric. There are several economic models which bear this out. Take Japan, following the oil price shock of the seventies, Japan seriously undertook the task of radically restructuring their economy. This formed the basis of their growth. More recently, Germany has undertaken an aggressive renewable energy programme. Korea has a green growth programme. There are enough details for developing a different energy path, and its benefits in areas like agriculture. On the road to Mexico, plan to address groups of government, civil society, the public and stakeholders and draw attention to the benefits of action."

Regarding IPCC plan to ensure that the intensity of climate change is mapped out better, he said, "The IPCC will work to strengthen the hands of sane elements. The recent spate of reports is part of a concerted effort to undermine science through trivial issues. The attacks have increased especially as there is a renewed political commitment to deal with climate change. There is now a US president who is committed to taking action on climate change that is big move from the eight years of the Bush administration. The IPCC is ready to listen to any ideas to strengthen it."

On climate change and finance, he said, "The emphasis of the IPCC is to carry out scientific analysis that is policy-relevant. There are countries that don't have the capacity to deal with impacts of climate change. In that sense the implications of climate change are far greater for the prosperous countries. In the Netherlands, 26 per cent of land is under sea level and 29 per cent is prone to flooding, given the lack of capacity. There is a need to realize that some countries face the real prospect of becoming failed states. We need to create an understanding that we are all together on this spaceship earth. And beyond a point we cannot go on as we are now. There is a need to convince the public, especially in the developed countries of these realities."

Climate Team Worried after Saran's Exit

News of the exit of Shyam Saran, PM's special envoy on climate change, has thrown the Indian climate team into turmoil.

Chandrashekhar Dasgupta, the senior most Indian negotiator and member of the PM's council on climate change told *TOI*: "I am deeply concerned that the per capita equity approach, which provides the foundation for India's position on climate change negotiations, is being questioned at the level of minister of state."

He pointed out that "equity demands the per capita emissions of developed countries should be sharply reduced so that they converge, over a period of time with rising per capita emissions of developing countries. Accordingly, PM has offered that our per capita emissions will not at any stage exceed those of developed countries."

The senior negotiator added, "Questioning this basic principle seriously weakens India's position. If the per capita principle is sacrificed, it would amount to 'decapitating' equity."

The disquiet over Saran's sudden exit is echoed by some sources in government who aver that the PM wanted to retain Saran and was quite willing to elevate him to MoS rank. But the former foreign secretary was clearly facing difficult odds as his approach was being challenged by Ramesh who was seen to be increasingly driving climate change policy.

Orders Study by Known Critic of 'Per Capita' Argument

Within a couple of days of the Prime Minister's Office announcing that Shyam Saran, PM's special envoy on climate change, was quitting, there was turmoil in the Indian climate team.

Indian negotiators were up in arms against minister of state for environment and forest commissioning a study and proposing a meeting of experts that could redefine India's fundamental principle of 'per capita emissions' norm while negotiating how the burden of reducing greenhouse gases was shared.

Saran's exit is being seen as heralding a swift change in India's stance on climate change. A pointer to this is seen in Ramesh's decision to commission Arvind Subramanian, an economist working with the Peterson Institute for International Economics, a Washington-based think tank, to undertake a study to define equity in the context of climate change.

Sources said, on the basis of this study, the minister is keen to call a meeting of experts to discuss 'equity'. What has caused consternation is Subramanian's view on the subject - in his published work, he has argued against the long-standing Indian per capita argument and the stand that national responsibilities must be divided on this basis.

The per capita norm, embodied in the Kyoto protocol, has been backed by successive governments.

Blatant error concerning Glaciers

In the weeks before and after the Copenhagen climate change conference, the science of climate change came under harsh attack by critics who contend that climate scientists have deliberately suppressed evidence and that the science itself is severely flawed. The Intergovernmental Panel on Climate Change (IPCC), the global group of experts charged with assessing the state of climate science, has been accused of bias.

The global public is disconcerted by these attacks. If experts cannot agree that there is a climate crisis, why should governments spend billions of dollars to address it?

The blatant error, concerning glaciers that appeared in a major IPCC report, it should be understood that the IPCC issues thousands of pages of text. There are, no doubt, errors in those pages. But errors in the midst of a vast and complex report by the IPCC point to the inevitability of human shortcomings, not to any fundamental flaws in climate science.

When the emails and the IPCC error were brought to light, editorial writers at *The Wall Street Journal* launched a vicious campaign describing climate science as a hoax and a conspiracy. They claimed that scientists were fabricating evidence in order to obtain government research grants—a ludicrous accusation— given that the scientists under attack have devoted their lives to finding the truth, and have certainly not become rich relative to their peers in finance and business.

But then this line of attack charging a scientific conspiracy to drum up "business" for science was almost identical to that used by *The Wall Street Journal* and others in the past, when they fought controls on tobacco, add rain, ozone depletion, second-hand smoke, and other dangerous pollutants. In other words, their arguments were systematic and contrived, not at all original to the circumstances.

We are witnessing a predictable process by ideologues and right-wing think tanks and publications to discredit the scientific process. Their arguments have been disproved repeatedly for 30 years, time to time, but their aggressive methods and public propaganda succeed in causing confusion.

Climate change science is a wondrous intellectual activity. Great scientific minds have learnt over the course of many decades to "read" the Earth's history in order to understand how the climate system works. They have deployed brilliant physics, biology, and instrumentation (such as satellites reading detailed features of the Earth's Systems) in order to enhance our understanding.

And the message is clear: large-scale use of oil, coal, and gas is threatening the biology and chemistry of the planet. We are fuelling dangerous changes in Earth's climate and ocean chemistry, giving rise to extreme storms, droughts, and other hazards that will damage the food supply and the quality of life on the planet.

The fact is that the critics, who are a few in number but aggressive in tacks, are deploying tactics that they have honed for more than 25 years. During their long campaign, they have greatly exaggerated scientific disagreements to stop action on climate change, with special interests like Exxon Mobil footing the bill. Many books have recently documented the games played by the climate-change deniers. *Merchants of Doubt* a (new book 'by Naomi Oreskes and Erik Conway released in the year 2010, is an authoritative account of their misbehaviour). The authors show that the same group of mischief-makers, given a platform by the free-market ideologues of *The Wall Street Journal's* editorial page, has consistently tried to confuse the public and discredit the scientists whose insights are helping to save the world from unintended environmental harm.

Today's campaigners against action on climate change are, in many cases, backed by the same lobbies, individuals, and organizations that sided with the tobacco industry to discredit the science, linking smoking and lung cancer. Later, they fought the scientific evidence that sulphur oxides from coal-fired power plants were causing "add rain." Then, when it was discovered that certain chemicals called chlorofluorocarbons (CFCs) were causing the depletion of ozone in the atmosphere, the same groups launched a nasty campaign to discredit that stance too.

Later still, the group defended the tobacco giants against charges that second-hand smoke causes cancer and other diseases. And then, starting mainly in the 1980s, this same group took on the battle against climate change.

What is amazing is that, although these attacks on science have been wrong for 30 years, they still sow doubts about established facts. The truth is that there is big money backing the climate change deniers, whether it is companies that don't want to pay the extra costs of regulation, or free-market ideologues opposed to any government controls.

The latest round of attacks involves two episodes. The first was the hacking of a climate-change research centre in England. The emails that were stolen suggested a lack of forthrightness in the presentation of some climate data. Whatever the details of this specific case, the studies in question represent a tiny fraction of the overwhelming scientific evidence that points to the reality and urgency of man-made climate change.

The IPCC and the climate scientists are telling us a crucial message. We need urgently to transform our energy, transport, food, industrial, and construction systems to reduce the dangerous human impact on the climate. It is our responsibility to listen, to understand the message, and then act.

Chapter - 6

Cancun Summit

Kyoto Protocol of 1997 on climate change is expiring in 2012 and time is running out fast. So, we should take the Cancun (Mexico) summit as our last chance to save the planet. From Bali in Indonesia (2007) to Poznan in Poland (2008) and to Copenhagen in Denmark (2009), developed and developing countries have been struggling to fix desired levels of carbon emission cuts that each other should adopt to ensure that global average temperature does not rise beyond 2° C (preferably, 1.5° C) by 2050. It is essential to save the world from calamity. Also, there is no clarity whether the US would commit to the quantum of emission cuts till its government passes legislation in this regard, which certainly would not happen before the Cancun summit. There are some other connected issues, too.

In view of the above grim scenario, we can't be hopeful of any universally acceptable solution at Cancun unless we change our strategy of combating climate change. For this, we need a paradigm shift in our thinking. We can explain this as follows:

Our carbon emissions are rising because most of our energy (say, about 80%) that we use comes from burning fossil fuels, viz., coal, oil, etc., and only about 20% of clean energy is available as hydropower, bio-fuels, nuclear, wind and solar power. Out of 20% of total global renewable and clean energy, only a small fraction (about 0.5%) consists of wind and solar energy. It is these two sources of solar and wind energies where there is a huge potential for development. If we focus on these two forms of energy, we would surely be able to turn the tables upside down in a few decades when we would be producing 80% clean energy from wind and solar sources with hydropower, nuclear power and in the form of bio-fuels and other clean energy.

With economies of scale, the cost of solar and wind energies may drastically come down even in comparison to the energy produced by fossil fuels. This may sound as a dream to some at the present juncture. It is possible to achieve provided we sincerely invest in R&D of these two wonderful and never ending resources of clean energy.

Two moot questions that now arise are: how much investment is required at the global level for R&D activity, and, who should fund this research? It has been estimated that an amount of 0.2% of world GDP, i.e., about $100 annually till 2050, would be required for R&D. This is well within the capabilities of G20 group of world's richest countries that account for 90% of the global earnings. This is not an insurmountable amount if there is a serious desire to mitigate global warming.

A recent publication *Smart Solutions to Climate Change* (Cambridge University Press) asserts that it would require emission reduction at global level by about 80% till 2050 to keep the rise in global average temperature below 2°C. This translates to the conclusion that while we can at the most reduce environmental damage to the tune of $1 trillion over the century, we would cut economic growth by nearly $40 trillion.

Thus, emission reduction appears to be a flawed strategy to mitigate climate change and we should rather resort to innovative R&D activity for producing affordable wind and solar energies. Simultaneously, let the countries do whatever reduction in emissions they want to match voluntarily without making. We have experienced that despite legally binding emission reduction of 5.2% below the 1990 levels (according to Kyoto Protocol) imposed on annexure-A countries, we could achieve very little till now.

Further, for achieving success at Cancun, monitoring, review and verification (MRV) of projects funded by developed countries need not be enforced as it can lead to unnecessary functional complications without serving any useful purpose. As responsible nations, let it be left to the nations to do self-monitoring of such projects as they do with their own self-funded projects.

Investment should be made in the R&D for producing cheap wind and solar energies for the benefit of mankind and other life on earth. This should not be taken as a liability; rather, it should be taken as a big business opportunity to enhance their economies to fight the current financial crises better and generate more employment in their countries.

Securing a global climate treaty this year in Cancun seems no more likely than it was last year in Copenhagen. Most countries see aggressive measures to reduce carbon emissions as a threat to their national economic development. Emerging markets feel the main burden of reducing emissions should fall upon the chief culprits - mature economies - who in turn argue they will be at a competitive disadvantage if binding agreements to reduce future emissions are not universal. Both have valid arguments, but an inability to compromise on either side is leading to paralysis.

The good news is that investment in emissions-free renewable energy is taking off anyway. In 2009, 62% of newly installed power capacity in the EU was renewable as was more than half the new capacity deployed in the US, while China installed a huge 37 gigawatts (gw) of renewable capacity. Last year, nearly 80 gw of renewable power capacity was installed globally, providing the equivalent power needs of 43 million European households.

Wind, solar, hydro and other non-combustible renewable energy sources still account for just 4% of the world's energy supply, while 80% comes from burning fossil fuels, the main source of carbon emissions.

Even at current rates of investment and with existing policies to promote renewable energy, the predicted growth in total energy demand by 2050 dictates, according to the International Energy Agency (IEA), would be a continued dependency on fossil fuels. Under this scenario, O_2 emissions would increase to two-and-a-half times the current levels. Faced with the urgency of climate change, our best hope of significantly reducing emissions is to use energy more efficiently. Projections by the IEA show that using energy more efficiently has more potential to curb CO_2 emissions over the next 20 years than all other options put together.

What's more, research by McKinsey shows that a number of existing technologies could save so much energy that they would pay for themselves within two-and-a-half years. These include building insulation, new types of lighting, and energy efficient motor and drive systems.

Economies taking advantage of this low-hanging fruit can achieve three major goals all at once. They can make more energy available without additional infrastructure, reduce emissions and save money.

One major barrier is the cost of energy. Energy leaders and professionals say energy is too cheap to make energy-efficiency an attractive alternative.

Another barrier, which generally affects mature economies more than emerging ones, is a reluctance to absorb the upfront cost of retrofitting equipment or installing new technology before older technology has reached the end of its productive life cycle.

The world's most energy-efficient economy, Japan, can give us some clues on how to overcome such barriers. Above all, the Japanese example shows that the role of the government is crucial.

A combination of standards, incentives, taxes, labels and mandatory targets pursued systematically since the 1970s has made energy productivity twice as high in Japan as it is in the US. For the same amount of energy used, Japan gets $2 of GDP for every $1 generated in the US. This efficiency is essential given Japan's lack of domestic energy sources.

A key to Japan's success has been the cooperation of government and businesses to define efficiency measures. Working together, they have created a framework that provides the long-term predictability that businesses need to estimate a return on their investment.

Japan's 'Top Runner' programme is one good example. Under this scheme, the most efficient product on the market becomes the new bench mark. Other products in the same category must then attain similar efficiencies within a fixed time frame, or face putting the company's brand image at risk when it fails to meet the target.

China lashed out at Japan, accusing it of attempting to kill off Kyoto Protocol. "Some countries don't like the Kyoto Protocol and want to kill it. This is a very worrying movement. The 1997 protocol is a milestone in our efforts to deal with climate change", China's special representative and deputy head of delegation Huang Huikang said in an obvious reference to Tokyo. Japan, which has taken on an aggressive stand against continuing with the Protocol beyond 2012, would like China to take on mandatory emission cuts under a new agreement.

Right on the very first day of 16th climate change conference in the beach resort town in Mexico, the representatives of the two countries did not lose any opportunity to take on each other. "Kyoto killing is a kind of propaganda wording. Japan does not want to kill Kyoto. Only developed countries should not be made to bear the burden of emission cuts. The largest emitter China and all other major emitters should take on cuts", said Akira Yamada, a senior Japanese negotiator.

While the focus has been on China, Tokyo would like the US to take on binding cuts as well. The US, which is not a signatory to the Kyoto Protocol, has sought to sidestep the issue by stressing on the need to "build on" the progress of Copenhagen. The US maintained that there is a need to ensure that "sharp difference of opinion over the 1997 agreement" doesn't kill off the progress made. The US special envoy for climate change, Todd Stem, said that it "would be a huge mistake to kill this conference".

"It may be that the Kyoto problems tie this whole conference up but I'm very hopeful that doesn't happen. The Cancun outcome hung in the balance", Stern said. Stepping in, the UN climate chief Christiana Figueres called for a compromise to help craft an outcome that would help deal with the adverse impacts of climate change - more floods, desertification and rising sea levels. "It is of course a position that is 180 degrees opposite", Ms Figueres said referring to reluctant Kyoto members Canada, Russia and Japan. "I don't think that it will be possible to guarantee a second commitment period here in Cancun. I know for sure that Cancun cannot obliterate the possibility", she said.

India's environment minister expressed his concern over the deadlock on Kyoto to conference's president Patricia Espinosa. The Mexican foreign minister is understood to have said that she was working on diffusing the situation. Jairam Ramesh said that while Japan's stance was not surprising, "they have been saying this for an year now", he was taken aback by the tone and tenor of their assertion in Cancun. "It is not surprising, Japan has taken this position for an year now. But what has taken me aback was their assertion that Japan would not agree to a second commitment period for the Kyoto Protocol under any circumstances", Ramesh said.

For now, the storm over Kyoto threatens to engulf Cancun. The Mexican presidency of the summit is working to find a way out.

America and India at Cancun

The climate conference in Mexico offers an opportunity further to take an important step to fight climate change. The US is helping developing countries reduce emissions and adapt to the adverse effects of climate change. Just as no nation can escape the effects of climate change, no nation alone can solve this problem.

America and India have expressed the importance of facing the challenge of climate change. They pledged that two countries will contribute positively to a successful outcome at the United Nations Framework Convention on Climate Change. These popularly elected leaders of the world's two largest democracies have recognised that around the world today, we are already seeing some of the damaging effects of climate change. The toll on shared planet will only get worse if the international community does not strengthen its efforts to address this problem.

The US is delivering on our fast start commitment to help developing countries reduce emissions and adapt to the adverse effects of climate change. This year alone, the US has significantly increased its climate finance to a total of $1.7 billion, $1.3 billion of Congressionally-appropriated assistance and $400 million of development finance - and export credit. The US is also working hard to reduce its own emissions and transition to a clean energy economy. President Obama's Recovery Act provided more than $80 billion in investments, loans and incentives to support a range of initiatives that are vital to this goal.

However, no country alone can meet the challenges of climate change. Recognising this, both countries agreed to strengthen US-India cooperation on energy and climate change through several initiatives. Two nations have formed a Partnership to Advance Clean Energy through an initiative supported by eight US government agencies and their Indian counterparts to promote research and deployment of renewable energy technologies throughout India. Under this initiative, both India and America are working with the private sector to fund R&D on potential breakthrough technologies toward 'green building' efficiency, solar energy, and advanced bio-fuels. They are also partnering to jointly develop, deploy, and commercialise innovative clean energy technologies to accelerate the transition to a low-carbon economy.

The US strongly supports sustainable, inclusive and comprehensive growth for developing countries. The Copenhagen Accord and the meeting in Cancun should be viewed as an important step in collective commitment to improve this transition to a cleaner, healthier planet for all countries.

Indian view

India made it clear that the onus of ensuring an outcome can't lie with the developing nations alone. Environment minister Jairam Ramesh stressed that the lack of progress on the $30 billion fast start finance, a key element of the grand bargain of Copenhagen was crucial for an outcome at Cancun. He said that a progress on a global monitoring system or international consultation and analysis was not possible without movement on the $30 billion that industrialised countries pledged to provide to 'vulnerable' countries.

The minister made it clear that there could be little progress on a global monitoring system if the industrialised countries did not meet their commitments. "You can't expect progress on international consultation and analysis without fast start finance. Fast-start finance is a key element of the

Copenhagen grand bargain. If it doesn't take off then one of the pillars of the bargain is missing", Ramesh said.

In drawing attention to the operational aspect of the "balanced" outcome in Cancun, Ramesh also sought to silence his critics at home. The minister has been under attack in India over his innovative proposal for a global monitoring system or international consultation and analysis. At Cancun, however, he was hailed for taking the initiative to break the logjam in the negotiations. He has been charged with toeing the US line and bartering away India's interests. In a message directed at his domestic critics, Ramesh laid out the three elements that form the basis of India's approach at Cancun. India's approach would be determined by the need to protect its economic interests, enhance its domestic environmental agenda and use climate change as a tool of global diplomacy to reposition New Delhi.

"There are clouds on an already cloudy Cancun horizon" Ramesh said in reference to the European Union's inclusion of loans in its contribution of fast start finance and the US's meager contribution of $1.8 billion which includes $400 million in export credits. "I am deeply disappointed", he said that as per the bargain in Copenhagen the industrialised countries had to put up $10 billion in the first year, that 2010. "That target is far from being met. The fast start finance is neither fast, nor has it started, nor is it finance". Ramesh was also critical of the "heavy dependence" on carbon markets for finance, saying that this was not the understanding that had been arrived at Copenhagen.

"At Copenhagen, the BASIC countries agreed to international consultation and analysis to ensure fast start finance. We also voluntarily gave up claim on the $30 billion over three years. Reserving the entire amount for the most vulnerable - Africa, small island developing states, and less developed countries", the minister said. India's reiteration that the entire fast start finance was reserved for the most vulnerable can be seen as part of its effort of reaching out to this segment of the G-77 grouping. As part of this effort,

India is signing an agreement offering capacity building assistance to the AOSIS countries.

Stepping away from the Cancun mantra of balanced outcome, Ramesh said that India would work towards "operationally meaningful decisions". "It has to be more than statements of principles. We don't want a Cancun version of Copenhagen. The minister stressed that New Delhi's approach to current talks would be "work towards a solution" and "not repeat mantras." "If we are serious about the outcome, we should keep pushing the frontier," Ramesh said.

Cancun Summit lays Ground for Future

Almost 194 nations agreed in the Summit to take modest steps to combat climate change, including a new fund to help poor countries, and put off major disputes until 2011 and beyond. "This is a new era of international cooperation on climate change," Mexican foreign minister Patricia Espinosa told delegates at the end of two weeks of talks after breaking the deadlock between rich and poor countries. The deal, reached at marathon overnight talks, comprises a plan to design a Green Climate Fund, measures to protect tropical forests and ways to share clean energy technologies and help developing nations adapt to climate change. It also reaffirmed a goal of raising an annual $ 100 bn in aid for poor countries by 2020.

The Cancun Agreements comprise understandings on a system of transparency, a fund to help developing countries, and a system of technology sharing and parameters for funding deforestation efforts in developing countries. The deal was adopted amidst standing ovations and applause for Mexican foreign minister and COP President Patricia Espinosa. The Cancun Agreement represent a step towards operationalising the Bali Action Plan.

India played a proactive role in the shaping of these agreements, contributed by outlining the framework for a global monitoring system for both developed and developing countries, a technology mechanism, bringing in the concept of equitable access to sustainable development. Most importantly, for the first time the agreement brings the United States into a regime that is comparable to that applicable to other industrialised countries. The US, a key player in hammering out this deal, ensured that while there was progress on all the elements on the Bali Mandate, the issue of transparency was given primacy. On the other hand, the European Union appears to have given up its leadership position in climate change negotiations and instead focused on broader goals. European Commissioner for Climate Change Connie Hedegaard said, "Europe continues to lead by example. We wanted a second commitment period for Kyoto protocol, and that has been worked out".

The importance of the agreements lies in the fact that for the first time, a United Nations document acknowledges that global warming must be kept below 2°C compared to the pre-industrial temperature. It also sets out 2050 as the target year when the global emissions would be at peak. The targets set by Industrialised countries to reduce emissions and steps taken by developing countries to reduce the growth of emissions will now be listed in the UN system. Not only this, a system has been put in place to efficiently track efforts to reduce and limit emissions as well. To enable these efforts, the Green Climate Fund is intended to be set up. The fund will raise and disburse $ 100 billion a year by 2020 to protect poor nations against climate impacts and assist them with low-carbon development. A new Adaptation Committee will support countries as they establish climate protection plans. A mechanism for improving forestry and preventing emissions building natural carbon sinks has also been put in place.

The only hold out to the process was Bolivia, which felt that the Cancun Agreements were not enough of a response to the environmental problem. For an agreement starved UN climate process, Cancun comes as good news. Environmentalists, however disagree. There is a strong feeling that while Cancun represents a political deal, it is rather low on the environmental integrity quotient.

Preliminary reports make it clear that the climate talks at Cancun have yielded an agreement essentially to continue talking and not give up the effort to curb man-made global warming. There is no successor agreement to the Kyoto Protocol that obliged some 40 developed countries to reduce their absolute levels of green-house gas emissions over 2008-12 with reference to the base levels in 1990. There is agreement to cut developed country emissions by 25% - 40% by 2020, but in the absence of any concrete mechanism to achieve the goal, the agreement stands in the company of sentiment, if not sanctimony. In any case, the United States, the biggest culprit in terms of emissions, both consumption and production are included, is pretty much determined not to do anything on the climate front, under pressure from Republican theologists. China, the other major emitter of gases that traps heat in the atmosphere, is also chary of any binding agreement. So, the best possible outcome at Cancun was to continue talking, and not give up the fight altogether as a hopeless project. This has been achieved, with the agreement keeping hope alive that the next Conference of Parties (CoP) in Durban in 2011 would achieve what Cancun could not. There is the added sweetener that there would be a global fund that developing countries can draw on to aid their mitigation/adaptation projects. What is increasingly dear is that a real breakthrough on the climate front would come from technological breakthroughs in creating renewable energy. Various ways of tapping the energy of the sun, the wind, ocean waves and of the earth's inner heat need to be explored with greater vigour, along with advances in nuclear energy, both fission and fusion. The bulk of India's funds for combating climate change must go to fund research and development in these areas.

Much has been made of India's offer at Cancun to accept binding obligations. Most critics have automatically assumed this to mean accepting emission cuts. India cannot curtail growth, so emission cuts are ruled out. But India can and should boldly accept verifiable, binding cuts in emission intensity.

With global warming on the rise and species and their habitats fast vanishing, changes for eco-system to adopt neutrality are diminishing. Recent years show increasing temperatures in various and increasing extremities in weather patterns. So, it is heartening that representatives of 194 member states at the Cancun Climate Change Summit reached a deal - a non legally binding, yet balanced package of agreement.

India is poised to become the third largest emitter of carbon dioxide in absolute terms and, therefore, it is high time that a solution has to be found in a pragmatic way. It is no good to be obstinate and to argue that developed countries have historically caused the present emission levels and hence, it is their turn to drastically cut to emission levels. Such an approach would help none. It is time for all countries to adopt legally binding cuts on carbon emissions as only concerted and determined efforts will save our planet.

Conclusion

Gandhi and Environment Growth

We can begin with an idea that the Mahatma considered a *mahavakya* (great saying) in the *Upanishads*. It occurs in the very beginning of *Isa Upanishad*, '*Tena tyaktena bhunjitha*. It is the identity of a steward for this world, rather than an owner who could do as he pleases with it. Its extended meaning, "Renounce ownership of the world and enjoy", embodied Gandhi's life. Ultimately, sustainable growth is about growth through stewardship and conservation of society, nature and its resources. This view has been an integral part of our culture for over 3,000 years. It is reflected in our innate thriftiness in everyday life, which Gandhi again exemplified through many stories of his frugality. It is also evident in the numerous professions that make a living out of recycling and reuse, such as the local *kabadiwala* on every street. However, as our culture becomes more oriented to acquisition, especially in a rapidly-growing economy, we risk letting go of these habits that have served us well in the past.

There is another analogy we can draw from *Upanishads* regarding unconstrained and sustainable growth. In *Katha Upanishad,* the god of death *Yama* tells the boy *Nachiketa* of two paths that lie before us, the path of pleasure (*preyas*) and the path of preference (*sreyas*). The former is sweet initially but soon turns to poison. The latter is like poison initially but then turns to nectar that provides sustained joy. *Yama* also compares this path to walking on the edge of a razor (*ksurasya dhara*), but it gets easier as we progress on it. This search for a greater path of conduct in life occurs throughout *Upanishads*. Sustainable growth is like this difficult path initially, but good for the world and good for the business enterprises that stay with it.

The sages who composed *Upanishads* over two millennia ago were visionaries like Gandhi. We can learn something enduring from them, and from this more recent Mahatma. While many leading Indian companies are making a good start, we need to build a broader base of support to scale these efforts throughout Indian businesses and consumers. By tapping into the sense of stewardship and conservation already embedded in our national culture, we can build a national identity around this greater path of sustainable growth.

We are now at a juncture on the road to growth where we face two choices. The first is an unconstrained economic growth that enables us to race ahead to the future, but with significant downsides such as weakened long-term economic security and well-being due to non-renewable resource constraints, climate change and environmental damage. The other path is sustainable growth, which is the use of sustainability-based innovations to develop products and services, business models and platforms, and infrastructure.

Sustainable Growth

Sustainable growth is about growth through stewardship and conservation of society, nature and its resources. This view has been an integral part of our culture. It is reflected in our innate thriftiness in everyday life. Innovation at leading Indian companies suggests that inclusive growth policies are beginning to have the desired effect in rural areas and on the urban poor. But much more is required from the government and industry.

Prof. CK Prahalad made one of his last contributions to management thought by introducing the notion of Gandhian innovation. These are business innovations that embody two core principles that Gandhi lived by affordability and environmental sustainability. We can add a third core principle in Gandhi's philosophy - freedom from authoritarian control and a general distrust of the central authority. Sustainable growth can be considered Gandhian growth because its business innovations are rooted in these three principles. The mid 1980s to the mid-1990s in India may be described as Sustainable Growth. In this period, easing of many government controls led to business, technology and policy innovations that initiated decentralised growth in the economy. These changes although partially implemented, illustrate the first core Gandhian principle - decentralised control. The adoption of these innovations then exploded in the next decade, 1995-2005, and resulted in a boom in economic growth. This decade also planted the seeds for innovation that initiated inclusive growth by making products and services more affordable to the vast majority of Indians. In turn, Sustainable Growth 2.0's rapid expansion will likely be the decade 2005-2015 in which we are halfway through, fuelled especially by business innovations that target bottom of the pyramid. It, therefore, illustrates the second core Gandhian principle, affordability, and has now become the national agenda.

It is encouraging that the government is finally putting together some of the policy pieces required for accelerating

Sustainable Growth 3.0. These include measures such as the carbon tax on coal to fund clean energy, the perform achieve and trade (PAT) mandate for energy-intensive facilities to reduce energy consumption, the National Solar Mission to implement 20 gw of solar power by 2022 and several other initiatives announced earlier this year. As Nandan Nilekani points out in his book, *Imagining India*, sustainable growth will be more effective when there is greater local control and clearer property rights over local environmental and energy resources. When it happens, it will represent a deepening linkage of the Gandhian principles of decentralised controls and affordable access with that of environmental sustainability. Sustainable Growth 3.0 is then likely to escalate rapidly in mid-2010s to mid- 2020s.

Drivers of Successful Change

Market demand influences new behaviours to a greater extent than regulations especially if the latter are poorly enforced. For Sustainable Growth 3.0 to accelerate, eco-friendly growth needs to be viewed as a business opportunity, rather than merely a reduction in risk from non-compliance. Sustainable Growth 2.0's lessons are instructive, that inclusive growth took off because companies realised it was a great opportunity to do well financially by expanding markets while simultaneously doing good to society. There is another big driver of change that Gandhi used, masterfully, which proponents of Sustainable Growth 3.0 could do well to emulate is the creation of an identity around the intended change that the average Indian could easily relate to during the Independence movements. It represented a fearless Indian throwing off a colonial yoke and was created through symbols such as the *charkha* and the lifting of sea salt at Dandi, new words and phrases such as *satyagraha* and Quit India, and by anchoring in values such as *ahimsa* that define our heritage. Perhaps we should take a leaf out of the Mahatma's notebook to locate where to search for such an identity. He did not believe that, traditionally, distinct spheres of life such as economics, nature, personal health and habits, and society should be kept separate in pursuing his work. Instead, he sought to integrate them into his way of being and doing. It is our own enduring Indian culture. More precisely, it is our ancient worldview found in the *Upanishads* relating humanity to nature, which transcends Hinduism itself and is secular in its outlook. It was the foundation of the Mahatma's life and guided his every action.

Europe's Determination to Decline

In a heroic case of finding a silver lining in the bleakest of all situations, the European Union climate commissioner has concluded that the global economic crisis and recession actually provided a lucky break for everyone.

Commissioner Connie Hedegaard says that the slowdown in economic activity will make it easier for the EU to achieve its 2020 goal of ensuring that greenhouse-gas emissions are 20% below their 1990 level. In fact, Hedegaard believes that cutting emissions has become so easy that European leaders should be more ambitious and unilaterally aim for a 30% reduction below the 1990 level an idea that has won support from David Cameron's new British government.

This may seem like good news, but it is not, because there is a strong correlation between economic growth and carbon emissions. For almost all countries, higher emissions come from higher growth rates. And if you restrict carbon emissions without providing affordable alternative energy sources, GDP will falter. In other words, by advocating even deeper cuts in emissions, Hedegaard is, in effect, calling for an even deeper recession.

It's worth noting that even before its current economic difficulties, Europe was unable to keep up with the growth rates of the US, not to mention the emerging economies of India and China. To stay in the game, the EU acknowledged a decade ago that it needed to become uniquely inventive. Hence, the European Council's Lisbon Strategy of 2000, which centred around a pledge to increase general research-and-development spending by 50% over the following decade. Unfortunately, Europe has done no such thing· if anything, R&D spending has actually declined slightly since then.

This is especially regrettable because R&D in green energy technologies is really the only viable long-term strategy for reducing fossil-fuel consumption without crippling the world economy.

European politicians instead seem to have become increasingly committed to the notion that global warming is the world's most urgent problem. Some conspiracy-minded commentators even suggest that this is related to Europe's lack of competitiveness: instead of trying to keep up, they say, Europe has decided to find a way to slow everyone else down.

One needn't accept this Machiavellian view to recognise that trying to cut back on the use of fossil fuels in the absence of practical alternatives is a recipe for economic stagnation.

This seems to be a driving factor behind China and India's refusal to go along with Europe's plans concerning at last December's global climate summit in Copenhagen. The German magazine *Der Spiegel* recently got hold of a tape of the final negotiating session. It is instructive to hear the baffled reactions of European leaders like Germany's Angela Merkel, France's Nicolas Sarkozy, and Britain's Gordon Brown as their developing country counterparts served notice of their refusal to consign their populations to continued poverty in order to solve a problem that the rich countries have created.

Attempts to rekindle commitment to a global carbon in 2010 emission deal had failed. Both the outgoing head of the UN climate change secretariat and Commissioner Hedegaard have admitted the obvious: a deal is extremely unlikely to be reached at the next major summit in Mexico at the end of the year.

Nonetheless, Europe has continued to pursue its quixotic course, even without a global treaty on reducing carbon emissions. And make no mistake about it: the EU's unilateral emission restrictions are not only economically destructive - likely to cost Europe an estimated $250 billion a year by 2020 - but are also astonishingly ineffective.

Climate models uniformly show that for all the economic havoc that such carbon cuts would likely wreak, they would have a negligible impact on global temperatures. The widely used RICE climate-economic model shows a miniscule drop of 0.05 degrees Centigrade over the next 90 years. Despite the huge outlay, the difference in climate by the end of the century would be practically indiscernible.

Unfortunately, it seems as if Europe has decided that if it can't lead the world in prosperity, it should try to lead the world in decline. By stubbornly pursuing an approach that has failed spectacularly in the past, Europe seems likely to consign itself to an ever-dwindling economic position in the world, with fewer jobs and less prosperity. Even the most optimistic-minded would struggle to find a silver lining in that outlook.

An Economy Enshrined in Nature

One hundred and twenty crore Indians cannot shift to urban centres and become software engineers, professionals and service providers. So, villages, forests, agriculture fields, rivers, hills and lakes need to survive in order to enshrine a large number of microeconomic activities.

Like rivers, forest has the potential to provide jobs to a large tribal population. As more jobs are lost due to the current economic downturn, sustainable forest management could become a means of creating millions of green jobs, thus helping to reduce poverty and improve the environment said Jan Heino, assistant director general of FAD's forestry department. A unique study - Green accounting for Indian states and Union Territories - found the value of our forest at Rs 88,60,259 crore in 2003. There are hundreds of minor forest products like cane, wood, bamboo, tendu leaves, tusks, medicinal plants and gums, etc, which have good demand in domestic and international market.

Transparent supply chain, healthy co-operative societies, dedicated extensions to the services of the government and political will could earn good amount of revenue for the state. The ILO Report 2009 estimates that the global market for environment products and services is projected to double to $2,740 billion by 2020 from the present $1, 370 billion per year.

Nearly 47.61 lakh artisans in India as per All India Artisan Census 1995-96 make high value addition to organic material available in nature. The artisans of Bastar make exotic wood craft, while the hill tribe in North-East India make hundreds of utility and decorative items from bamboo and cane. Handicraft was the major items of export from India in the past. Pliny, the Roman officer and Encyclopedist (23-79 AD) complained Indian luxury trade was depleting the Roman treasury to the extent of 50 million sesterces annually. As per the Union government's Foreign Trade Policy 2009-10, all handicraft exports are to be treated as special focus products and entitled to 5% duty credit scrip. This may help the exporter to access world export market for handicraft worth $350 billion.

India can make use of its 20 agro ecological regions and 60 sub-regions which produce a large number of crops. Agricultural sustainability should be the theme of agriculture planning. G-8 'L' Aquilla Food Security Initiative, concluded on July 10, 2009, has committed $20 billion to sustain agricultural development in the developing nations in the next three years. The commitment, has the apprehension that extreme poverty would grip 90 million more people across the world due to global slowdown. In fact, the food security initiative is a measure to correct the wrong done in the beginning of the 20th century. Farming, forestry and fishing in 1913 accounts for 28% of employment in the US, 41 % in France and 60% in Japan and 12% in the UK. Their dependence on those sectors has gone down to 6% now ultimately leading to job loss in natural sectors.

In India's vast and complex economy, conscious policy intervention is required to maintain a sustainable balance amongst industry, agriculture, trade, services and the natural sectors.

Equitable Sharing of Carbon Space

The third meeting of the BASIC (Brazil, South Africa, India and China) ministers on climate change was held in Cape Town. The joint statement, released at the end of the meet, emphasised on equitable sharing of carbon space. This seems to be the core issue in climate change negotiations.

According to the fourth IPCC report on climate change, a temperature rise above 2 degree Celsius from 1990 levels might not be ecologically sustainable. There are detractors. But it seems there is a majority consensus globally that attempts should be made to keep the temperature at 2 degree Celsius. This upper bound on temperature increase translates into an upper bound on greenhouse gas (GHG) emissions. This is where the difficulty arises. Curbing emissions in the absence of technological advancement translates into hurting industrial growth. The crucial question that emerges then is how to decide on the distribution of emission levels among economies. Developing countries argue that since historical emissions of GHGs by developed economies are a major cause for the precarious climate change scenario, the moral responsibility of taking the bigger burden on curbing emissions rests on them.

The Kyoto protocol tried to deal with this by dividing economies into Annex-I (developed) and non-Annex (developing and LDCs). The former had to make legally binding commitments on their emission cut targets. But the Kyoto protocol, which expires in 2012, has not been very successful since not many Annex-I members have managed to meet their bound targets. Further, the US, one of the largest emitters of GHG, did not ratify the protocol. Neither did it make commitments to meet the targets.

The Copenhagen accord, a non-legally binding text, follows the principle of voluntary pledges of reduction commitments. These commitments fall short of the required levels to meet the 2 degree Celsius target.

India's stance traditionally has been that carbon space should be decided on the basis of per capita emissions. India is the 5th largest global contributor of CHG emissions as per estimates of the World Resources Institute. But if per capita emissions is considered, India's global ranking falls to 124. This is extremely low when compared to economies such as the US and EU. In the recent past, though, there seems to have been a change in the government's thinking, with environment minister Jairam Ramesh speaking about options other than per capita for carbon space sharing. Also, economists Aravind Subramanian and Aditya Manoo argue that developed economies may not accept a simple per capita approach since it could be argued that if culpability for past actions is to be taken into account, it should depend on intent.

Given that the adverse impact of GHG emissions has become evident only over the last two decades or so, the responsibility of industrial countries for their cumulative emissions should pertain to this shorter period. Countering this is Jagdish Bhagwati who cites the US domestic laws on pollution where the tort liability is 'strict'. This debate basically emphasises that it is tough to reach a mutually agreeable formula on sharing carbon space.

However, once the method of burden sharing is agreed upon, there is a chance that everything else would fall in place. Else, there is the danger of economies implementing unilateral measures such as carbon border measures to deal with the emissions. These proposed border measures are an indirect way for the developed economies to capture carbon space. The measures envision imposing taxes or other forms of border adjustments on imports from economies that do not have comparable standards of climate change adaptation to prevent carbon leakage.

Basically border measures would be used to ensure that stringent domestic policies would not lead to losing on carbon space. The danger with these proposed measures is that, though guised under environment protection, the intent is often trade protectionism. In fact, this is emphasised by the fact that the EU benchmarking of sectors prone to carbon leakage is mainly on the basis of trade intensity rather than GHG intensity.

All this underlines the importance of economies reaching an equitable burden sharing paradigm. It is essential that while historic responsibility is taken into account, the emphasis should not be purely on developed economies. The possibility of an agreement coming into place without the BASIC economies also being proactive and willing to shoulder some of the burden is highly unlikely. Developing countries would get negatively affected by both the environmental costs and also the economic costs of trade measures. So, the onus lies on us to take the initiative for reaching such an agreement.

By thinking out of the box, India can break stalemate on fighting climate change.

Politics notwithstanding, the world cannot wait for a deal on climate change. The cost of inaction and the harm caused by climate change will affect poor countries disproportionately. The time for them to act is now. With its growing economic clout and international stature, India is uniquely positioned to take the lead and break the stalemate with an out-of-the-box proposal. It can do this without sacrificing its goals of sustainable development and of eliminating energy poverty (56 per cent of rural Indian households lack access to electricity). It can also do this without abandoning its long-held and legitimate position of equity in 19 per capita emissions.

The point often missed in terming China and India as big emitters is that global warming is not caused by current emissions of GHGs but by their accumulated stock in the atmosphere. Once released, these gases can stay in the atmosphere for up to 100 years. A tonne of CO_2 emitted by industrial revolution-era Britain in the late 1800s is almost as bad as a tonne of CO_2 emitted by China or India today. So, EU with 16 per cent of current emissions accounts for nearly 27 per cent of cumulative emissions, ranking second only to the US. For the UK, an early industrialiser, the difference is even more pronounced. Its historic share is nearly three times its current share. Conversely, the historic share for many developing countries is sharply below their current share of global emissions. China's and India's cumulative shares (7.6 per cent and 2.2 per cent, respectively, since 1850) are only half their current shares.

India needs to couple its stance on equity with the market based approaches western economies so vigorously proselytise. Global emissions trading whereby each person on the planet would have an equal quota/ entitlement to emit GHGs offers a win-win opportunity. While this means India would take on a cap or ceiling on its total emissions, it would be non-binding since its current emissions are well below what it would get on the basis of a per capita allocation (especially one that also took into account historic contributions). For carbon dioxide alone, while an average American emits 20 tonnes each year, an average Indian emits only 1.1 tonnes and the world average is about 7 tonnes. Cutting the latter amount by half and setting the 'safe' limit at about 3-4 tonnes of CO_2 per person would still give India a comfortable buffer.

Giant CO_2 'burp' started warming 20000 years ago

According to a new study a giant "burp" of carbon dioxide stored under the ocean between South Africa and Antarctica may have helped end the last ice age more than 20,000 years ago. The study led by a scientist from Cambridge University, is "the first concrete evidence that carbon dioxide was more efficiently locked away in the deep ocean during the last ice age".

The team made its discovery by doing radiocarbon dating on shells under the Southern Ocean from tiny foraminifera creatures, says the study; which will be published in Science magazine.

Luke Skinner's team measured carbon-14 levels in the shells and compared this with carbon levels in the atmosphere at the time to work out how long the CO_2 had been locked in the ocean.

"Our results show that during the last ice age, around 20,000 years ago, CO_2 dissolved in the deep water circulating around Antarctica was locked away for much longer than today", Skinner said. This could clarify "how ocean mixing processes lock up more carbon dioxide during glacial periods", he said.

According to the study "Pulses or 'burps' of CO_2 from the deep Southern Ocean helped trigger a global thaw every 100,000 years or so. The size of these pulses was roughly equivalent to the change in CO_2 experienced since the start of the industrial revolution".

"If this theory is correct, we would expect to see large transfers of carbon from the ocean to the atmosphere at the end of each ice age".

Skinner said the findings will help understand the feasibility of proposals to tackle global warming by pumping carbon dioxide into the deep sea. "Such CO_2 would eventually come back up to the surface, and the question of how long it would take would depend on the state of the ocean circulation, as illustrated by the last deglaciation", Skinner said.

Green Revolution

British Petroleum is going to great lengths to salvage its image-buying every possible term in the vicinity of 'oil spill' from search engine providers and spending millions on advertising to bolster its image after the crisis in the Gulf of Mexico. But the green consumer is not buying.

According to Lulu Raghavan, country director, Landor, India is part of a fundamental shift in consumer behaviour that began over a decade ago. Sure, there are several grey areas in the field. To begin with, consumer perception of a green brand is quite multi-dimensional - a company that manages resources better or associates with an environment protection organisation or introduces a green product in the market place. But overall it bubbles up to responsibility. Over 60% of consumers in the countries included in the survey - the US, the UK, France, Denmark, Australia, China, India and Brazil- want to buy products from environment friendly companies. However, the Indian consumer's green ambitions a fair share of challenges face 72% have a limited selection and cost are concerning the eco-friendly products. But there's a solution. "Not only must companies have their green credentials straight but the way ahead is through innovation," says Raghavan. Greenwash won't work on a savvy consumer. But they would generally trust advertising, especially in developing nations.

Innovative Engineering Solution for Clean and Green Energy.

Energy efficiency is emerging as a critical piece in the entire clean technology ecosystem. The government offering support, the sector has become prime entry point for new business.

More entrepreneurs across the country are buying from this point of view, as they set up startup enterprises in areas such as solar energy development, waste management, LEDs, bio-fuels and diversified clean energy. Green is in, as the country grapples with multiple issues from crippling power deficiency to high pollution levels.

At a time when the domestic economy is poised to grow at 8.5% and the government is focusing on financial inclusion, renewable energy offers enormous potential to bridge India's energy demand-supply gap, which would be required to maintain this projected economic growth. Almost half of India's 1.2 billion people have no access to grid or power supply. Of the 160,000 mw of power generated in the country, about 18-20% is lost due to inefficient grid and power distribution infrastructure. Much effort to drive a green agenda in the country is also coming from the government, which is planning to make it mandatory for firms to disclose "green initiatives" in their annual reports taken by them to move towards green technology in their annual reports. This slew of preferential fiscal and regulatory incentives from the government, besides the rising concerns around energy security, is prompting growth in the sector. High availability of resources, especially in waste management, and the macro-level investment buzz around the sector are some of the key factors that are driving significant entrepreneurial interest. Established in 2004 to support the development of clean development mechanism projects in the carbon market, the firm specialises in areas of wind, biomass gas, biomass combustion, solar and waste management. The company is backed by IDFC Private Equity.

Ours is a country that has the ideal environment to capture sunlight and generate enough solar energy to meet all its needs. Over the next 15 years, India will add about 300gw of power. The cost should be down considerably to play a major role in power addition. Otherwise, as a country, we risk our environment and our health.

Our job is to ensure that the power being used is of good quality and highly reliable, consequently reducing operational costs and improving overall electrical infrastructure - efficiency for the industry. With the increasing automation in the industrial and commercial sector, equipment has become sensitive to the quality of power supplied to them. The power disturbances can result in tremendous increase in the operational and maintenance cost for any industry. The system that we install seeks to identify power quality issues right at the source level and eliminate them at that point itself, helping you reduce your operational costs and become more competitive.

Index